Institutional and Organizational Transformations in the Robotic Era:

Emerging Research and Opportunities

Albena Antonova
Sofia University, Bulgaria

A volume in the Advances in Business Information Systems and Analytics - IGI Global - Electronic Resources (ABISA) Book Series

IGI Global
DISSEMINATOR OF KNOWLEDGE

Published in the United States of America by
IGI Global
Business Science Reference (an imprint of IGI Global)
701 E. Chocolate Avenue
Hershey PA, USA 17033
Tel: 717-533-8845
Fax: 717-533-8661
E-mail: cust@igi-global.com
Web site: http://www.igi-global.com

Library of Congress Cataloging-in-Publication Data

Names: Antonova, Albena, 1978- author.
Title: Institutional and organizational transformations in the robotic era : emerging research and opportunities / by Albena Antonova.
Description: Hershey : Business Science Reference, [2018]
Identifiers: LCCN 2018006309| ISBN 9781522562702 (hardcover) | ISBN 9781522562719 (ebook)
Subjects: LCSH: Organizational change. | Information technology--Social aspects. | Sustainable development.
Classification: LCC HD58.8 .A72878 2018 | DDC 303.48/3--dc23 LC record available at https://lccn.loc.gov/2018006309

This book is published in the IGI Global book series Advances in Business Information Systems and Analytics (ABISA) (ISSN: 2327-3275; eISSN: 2327-3283)

British Cataloguing in Publication Data
A Cataloguing in Publication record for this book is available from the British Library.

Advances in Business Information Systems and Analytics(ABISA) Book Series

ISSN:2327-3275
EISSN:2327-3283

Editor-in-Chief: Madjid Tavana, La Salle University, USA

MISSION

The successful development and management of information systems and business analytics is crucial to the success of an organization. New technological developments and methods for data analysis have allowed organizations to not only improve their processes and allow for greater productivity, but have also provided businesses with a venue through which to cut costs, plan for the future, and maintain competitive advantage in the information age.

The **Advances in Business Information Systems and Analytics (ABISA) Book Series** aims to present diverse and timely research in the development, deployment, and management of business information systems and business analytics for continued organizational development and improved business value.

COVERAGE

- Business Information Security
- Forecasting
- Big Data
- Algorithms
- Business Models
- Business Process Management
- Statistics
- Data Management
- Decision Support Systems
- Data Analytics

IGI Global is currently accepting manuscripts for publication within this series. To submit a proposal for a volume in this series, please contact our Acquisition Editors at Acquisitions@igi-global.com or visit: http://www.igi-global.com/publish/.

The Advances in Business Information Systems and Analytics - IGI Global - Electronic Resources (ABISA) Book Series (ISSN 2327-3275) is published by IGI Global, 701 E. Chocolate Avenue, Hershey, PA 17033-1240, USA, www.igi-global.com. This series is composed of titles available for purchase individually; each title is edited to be contextually exclusive from any other title within the series. For pricing and ordering information please visit http://www.igi-global.com/book-series/advances-business-information-systems-analytics/37155. Postmaster: Send all address changes to above address.

Titles in this Series

For a list of additional titles in this series, please visit:
https://www.igi-global.com/book-series/advances-business-information-systems-analytics/37155

Social Network Analytics for Contemporary Business Organizations
Himani Bansal (Jaypee Institute of Information Technology, India) Gulshan Shrivastava (National Institute of Technology Patna, India) Gia Nhu Nguyen (Duy Tan University, Vietnam) and Loredana-Mihaela Stanciu (University Timisoara,Romania)
Business Science Reference • ©2018 • 321pp • H/C (ISBN: 9781522550976) • US $215.00

Harnessing Human Capital Analytics for Competitive Advantage
Mohit Yadav (BML Munjal University, India) Shrawan Kumar Trivedi (Indian Institute of Management Sirmaur, India) Anil Kumar (BML Munjal University, India) and Santosh Rangnekar (Indian Institute of Technology Roorkee, India)
Business Science Reference • ©2018 • 367pp • H/C (ISBN: 9781522540380) • US $215.00

Corporate Social Responsibility for Valorization of Cultural Organizations
María del Pilar Muñoz Dueñas (University of Vigo, Spain) Lucia Aiello (Sapienza University of Rome, Italy) Rosario Cabrita (University Nova de Lisboa, Portugal) and Mauro Gatti (Sapienza University of Rome, Italy)
Business Science Reference • ©2018 • 328pp • H/C (ISBN: 9781522535515) • US $215.00

Contemporary Identity and Access Management Architectures Emerging Research and ...
Alex Chi Keung Ng (Federation University, Australia)
Business Science Reference • ©2018 • 241pp • H/C (ISBN: 9781522548287) • US $175.00

Research, Practices, and Innovations in Global Risk and Contingency Management
Kenneth David Strang (State University of New York, USA & APPC Research, Australia) Maximiliano E. Korstanje (University of Palermo, Argentina) and Narasimha Vajjhala (American University of Nigeria, Nigeria)
Business Science Reference • ©2018 • 418pp • H/C (ISBN: 9781522547549) • US $245.00

For an entire list of titles in this series, please visit:
https://www.igi-global.com/book-series/advances-business-information-systems-analytics/37155

IGI Global
DISSEMINATOR OF KNOWLEDGE

701 East Chocolate Avenue, Hershey, PA 17033, USA
Tel: 717-533-8845 x100 • Fax: 717-533-8661
E-Mail: cust@igi-global.com • www.igi-global.com

Table of Contents

Preface

During the last years, digital transformation became part of the daily agenda for practitioners, politicians and scholars. The literature in the digital field rapidly explodes, providing empirical evidences, good practices and managerial insights. Technology companies and innovative start-ups, universities and research organizations lead this trend, reporting weekly new breakthrough discoveries. The number of conferences about digital transformation globally expands, attracting cohorts of innovation experts, digital entrepreneurs and investors. The crucial role of institutions and regulators to support and encourage faster diffusion of innovations in real-life settings gain wide acceptance. The forms of university-industry-government cooperation, based on the triple helix model (Leydesdorff, 2012), evolved to quintuple helix model (Carayannis, Barth, & Campbell, 2012) and finally to ecosystem as a helix model (Carayannis, Grigoroudis, Campbell, Meissner, & Stamati, 2018). Based on these concepts, institutional arrangements aim to facilitate the conversion of new technological knowledge into innovations and economic growth.

Already used to the pace of technological innovations, ubiquitous and omnipresent, people and companies now prepare to ride the next digital wave. Mass economy digitalization become popular as Industry 4.0, robotic era or smart manufacturing. The emerging technologies behind this term comprise a large set of cobots, advanced cyber-physical systems, autonomous vehicles and drones, internet of things (IoT), big data, augmented and virtual reality, deep learning and artificial intelligence. Robotic era is expected to fuel the next economic cycle. In one simplistic scenario, the world economy will move fast to reach a new stage of technology maturity, meanwhile automatically adjusting to the necessary social and institutional changes. Organizations will disrupt, continuously improving industry performance, business models efficiency and value adding. In the same time, institutions will follow the economy boom, adopting gradually to the new lifestyles, new mental models and new cultural mindset, deploying smoothly the next "golden age", based on the model of Perez (2010).

However, the reality shows that technology innovations and the fast economic growth lead to grave social challenges and institutional struggles. As an illustration of that, lately populism rises globally (Moffitt, 2016), eroding public support and trust in institutions, undermining human rights and democratic freedoms (Roth, 2017). Recent econometric analysis of factors for rising populism, find out the dominance of economic reasons (Algan, Guriev, Papaioannou, & Passari, 2017) over the cultural backlash (Inglehart & Norris, 2016). In this perspective, scholars prove the role of economic insecurity, unemployment and globalization, leading to general reaction against progressive change of culture and values. The mass votes for non-systematic political parties, populists or autocratic leaders, or favoring either left-wing populism (against elites) or right-wing populism (against minorities and migrants), manifest the demand for new institutional settings. All evidences from the last years' elections around the world come to show that the crisis of trust in traditional institutions is global. The demand for new institutional arrangements and new social rules and agreements is clearly manifested. Can we avoid costly social conflicts and political struggles, by adapting new institutional and organizational settings?

The present book aims to discover how technological innovations lead to new institutional changes and organizational transformations. Stepping on the analysis of characteristics of new technology features, there will be explored the models of institutional transformation and types of evolution of business organizations. Further we will propose an alternative model for new institutional design. The main objectives of the book is not only to explore the questions how to design the new "rules of the game" based on (North, 1990), but how to make the new "game" (and the new social arrangements and social models) in the robotic era meaningful, fair and purposeful for all.

Generally, every new technology enlarge the domain of the "feasible" solutions in a simple and mechanic way. Every new or enhanced instrument give an advantage of a person to overcome a physical or real-life constraint, gaining more power over the nature. This way, technologies expand the limits of possible choices to respond on specific personal or public needs and to attain specific goals. In this perspective, new technologies enlarge the domain of "what can be done", "what can be improved", "what can be achieved" within the same constraints of the physical world, improving the options to cope with limited resources and physical barriers. For example, the physical reach of specific location nowadays is only a function of disposable technology that can range from bicycle and car to ship, bus, airplane, or even a spacecraft. Therefore, the main purpose of any technology is to increase the number of solutions and alternatives, expanding the domain of possibilities and choices.

On the other hand, new technologies per se cannot automatically lead to social or institutional changes. In order to be successfully implemented in people's life, new technology outcomes have to be transferred to specific market offerings such as new products or services. Different analysis focus on the knowledge conversion models, revealing the factors facilitating this process. In this phase, additional forces determine its success, as for example the market positioning, competition, demand and supply, learning curve, alternatives and not last – institutional support. As illustration of the need new technologies to be implemented in attractive market offerings, we can name the project *Google glass*. Google officially abandoned its augmented reality glasses in 2015. Among the main reasons for that were the lack of competitive price offering, privacy concerns and limited demand from the public. In 2017 the modified AR device was re-launched, this time as a focused business offering *Glass enterprise edition*. The new Google glass device address specific professional applications in medicine and manufacturing. Thus, in order that a new technology become a successful product or service, many additional efforts are needed, concerning customers segmentation, market dynamics, price options, potential demand, competition and supply chain. In many other cases the complex value-chain offering include a long vertical integration of companies, combining logistics, infrastructure, related products or services, context and specific business offers, and accessible price offering for the end-user. Therefore, organizational role is to transfer the successful technology innovations (what can be achieved) into an appropriate market offering. It is explained by the question "*why*" (the customer will choose our product, the customer will pay the price, the customer will prefer the product over the competition and others).

Finally, the role of institutions is to define the general framework of social rules and good practices for living together with the new emerging technologies. Safety, privacy and protection of the public interest are among the first issues of discussion behind any technology implementation. Institutions have to adopt new regulations following the question "*how*". How to ensure that new technologies do not harm the interests of the citizens and do not outstep the social order, how to protect and ensure the basic human rights. In the same time, as the domain of the "possibilities" behind new technology implementation increases, this enlarge the responsibilities of the users and owners of the new technologies. There emerge the demand for new set of rules and regulations, corresponding better to the realms of the new social arrangements. That is why from institutional perspective, new technologies demand redefined social processes, new social policies and new social rules.

One of the main questions today is how existing economic and political institutions should transform and adapt to the new digital transformation realms. The present book aims to explore the possible paths of transition to the new social institutional and organizational transformations toward the robotic era. It is not a "prophecy" or vision of strategic development and it will not provide guidance and practical to-do lists. Based on the review of theoretical findings and analysis of the past, we will try to identify analogies, similar models and path dependences that can help us to detect the new patterns of next social norms. Technology innovations or extended possibilities of the few cannot automatically lead to more efficient and just social and economic systems. Institutions and social norms are part of complex social agreements and all of them have to be reconsidered and evaluated in the changing realms. New technologies require new cooperation models and provide opportunities to develop new social frameworks of interaction.

In the same time, it has to be considered that new technologies need time and efforts to diffuse and to transpose the changed ideology and mental models from one complex social system to another. Therefore, it is interesting to explore the evolution of the new mental models and ideologies, preparing the society for the new forms of organization and social development. As Perez (2010) underlines, the economy of scale predefined the institutional logic of the Industrial era. It transferred the economic paradigms of mass production to all forms of mass organization of the social life – mass political regimes, mass culture, mass educational, healthcare and social systems, mass state administration, mass logistics, mass transportation and retail, and even mass tourism and mass entertainment industries. The model of economy of scale dominated the industry efficiency and became the main social norm for the last century. Now new technologies open the floor to very new type of institutional logic. It include new mental models and ideology trends, exploring niches, promoting individualism and "long tail" approaches. Personalization, customization and service-oriented paradigms are entering into the business and institutional realms, deeply influencing all economic and social trends. Individuals: customers, citizens or employees became part of complex value chains. Service-dominating (S-D) logic brought a new vision for the role of the end-user, defining him as an important factor for value co-creation (Vargo & Lusch, 2016). New technologies explore different models to contextualize, to personalize and to adapt products and services to specific individual requirements. For example, the last advancements in medicine and nanotechnologies, along with personalized pills and healthcare services, promise to extend substantially life-span expectancy. Many new practices show how personalization already pave its way to larger changes, affecting traditional sectors such as manufacturing, education, trade and entertainment. More importantly, personalization as emerging cultural paradigm gradually expands to become an expected norm and rule even in conservative social systems. In the same time, the rise of personalization and individualism brought new social phenomena. Issues such as loneliness, technology isolation, lack of human contact and empathy, changed family patterns and lack of social connections and safety nets become omnipresent. The old social norms, connections and habits gradually dissipate, requiring new solutions and practices. As illustration of the impact of these phenomena is the recent appointment of the first *Minister of loneliness* in UK.

Evaluation of different recent issues come to prove that this time new coming technology boom needs specific considerations. People are used to take technology innovations as instruments improving life and organizational practices, without changing social rules and norms. Even more, many of the discussed "new" technologies existed in the research laboratories and universities since decades. Can we find specific correlation or cause-effect relation between specific new technologies and new experienced social changes? The Figure 1 provides a visual representation of the relationship between new technologies, organizational settings and institutions and the evolved demand for new social arrangements. It shows the mechanisms how technologies accumulate the changes and lead to transformation or disruption in social institutions. Making an in-depth analysis of institutional change and revolutionary processes in a larger perspective is an attempt to explain the next movements to institutional transformation. Identifying the roots and phases of the revolutionary cycle can help us to predict institutional path and transition to new stages of stability.

It has to be admitted that a book about organizational and institutional transformation cannot present a neutral prediction or "wishful" vision for the future. Social transformation is not an easy process as social dynamics and social forces can act counterintuitively and unpredictably in situations of raising uncertainties. In fact, many organizations initiate transformation processes and fail, despite their efforts, dedicated resources and careful planning. The history shows many harmful and traumatic revolutionary changes, leading to rearrangements of the social contract on a costly human price. Institutional transformation go beyond the need to define more effective social arrangements.

Figure 1. Visual representation of the cycle of deployment of emerging technologies, diffusing via organizations and institutional settings

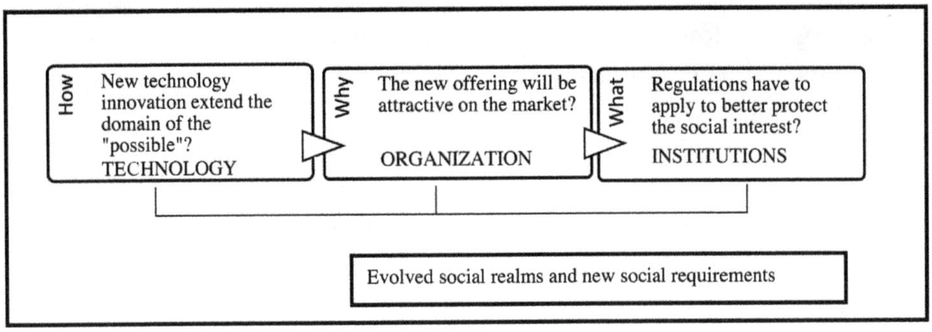

It affects power distribution, social standing and social status, shared mental models, access to resources and support of external alliances. Any change in the rules has a considerable impact on the social positions of the interlinked social actors. That is how institutions both influence and resume the complex social relationships and social movements.

This is the reason the present book proposes another model of institutional change focusing on smooth and iterative transformational approach. Based on an overview of the complex socio-technical factors leading to institutional transformation, we conclude that forming a new set of social rules is not a matter of choice. Conservative revival, opposition to the new trends and the culture of resistance can only temporally offer a safe place from the disruptive changes. New technologies will not only transform the economic contexts, but they will further expand the horizons of the “possible”. That is the reason, soon or late, institutions, organizations and social systems to adapt the opportunities of the “possible”, and to support the values shared by larger group of change agents, economic actors and new generations. In this moment, a new social contract needs to be negotiated, reflecting the evolved social standings and making new social agreement. Further, new understanding needs to be applied on phenomena such as the role of the work, the life models and life choices, the educational system, the meaning of social protection, the role of the state, the social services. These new realms will require definition of new paradigms and will promote new types of thinking for the social arrangements. Some of the answers and future trends are already present but still invisible. Therefore, the main issue today is to prepare the next institutional changes, firmly resuming the chance to improve the “*game*” but adapting smoothly the existing institutional systems.

The present book includes six chapters, structured as follows:

- Chapter 1 makes an analysis of the new emerging technologies and enlarge the domains of the "possible". It explores the main technology trends and its potentials to shape the new robotic era and its impact on the complex socio-economic systems.
- Chapter 2 provides the main definitions of institutions and analyzes its origins and complex roles in the society. There are explained the main institutional characteristics, including institutional functions, rules and regulations.
- Chapter 3 assumes the general mechanics and mechanisms of evolutionary institutional change. There are presented the main theories and characteristics of institutional transformations, explaining some of the key processes, such as institutional constitution, its smooth transformation and actors, institutional entrepreneurship and institutional patchwork.
- Chapter 4 revises the theories behind revolutionary changes. It defines revolutions in variety of contexts, including social and political revolutions, science revolutions, technology and industrial revolutions, outlining its deployment models, phases and evolutionary types.
- Chapter 5 covers the issues of organizational change and analyzes the theory of change management. Following the methodology of case studies and best practices, there are identified the main transformational processes enabling complex organizations to evolve and survive in a fast changing environment. Finally, some recent aspects of the digital transformation in businesses are explored in details, providing thoughts for new coming robotic era.
- Chapter 6 proposes an alternative approach for institutional design. Exploiting the metaphors of the "game" (ecosystem) and the "rules of the game" (institutions), there are analyzed the main processes and mechanics for (computer) game development. The overview of the (computer) game design demonstrates an alternative model to structure social processes in an open and enriching way. Applying the findings of the game mechanics for designing new socio-economic ecosystems can result in better performance and economic output. This way many social interactions can transform to enjoyable social experiences, enriched by gamification elements and limiting the forms of domination, the use of violence and coercion. Transposing the logic

of game mechanics to institutional logic can allows us to figure out and envision new models of institutional design.

- The final section makes a general conclusion, providing an overview of the next challenges and open issues. Adopting better transformation processes and practices can lead to smooth, relaxed and better adapting social systems. In this perspective, the most crucial institutional transformational process is social learning and change acceptance. That is how the concepts of the learning organization of (Senge, 2014) can improve institutional transformation processes, opening to knowledge sharing, discovery, learning and making it continually improving.

With new technologies, the dominant paradigm of the "economy of scale" behind the existing institutional settings gradually becomes obsolete. The humanity needs to reconsider its further survival, outperforming unsustainable economic and social practices. Therefore, the demand for new forms of institutional and organizational settings, new rules of the game and new models of lifestyle are already manifested. In the attempt to make the society more efficient and fair, many people look for new political solutions, new alternatives, and new forms of social change. The emerging technologies already expanded the limits of the "possible". The debate for the future of work and the jobs of the future will soon be resumed. On one hand, in the new coming robotic era, people will operate and interact with more sophisticated machines. On the other hand, new professions will emerge, favoring and valuing social aspects of the human interactions. Many jobs and occupations will change its nature, transforming into digital-enhanced platforms of interactions, emotional engagement and personal touch. This way, new social norms will restore the connections and context of the social groups, revaluating the human interactions: taking care, motivating, teaching and expanding personal and individual skills and abilities, enriching experiences, self-actualization and socialization.

Organizational and institutional transformation in the robotic era is the demand to redefine the rules of the game in order to reconsider the social order and to adapt to more sustainable and responsible solutions. Making new institutional arrangements and transforming the social interactions to enjoyable experiences, enriched by gamification elements, can give birth to new growth potential and enhance economic and social performance beyond the existing models of violence and coercion.

REFERENCES

Algan, Y., Guriev, S., Papaioannou, E., & Passari, E. (2017, Fall). The European trust crisis and the rise of populism. *Brookings Papers on Economic Activity.*

Carayannis, E. G., Barth, T. D., & Campbell, D. F. (2012). The Quintuple Helix innovation model: Global warming as a challenge and driver for innovation. *Journal of Innovation and Entrepreneurship, 1*(1), 2. doi:10.1186/2192-5372-1-2

Carayannis, E. G., Grigoroudis, E., Campbell, D. F., Meissner, D., & Stamati, D. (2018). The ecosystem as helix: An exploratory theory-building study of regional co-opetitive entrepreneurial ecosystems as Quadruple/Quintuple Helix Innovation Models. *R & D Management, 48*(1), 148–162. doi:10.1111/radm.12300

Inglehart, R., & Norris, P. (2016). *Trump, Brexit, and the rise of populism: Economic have-nots and cultural backlash.* Academic Press.

Leydesdorff, L. (2012). The triple helix, quadruple helix,…, and an N-tuple of helices: Explanatory models for analyzing the knowledge-based economy? *Journal of the Knowledge Economy, 3*(1), 25–35. doi:10.100713132-011-0049-4

Moffitt, B. (2016). *The global rise of populism: Performance, political style, and representation.* Stanford University Press. doi:10.11126tanford/9780804796132.001.0001

Perez, C. (2010). Technological revolutions and techno-economic paradigms. *Cambridge Journal of Economics, 34*(1), 185–202. doi:10.1093/cje/bep051

Roth, K. (2017). The dangerous rise of populism: Global attacks on human rights values. *Human Rights Watch World Report, 2017*, 12.

Senge, P. M. (2014). *The fifth discipline fieldbook: Strategies and tools for building a learning organization.* Crown Business.

Utterback, J. M. (1971). The process of technological innovation within the firm. *Academy of Management Journal, 14*(1), 75–88. doi:10.2307/254712

Vargo, S. L., & Lusch, R. F. (2016). Institutions and axioms: An extension and update of service-dominant logic. *Journal of the Academy of Marketing Science, 44*(1), 5–23. doi:10.100711747-015-0456-3

Chapter 1
Introduction to Digital Transformation in Era 4.0

ABSTRACT

The robotic era currently attracts the attention of experts and professionals in the digital fields. Policymakers, leaders, scholars, and public authorities and experts have to make decisions and formulate what will be the next digital transformation. In the first chapter, the author proposes an overview of the basic technologies and digital concepts, defining Industry 4.0 and its potential as source of disruptive changes. The chapter is structured as follows. First there are the main concepts behind Industry 4.0 technologies and the characteristics of the digital technologies. Then there are conceptualized some of the unique technology elements, functionalities, and implementations, outlining their disruptive potential to outperform the existing paradigm. Finally, there are identified some general complex system applications and implementation models, focusing on their impact to transform dominant mental models and institutional bases.

INTRODUCTION

During the last few years, economy digitalization became the dominant topic of public discourse. It is interesting to follow how policy makers, professionals and scholars took their role in the public debate for digital transformation. The term *Industrie 4.0* was first coined in the political program of the German government in 2011, focused to encourage investments in the next-

DOI: 10.4018/978-1-5225-6270-2.ch001

level manufacturing industry technologies (Kagermann, Helbig, Hellinger, & Wahlster, 2013). In parallel, other competing terms and policy concepts emerged such as *Industrial Internet*, *Advanced Manufacturing*, *Smart Industry*, *Smart Manufacturing* and *Smart Factory* (Hermann, Pentek, & Otto, 2016). In the beginning of 2016, the president of the World Economic Forum, Klaus Schwab, for the first time in Davos publicly used the term *Fourth Industrial Revolution* to describe the new coming irreversible and global economic shift. In December 2016, the US President Executive Office published the report *Artificial Intelligence, Automation and Economy* (EOP, 2016). The EU commission launched *European platform of national initiatives* with the goal to facilitate and to encourage digital transformation, by best practices' sharing, collaboration, joint investments, exploring common approaches to regulatory problems, and reinforcing the re-skilling of the workforce (EU, 2018). By 2018, 15 countries among the EU members-states already has adopted different *Industry 4.0* or *Smart Manufacturing* policies, following USA, China and Japan.

In the same time, many leaders and scholars warned that the expected transformations can have a costly social price. The Microsoft' founder, Bill Gates stated in media that *robots really are about to take your job* (Reed, 2014, in press). Soon after him, Elon Musk and Steven Hawking took the word to oppose to the fast developments in AI (Williams, 2017, in press). In 2015, an *Open letter on the Digital economy* was issued in MIT (Brynjolfsson, McAfee, & Jurvetson, 2015). More than 1000 scholars, leaders and ICT professionals around the world has currently signed it, insisting for better models of "inclusive growth" and for "set of basic public policy changes" limiting the economic and social struggles, expecting to result from wider implementation of new technologies. Meanwhile, the public discussions in the framework of *Era 4.0* intensified, covering daily a wide range of issues like robot-tax, cybersecurity and cyberattacks impact and digitalization race, just to name a few... All this come to show that new emerging digital phenomena bring many new ethical, economic, social and moral questions that need to be resolved. Furthermore, it is important to highlight that all these public debates, policy initiatives and publications are part of larger socio-economic transformational processes.

Internet and information technologies provoked substantial transformation in the global economy twenty years ago, so the new coming technologies are expected to make the same shift in the economic structure and functioning social models. On one hand, new technologies are digital and smart. They are ubiquitous, omnipresent, multitasking, self-learning, ensuring data and cloud interconnected operational units. On the other hand, they are autonomous, intelligent and self-directed, converging digital and physical space, outperforming human abilities, skills and knowledge. Is this the end of the human labor? What makes Industry 4.0 or smart factory technologies so unique? Defining the mechanics of these new technologies and discovering its potentials will help us to figure out what is their disruptive impact and how they will dominate the new economic models. Looking for appropriate answer to these questions, the first chapter will identify the key technologies behind digital transformation, their impact and their role to serve as catalyst of evolutionary and revolutionary changes.

Today, digitalization and digital transformation are highly ranged in organizational and policy development roadmaps, as triggers for further economic growth and social success. As highlighted by Saldivar et al., (2015), the new manufacturing paradigm (Industry 4.0) is targeting innovations, low costs, better customer focus, optimal technology solutions, intelligent systems and alternatives towards on-demand and personalized products. In the same time, investments and risk-taking in digitalization and digital transformation programs and complex ICT projects seems persuasive and rational undertakings, opening the way toward new knowledge-based growth. However, many economic, political and social processes just highlight some of the positive aspects (benefits, advantages and values) from applications of the new technology solutions and ignore the broad picture and more complex and systematic cost-benefit analysis.

In order to illustrate the complex link between technology innovations, market dynamics and institutional arrangements, we will discuss the following example. During the last few years, the fast expansion of the cryptocurrency market capitalization draw the interest of many individual and institutional investors (Sovbetov, 2018). This triggered additional interest for better national and international institutional policies, as Lansky (2018) provides a good overview in the field. In the same time, the main factors behind value formation on the cryptocurrencies are market dynamics, volume and volatility, level of competition and rate of unit production (Hayes, 2017). However, further studies reveal that cryptocurrencies, being decentralized, anonymous and hard to follow, are widely used for schemes of money laundering, illegal trade of weapons and drugs, human traffic, terrorism and further criminal activities (Trautman, 2014). In this context, Gladden (2015) opens the debate if money can have "ethical value" and "moral" side. Based on AI, cryptography, neurocybernetics and quantum computing, he develops a technological framework for intelligent cryptocurrency. This new cryptocurrency could be used in transactions that only respond on basic ethical values, largely diffusing ethical principles and acceptable social standards (Gladden, 2015). This example with cryptocurrencies development illustrates that new technology solutions can radically extend the domains of the "possible", bringing both positive and negative outcomes. In the example above, financial investors act rationally, looking for better returns on investments and fuel the cryptocurrency growth. On their turn, state institutions consider mainly how to tax the incomes from cryptocurrency activity (Lansky, 2018). However, neither economic logic provides the desired growth potentials; neither institutional nor political organizations look to protect further the general social interest.

That is why, before making an in-dept analysis of institutional and organizational transformations, we need to gain better understanding of the sources of new technology shifts. Considering the multitude of options behind new technology solutions and their practical implementations will be the first point in our research. Therefore, the first chapter aims to outline how new technologies extend the domain of the "possible" and outperform the existing alternatives. It will investigate the traits of digitalization processes and the key features of new technologies, converging and changing the dominant institutional logics. Furthermore, there will be outlined the main characteristics that make new technologies disruptive, influential, and crucial.

The structure of the first chapter is as follows. The first part resumes the key concepts behind Industry 4.0 technologies eruption and the main characteristics of the digital technologies backbone. Based on architectural view of the Industry 4.0 paradigm, it is developed a new holistic perspective for technology presentation. Then there are conceptualized some of the unique technology elements, functionalitics, and implementations, outlining their potential to outperform the existing paradigm. Finally, there are discussed some complex system applications and implementation models, focusing on their impact to transform dominant mental models and institutional bases.

BACKGROUND

Digital transformation and economy digitization in a broader societal context is defined as an economic and social transformation triggered by the massive adoption of digital technologies that generate, process, share and transact information (Katz, Koutroumpis, & Martin Callorda, 2014). Saldivar et al., (2015) states that actually Internet is the key enabler of all digitalization processes, ensuring communication platform between humans and machines in Cyber-Physical-Systems (CPS). Industry 4.0 technologies serve as general-purpose technologies, used as "door-opening" versus "gaps-filling" and converge both technological and organizational innovations. Almada-Lobo (2016) defines Industry 4.0 manufacturing transformation based on Cyber-Physical Systems (CPS) and Cyber-Physical Production Systems (CPPS). It is based on mass customized, decentralized, vertically integrated, connected, mobile, cloud computing and advanced data analysis approach. In Industry 4.0 products and production systems including machines, warehouses, and operating resources are enhanced to CPS (Kagermann, Helbig, Hellinger, & Wahlster, 2013). Rüβmann et al. (2015) include in Industry 4.0 nine specific digital industrial technologies such as embedded sensors, connected products and devices (IoT), collection of data and real time data analytics (Big Data and Analytics), autonomous robotics and advanced manufacturing (3D printing). Additionally the model include AR/VR, Simulations, Cloud computing, cybersecurity and horizontal and vertical system integration that have the potential to lead the next industry growth and transformation. Further, Gawer and Cusumano (2014) determine the role of Industry 4.0 as platform of value chain organizations and complex management system along the lifecycle of products. Industry 4.0 combines advanced technologies with new organizational forms and management models to decentralize intelligence, enhance object networking and independent process management, and paradigm shift from "centralised" to "decentralised" production.

Digital transformation in manufacturing and adoption of smart factories started simultaneously in different contexts in global perspective. Furthermore, Industry digitalization together with its complex value chains is the main backbone of economy digitalization and lead further larger-scale socio-economic processes. Different sophisticated systems, including e-government, smart city, smart mobility, e-banking, e-health systems and its applications put additional layers over the main business processes. Hermann et al. (2016) in the literature review find out that the terms "Fourth Industrial Revolution" and "Industry 4.0" are often mixed. Confirming this, Saldivar et al., (2015) find the same for the terms "Smart Industry" and Industry 4.0, describing complex manufacturing systems and emerging CPS. Based on that, we can state that Industry 4.0 and smart factories concept designate the reversal of the production processes logic through extended smart and connected technologies. It combines both organizational and technological innovations and in the following paragraphs, we will make an overview of these two interconnected perspectives.

Most of the studies in the field of industry digitalization highlight its potential to lead to huge economic impact. On the first place, industry digitalization shall substantially increase operational effectiveness, to develop entirely new business models, new services, and products (Hermann, Pentek, & Otto, 2016). On the second place, it will provide a new ecosystem approach to vertical and horizontal industry integration. The adoption of digital technologies will produce larger effects on the ecosystem, including customer' role, logistics and supply chain, rather than just on the company. This way it increases opportunities from synergy effects between different stakeholders in horizontal and vertical integration. Finally combining technologies with new ecosystem cooperation and management models can lead to improved data analysis models, better forecasts and prognosis and further level of value chain and cross-sectoral integration. The mass customization and decentralization are state-of-the-art production paradigm to produce individualized, variant products and services with nearly mass production costs (Tiihonen & Felfernig, 2017). Mass customization rely on the model of long tail, exploiting further market demand and increasing value for customers. Furthermore, decentralization explore the models of products co-creation, open-innovation and user-oriented approach.

From technological point of view, Industry 4.0 stays for digital technologies such as: Cyber Physical Systems, Industrial Internet and Internet of things (IoT and IIoT), embedded systems, adaptive robotics, cyber security, augmented reality, data analytics, artificial intelligence and additive manufacturing. Rüβmann et al. (2015) selects the nine building blocks of Industry 4.0 technologies, completing the list with simulations, cloud computing, horizontal and vertical system integration and virtual reality. Recently, wider adoption and applications of blockchain technologies are discussed in various use cases as bank and insurance industry and digital supply chain transformation (Korpela, Hallikas, & Dahlberg, 2017). However, all these technologies converge in complex digital architectures in order to provide more productive systems, combining smart products, smart processes and smart factories. Furthermore, Industry 4.0 combines the principles of individualization, virtualization, hybridization and self-optimization (Brettel, Friederichsen, Keller, & Rosenberg, 2014). The key components of Industrie 4.0 are: Cyber-Physical Systems, Internet of Things, Internet of Services, and Smart Factory (Hermann, Pentek, & Otto, 2016). Based on them the following six design principles emerged: Interoperability, Virtualization, Decentralization, Real-time Capability, Service Orientation and Modularity.

Further, the recent study of Reich et al. (2017), proposes the following classification:

- **Smart Factory:** Digitally networked and automated production based on cyber-physical systems.
- **Smart Operations:** Processes and products are digitally mapped and can be managed using ICT systems and algorithms in a virtual world.
- **Smart Products:** Products can be controlled with IT and can thus communicate and interact with higher-level systems in the value chain.
- **Data-Driven Services:** Information-based services that can only arise when production, products and customers are networked.

It is interesting to mention as well the smart product evolution model (Reich, Gleich, & Sauter, 2017). The logic behind provides information about whether the technologies are basic technologies or expansion steps. On first place, the product include a basic technology such as sensors and actuators for examples. The second step is for intelligent product such as automated intralogistics, technologies for optimizing energy use, or predictive maintenance. The third step includes networking technologies as M2M communication, cyber security concepts as well as communications and interface systems, for example. Finally, the fourth step is a holistically connected product system as robot farming, Human Machine Interfaces and interaction.

KEY CHARACTERISTICS OF INDUSTRY 4.0

In order to analyse and define the main characteristics of Industry 4.0 technologies we will investigate how they extend the domain of the "possible". Therefore, we will analyse their impact and ability to transform and manipulate both the physical world and the virtual reality, by combining real-time data processing with interconnected machines along with devices, smart fabrics and complex solutions, artificial intelligence and people. Cyber-physical systems, Internet of things, Big Data, virtual reality technologies, 3D printing, artificial intelligence, robots and its derivatives such as drones, autonomous vehicles and others are among the complex solutions taking part of the Industry 4.0 (Strange & Zucchella, 2017). As they represent reliable, interoperable solutions that integrate the production facilities with the environment, they cover elements such as integration of data, cyber-security, integration of legacy systems and Big Data.

The expected effects of the new technologies are already discussed as: more innovative services, models and practices, optimization in manufacturing and logistics processes; a better and faster response to market changes, more sustainable processes, technology platforms for testing innovative applications, including design and manufacturing, rapid prototyping, scalable, modular systems, HPC and Cloud-based modelling and simulations. Saldivar et al., (2015) summarize that Industry 4.0 leads to a paradigm shift from centralized to decentralized manufacturing, based on customer-triggered autonomous processes of cyber-physical systems. On first place, Industry 4.0 technologies lead to the development of new content- and context-rich connected physical environments and "smart" objects, adding many Internet functions and computational services to "real world" things and objects, connecting them with people and interactive landscapes. These new functions bring substantial impact on business transformation. By collecting and processing real-time data and by performing different autonomous and independent actions, smart devices can improve further costs and business performance. Second, many successfully tested use cases exists, making them ready for the market. Moreover, all these technologies will influence the main business processes, and will reshape value-offering mechanisms in organizations (Saldivar, Li, Chen, Zhan, Zhang, & Chen, 2015).

Investigating the main characteristics and effects of Industry 4.0 technologies, there are identified the following:

- **Ecosystem Effects:** Including different stakeholders (customer' role, logistics and supply chain) and increases synergy effects in horizontal or vertical integration. Further it builds on evolving communities, discovering opportunities for process optimization, value development, innovations;
- **Localization Effects:** Smart factories involve CPS, combination of software and hardware embedded systems. Thus, mass exports to low-cost countries become obsolete due to the need to be close to the end-user and its respective ecosystem and market.
- **Economy Effect**: The emerging Industry 4.0 technology paradigm imposes new cooperation models in "smart manufacturing" and "smart factories" taking into account the overall product lifecycle. Organized around big data, connected technologies, cyber-physical systems, Internet of Things, 3D printing, cloud computing, artificial intelligence and robotics have the potential to disrupt value creation along different

industries and become the key ingredients of new business models and business processes.

However, Sommer (2015) makes the warning that Industry 4.0 can change the structure of the business landscape, leaving small and medium companies behind. He considers that digital transformation is a costly transitional process, and companies will need to adapt and invest in order to respond on the new-coming business realms.

In order to understand better Industry 4.0 technologies and their further impact there are identified different classification models. As stated in (Bartodziej, 2016), there exists many alternative Industry 4.0 classification models, based on technology stage of development (maturity level), industry specifics or life-cycle models. The life-cycle models represent a generalization of concrete time-dependent observations of technology developments. Some of the most popular maturity and technology life-cycle models are the Gartner's Hype Cycle Model, Ansoff's technology life cycle model and others. Bartodziej (2016) further proposes more expedient technology innovation-oriented classification of technology types, identifying pacemaker technologies (early stage technologies), key technologies (leading the hype) and basic technologies (already adopted and industry standard).

DIGITAL TECHNOLOGIES

Cyber-Physical Systems (CPS)

An important component of the Industrie 4.0 is the fusion of the physical and the virtual world, made possible by Cyber-Physical Systems (CPS). Monostori (2014) defines Cyber-Physical Systems (CPSs) as systems of collaborating computational entities, which are in intensive connection with the surrounding physical world and its on-going processes, providing and using, at the same time, data accessing and data processing services available on the Internet. Further Cyber-Physical Production Systems (CPPSs) rely on the newest and foreseeable further developments of computer science and ICT on the one hand, and on manufacturing science and technology, on the other. Thus, CPS are integrating both computation and physical processes. There are three CPS generations (Hermann, Pentek, & Otto, 2016). The first generation of CPS includes identification technologies like RFID tags, which allow unique identification and storage, while analytics are centralized service. The second generation of CPS are equipped with sensors and actuators with a limited function. Finally, the CPS of the third generation can store and analyse data, and has with multiple sensors and actuators that are network compatible. Further Monostori (2014) set out the next coming challenges in front of CPS development such as- context-adaptive and autonomous systems, cooperative production systems, identification and prediction of dynamic systems, robust scheduling, fusion of real and virtual systems and human machine symbiosis. The model of Lee et al., (2015), shows the architecture model of CPS and Industry systems (Figure 1). Finally, Wang et al, (2015) determine three main processes of Industry 4.0 integration – horizontal integration through value networks, vertical integration and end-to-end digital integration.

Artificial Intelligence and Advanced Robots

Based on observations from scholars and practitioners, in the next 10 to 15 years, robots and AI are expected to become the main technology disruptors, leading to profound economic, social and political implications (Agha, Cabibihan, Howard, Salichs, & He, 2016; LaGrandeur & Hughes, 2017; Sirkin, Zinser, & Rose, 2015; Leonhard, 2016). Kaplan (2015) explains that work in AI advances on two fronts. The first includes new and sophisticated algorithms for "learning from experiences", covering visual, media and auditory signals, information and data, machine learning, deep learning, neural networks, cognitive systems and genetic algorithms, further defined as synthetic intellect (Kaplan, 2015; Neapolitian & Jang, 2013). AI is not

Table 1. The classification of Industry 4.0 technologies, based on the architecture of (Lee, Bagheri, & Kao, 2015)

Layer	Technology	Level of Decision
Configuration and control	Artificial Intelligence (AI)	Self-optimization and self-adjusment; Control, vertical integration, adaptation and improvement;
Cognition	Artificial Intelligence (AI), Big Data, Cloud computing	Decision support; Best practices sharing and learning; self-service and service automation;
Cyber physical system	Robotics, IoT, and CPS	Information hub; Maintenance; Self-service automation; Planning, resource optimization;
Conversion	Actuators & controllers; IoT	M2M communication, data to physical
Connection	Sensors and basic infrastructure	Data acquisition and transfer

programmed in conventional sense but it evolves and improve from work experiences and deep learning models. In the same time, the second class of AI systems arises from the combination of robotics (dynamic systems with movable parts), sensors (data collection) and cloud computing (analytics). The notion of robotics is recently changing drastically as there emerge new forms of social robots, ubiquitous roboting, diffused and collective automation systems and "smartified" environments (Barile & Sugiyama, 2015). All these largely dismiss the stereotypes of autopomorfing or zoopomorphing automata. Implemented as bots, interconnected systems, personal virtual assistants and AI-based applications such as Cortana and SIRI, robots and AI invisibly take new roles. The impact of robots and AI systems recently increases in various industries and processes such as manufacturing, transportation and logistics, warehousing, agriculture, medicine, hospitability, journalism, marketing, communications, finances, healthcare and education (Kaplan, 2015; Ivanov, 2016). Robots and cobots include a wide range of humanoids, industrial robots, autonomous vehicles (Maurer, Gerdes, Lenz, & Winner, 2016), drones, and collectively programmed "swarm" robots, microscopic nano-robots and nano-bots. With new implementations, it becomes even more difficult to define a new system as a "robot". One of the common issues is that robots usually have moveable parts.

Advanced robots are among the key Industry 4.0 technologies and are widely discussed for their impact on the future of manufacturing (Sirkin, Zinser, & Rose, 2015). While in the past, industrial robots were mainly adapted to monotonous work and transaction processes, their role and functionality gradually expands from fully autonomous to semi-autonomous systems. In parallel, service robots take the floor (IFR, 2016), professionally adapting to many new industrial applications and especially in fields as medicine (Da Vinci robot). On other hand, consumer robots (ranging from autonomous car to smart refrigerators) and their extended functionality and capacity to interact autonomously raise further issues how they will be programmed to plan, organize and undertake actions (Ivanov & Webster, 2017).

In general, scholars reports that larger implementation of robotic and AI systems in Industry 4.0 settings increases productivity, improves quality and works conditions and company competitiveness and has a positive impact on wages. According to IFR (2016), by 2019 the number of industrial robots installed globally in factories will reach about 2,6 million, mainly in the automotive, electrical/electronic and metal and machinery industries (IFR, 2016).

Although the raising debate in academic research and media (LaGrandeur & Hughes, 2017, Leonhard, 2016) the future of work is robots and humans working together. Robots extend the human possibilities by improving quality of work and taking over dangerous, tedious and dirty jobs, and repetitive, boredom and heavy tasks. Enhanced with AI and self-learning capabilities, general-purpose robots will become more autonomous, flexible, and cooperative. However, evolution and wider implementation of robots will bring further opportunities and challenges (Decker, Fischer, & Ott, 2017).

Big Data and Business Analytics

Adoption of Big data or advanced data analysis plays a crucial role in Industry 4.0 and the digital transformation. As outlined in the whitepaper of Fraunhofer' Institute (Otto, Juerjens, Schon, Auer, Menz, Wenzel, & Cirullis, 2016), data has changed its economic role in industry from "data as a process outcome" to "data as a process enabler" to become "data as product enabler" and finally transforming to "data as a product". This is confirmed as well by (Ylijoki & Porras, 2016), stressing on that big data has disruptive effects on firms, ecosystems and businesses, leading to emergence of new business models and value-creation mechanisms. The accumulation and integration of big data, coming from different sources is seen as a must for developing adaptive, smart, customer-oriented business models and processes. Therefore further approaches have to be developed enabling companies to integrate both data from internal processes as ERP/CRM/SCM systems, IoT sources and private clouds with industry data, social media, open government data and open public data, scientific data, partner's/ suppliers/competitor's/ecosystem data and others. Thus, the role of big data and data analysis for companies will change substantially during the stages of digital transformation, leading to further impact on industries and economy as a whole.

The main data value-driven models are based on business analytics or data analytics methodologies, aimed to analyse, predict and control processes in business and industry (Coleman, Göb, Manco, Pievatolo, Tort-Martorell, & Reis, 2016). The main three subcategories of business analytics are:

1. Descriptive analytics (summarize, condense and aggregate data from complex data sets, using graphics and aggregated statistical metrics);
2. Predictive analytics (enable forecasts of future effects based on historical data, comprising statistical learning, machine learning, data mining and knowledge discovery from databases);

3. Prescriptive analytics (transforming the results of descriptive analytics and predictive analytics into business decisions, based on optimization theory and operations research and quantitative tools) (Coleman, Göb, Manco, Pievatolo, Tort-Martorell, & Reis, 2016).

It should be outlined as well that a substantial pre-condition for any data-based models and analytics is the good data quality (Baesens, Bapna, Marsden, Vanthienen, & Zhao, 2014). For these reasons, the data-value chain should include careful procedures and oversights to ensure high data quality through all data steps: (1) initial collection; (2) storage and updating; (3) retrieval, and; (4) processing and preparation for analysis.

Augmented Reality/Virtual Reality

Implementation of Augmented reality and virtual reality technologies in Industry 4.0 context is widely discussed in the recent studies of Blanco-Novoa et al., (2018), Choi et al., (2018) and Fraga-Lamas et al., (2018). AR and VR in Industry context form a class of solutions, aiming to extend and mix both real and virtual world. Augmented reality (AR) does not describe a specific technology, but a model to virtually "extend" the reality, enriching it and merging real and digital experiences. AR allows on demand access to digital content, Internet and computational services, enhancing real-life objects, tasks and contexts. Recently Hololens, Google Glass, and Oculus Rift to name a just a few, provides new cases of AR/VR implementation, improving access to digital content, self-service and service experience. From manufacturing point of view, there are a number of advantages for implementing AR to help industrial designers to experience a product's design and operations, comparing digital mock-ups with physical mockups for efficiently finding discrepancies between them. AR can help as well to facilitate collaboration, improving communication among distributed team members in a work force. AR can include brainstorming and discussion meetings utilizing common visualization via touch screen tables, interactive digital whiteboards, shared design spaces, and distributed control rooms. The recent industry research of Reich et al., (2017) expect virtual and augmented reality to increase significantly in the next years to come.

Internet of Things

The Internet of Things (IoT) recently exploded and is defined as the backbone of the Industry 4.0 revolution (Gilchrist, 2016; Lee, Bagheri, & Kao, 2015). It refers to new forms of digital technologies, connecting physical objects and devices with sensing, computing, and communication capabilities, connecting them to form a network and making use of the collective effect of networked objects (Guo, Yu, Zhou, & Zhang, 2012). The term "Internet of Things" was coined in 1999 by Kevin Ashton from Procter and Gamble. Today, Internet of Things (IoT) is an integrated part of the Future Internet and Industry 4.0 (Luthra, Garg, Mangla, & Berwal, 2017). Atzori et al. (2010) defines three main perspectives of IoT, based on things (RFID, NFC, WSAN, WISP), on Internet (Web of things) and on Semantics (Semantic technologies). The authors further describe IoT three main tenets: 1) sensors; 2) smart connected objects, using m2m communications, and; 3) data analytics and semantic technologies. Smith (2012) further explained the potentials of IoT to transform business and social patterns.

In the context of Internet 4.0 IoT represent the dynamic network infrastructure with self configuring capabilities based on standard and interoperable communication protocols where physical and virtual 'things' have identities, physical attributes, and virtual personalities and use intelligent interfaces, and are seamlessly integrated into the information network. Furthermore, 'things' covers different objects that can take active position in business, information and social processes. They can interact and communicate among themselves and with the environment by exchanging data and information 'sensed' about the environment, while reacting autonomously to the 'real/physical world' events and influencing it by running processes that trigger actions and create services with or without direct human intervention. RFID and sensor technology enable computers to observe, to identify and understand objectivity without being biased from humans.

Additive Manufacturing (3D Printing)

Additive manufacturing (3D printing) raised in the last decade to transform to another crucial Industry 4.0 application. Muller et al. (2018) define it as a revolutionary technology both for design and for manufacturing processes, affecting all product life-cycle phases. 3D printing enable conversion of any digital file into a three dimensional physical object, built up in thin layers. The

3D printers' applications today range from food-processing models (pasta, chocolate, pizza), to fashion and jewelry, to house-building and wide range of medicine applications (personalized medicine -prosthesis, organs and pills). The materials in 3D printing largely vary, including metal, plastic, paper, food and sand. Berman (2012) makes an overview of 3D printing, highlighting his emerging economic value for companies. He compares 3D printing to other manufacturing methods, such as mass customization, injection molding or machining/subtractive technologies. In many cases, 3D printing proposes cost effective solution, increasing the speed of production, limiting the waste of raw materials and reduction the need for distributing workload in low-wage countries. 3D printing technologies are largely automated and based on CAD software that doesn't require further specialized work.

Berman (2012) identifies 3 main phases for 3D printing implementation. The first stage includes rapid prototyping and bridge manufacturing, where 3D models are used to improve the design and development of mass products in companies. The second stage is for final product manufacturing, which is expected to reach about 50% of the market in 2020 ("3D Printing: The Printed World," 2010). The last stage consists of end-user manufacturing, where users will own and produce products in their homes, using pre-programmed or customized paid or open patterns. Berman states that when the price of the 3D printers becomes around USD 300, then it will enter the consumer market. Therefore, it can be expected that 3D printing can lead to a personal fabrication (Fab) revolution. It was defined by prof. Gershenfeld from MIT in his influential book "How to make almost everything". Fab Revolution describes the transfer of the digital revolution to the real world. This trend has been largely analyzed by Gershenfeld (2012). Some of the main trends resulting from 3D printing evolution, identified by the recent reports of Explaining the future®, are as follows:

- **Decentralized Production:** Anyone can now become a producer or a part of production process.
- **Mass Customization:** Using the advantages of mass production and meeting the customers' growing needs for personalization of products.
- **Product Hacking:** The need to protect digital data and making systems that cannot simply be "hacked", and prevent products to be copied, modified and reproduced (as today - digital content).
- **Home Fadding:** 3D printers are becoming more and more affordable and thus product production is therefore shifted from factories to people's home desktops (desktop manufacturing).

Birchnell and Urry (2013) discuss several scenarios based on the adoption of 3D printing technologies at home that can range from total replacement of the production facilities with 3D devices, to the situation where personal 3D printers remain partially used as in rapid prototyping.

DIGITAL DISRUPTION AS NEW PARADIGM

Disruptive Technologies and Their Economic Impact

The term "disruptive technology" as defined by Christensen (1997) refers to any technology innovation having lower cost and performance, measured by traditional criteria, but possessing higher ancillary performance. Christensen (1997) finds out that disruptive technologies may enter and expand emerging market niches, improving with time and ultimately attacking established products in their traditional markets. Nowadays existing businesses are largely threaten by digital disruption, as new technology innovations outperform business offerings. Thus disruptive technologies can make substantial difference as unseen competitors from other industries can become a real menace overnight. Digital disruption technologies can transform not only the way products are designed and manufactured, but they will influence the customers' expectations and further company transformation models. However, the recent research of Coccia (2017) comes to show that even when new entrants on the market can generate disruptive technologies, their wider diffusion and success depends on market and economic barriers. Furthermore, the author proves that larger industrial changes are driven not by disruptive technologies, but by disruptive companies (Coccia, 2017).

Digitization, as a social process, refers to the transformation of the techno-economic environment and socio-institutional operations through digital communications and applications. Digitization builds on the evolution of: network access technologies (mobile or fixed broadband networks), semiconductor technologies (computers/laptops, wireless devices/tablets), software engineering (increased functionality of operating systems) and the spillover effects resulting from their use (common platforms for application development, electronic delivery of government services, electronic commerce, social networks, and availability of online information in fora, blogs and portals). Disruptive technology trends have a larger impact not only on production and logistic processes but also on political and economic processes. As it focuses on localization, adaptation and customization in local production-delivering facilities, based on universal raw materials it will further affect the complex supply-chain. At the same time, "dehumanization" of the service sector increases, and thus customers will soon rarely find a real person, but increasingly will need to interact with different types of kiosks, vending machines, cash-management and universal service desks, specialized service robots or automated and computerized smart objects.

Transformed Value Adding Models

New technologies decrease the overall production and transaction costs in companies and in economy as a whole. They improve quality and product customization, logistic chain, inventory management and resource use. As customers increasingly prefer online and e-commerce services, firms have to further digitize their product offerings, limiting physical presence and operating with little inventory. Digital transformation requires better personalization and active involvement of the end-users in the process of value-co-creation. Improving manufacturing models and adapting its business processes and applications to the end-users requirements, they can bring new technologies to the end users, providing them with customized design applications (CAD-CAM), best practices, tutorials and patterns, facilitating their DIY efforts and supporting them with professional advice and expertise.

- **ICT Infrastructure and E-Business Architecture in Companies:** While in traditional e-business models, company data base systems are accessed by different application software packages (as ERP, CRM, SCM, BI and others). It can be expected that in the new realms, IoT and embedded technologies will provide the basic communication layer functionality, providing better options for collecting and analysis of real-time data. The contact with customers should increasingly personalize, including various interaction models and automated platforms. Therefore, the points of contact should be transformed to value-formation models, better adapting to personal and customized experience. Further automation and AI applications can define new patterns, facilitating autonomous decision-making and functioning in context-related situations.

- **Changed Manufacturing Models:** It can be expected that the overall production costs will decrease because of the introduction of new technologies, improving quality, logistic models, inventory and resource usage (robotics, 3D printing, complex automated systems and others). For example, 3-D printing has many advantages comparing to other manufacturing methods, as for example mass customization, injection molding or machining/subtractive technologies (Berman, 2012). Therefore it will definitely change the life-cycle design, production and usage of products and services.
- **Experience-Oriented Services:** The ubiquitous technology development will lead to more automated and technology-enabled services and self-services. Improving customer experiences, and value co-creation will lead companies to transform its value-adding mechanisms. The new emerging technologies as AR/VR and IoT will soon provide more context-based information and advices, contextualized in space, time, and customer preferences. In these realms the self-services will play an increasing role, as users will be able to customize their own experience by adding new digital layers to their activities. For example with the immersive technologies users can enrich their experiences while playing a sport, travelling, or working. Moreover, new complex product-service packs will intensify the self-service model, exploring new ways of service use and conception.
- **The Future of Work and Digital Skills:** The wide adoption of smart technology solutions will change the labor markets demands. Historically, implementation of new technologies and innovations initially results in a social price due to the changing labor needs (Kaplan, 2015). With new emerging technologies, AI, smart devices and robots, the company performance will be further improved due to optimization of internal processes, better adapting to market demands. However, sophisticated technologies cannot replace humans. Creativity, adaptability, knowledge and expertise, flexibility and dreaming make people unique resource on the market. As happened in the past, new professions will soon emerge, requiring new types of qualification and expertise. In the context of changing manufacturing models and automated services, we can expect a shift toward creative and art-focused professions, requiring high-order and out-of-the-box thinking, empathy and emotional intelligence, research skills, risk taking, working in complex systems and adaptability to change. As

educational and social systems adapt slowly to the imposed market fluctuations, the society as a whole will have to wait for further economic growth. Neither politicians nor educational institutions will be able to overcome the gap on the labor market. Therefore, companies will have to lead the change, better preparing to turn technologies into business opportunities and new business offerings, successfully overcoming and minimizing the imposed social price.

During the last decades many new digital technologies emerged, smoothly implemented in the framework of the Industrial society. However, this time, in order to survive, even traditional businesses need to prepare. Companies, institutions and social organizations should prepare to new dramatic changes provoked by digital disruption. After decades of ICT technological innovations, new disruptive solutions come to change large number of products and services, organizational processes and logistic chains. For example, blockchain technologies just for few months reshaped conservative financial and insurance industry. Their revolutionary impact is fast spreading over the working styles, organizational and personal development, and social cooperation. The influence of the new technologies is fast and wide. The economy polarization and social inequalities extend. Many elements of the existing economic systems defined in the Industrial era do not respond to the current realms and need to be reevaluated and transformed.

Digital technologies will further evolve connecting wider complex and holistic smart systems as: connected homes and buildings, smart factories, farms, smart grids and entire smart cities, reconfiguring value chains and focusing on pressing problems with systems inefficiencies, climate change and resource depletion. Concurrent to this technological revolution there is a set of broader socio-economic, geopolitical and demographic developments, each interacting in multiple directions and intensifying each another (Schwab, 2016). Thus along with the new technology advances, many social issues as accumulating public debt, raising inequalities and shrinking middle class rise globally. Many authors such as Kaplan (2015), LaGrandeur and Hughes, (2017), and Leonhard (2016), point out some key issues of the new robotic era such as mass unemployment and rising inequality. The book of the futurist Gerd Leonhart "Technology versus Humanity" (2016) underlined the crucial role of new technologies implementation for deployment of possible scenarios and transformative changes ahead.

Digitalization is commonly considered as source of the next growth cycle. The main digital transformation efforts today stands for designing new social and economic systems. Industry 4.0 describes how organizations can integrate and survive. Digitalization is for country positioning and capacity to follow the fast-changing environment. New technologies not only converge the digital and physical space, but more importantly, they provide competitive advantages for lock-in and path-dependency effects for the future. However, there still lack convincing proofs of concepts and economic effects such as real use cases, sustainable business models and stable economic returns. The economic value of digital investments is hard to be measured with key economic and performance indicators. Even the success rate of rising entrepreneurship, boosting digital startups and the number of innovative projects is not persuasive. Currently, even leading Industry 4.0 promoters cannot provide convincing evidences and practical insignts but only general visions and recommendations (Hermann, Pentek, & Otto, 2016). The achieved results largely differ from expectations. For example, the public effect of wide scale initiatives such as open data (opening the government data to the public) remain inefficient and lower than expected. Therefore, it has to be recognized that all interest for digitalization actually do not rely on economic performance, nor on evidences for new employment prospects or economic growth. Neither people discuss their capacity to improve productivity and to boost efficiency in science development, environmental protection or poverty alleviation.

That is why we can conclude that digital technologies such as new "tools", "instruments" and "solutions" are just marginal part of the political and public discourse. Digitalization and widely adoption of digital technologies, Industry 4.0 or smart factories serve today as new political ideology, rising concerns and preparing wider social processes and transformations.

CONCLUSION

Disruptive technologies are gradually changing our society and its economic paradigms, requiring individuals, companies and social institutions to adjust and adapt. On one side, it is expected that the Fourth Industrial revolution will soon provide more intelligent and smart, upgraded and modernized products and services. On the other side, it will take time and efforts as companies and individuals are still not prepared. In order that companies redefine their business models, adopt new technologies and reorganize its value-offering with digital services, they have to learn, to experiment and adjust. New disruptive technologies theoretically propose many opportunities. However, the literature review shows that there still miss practical and theoretical knowledge. Therefore, we will have to fill the gaps, experimenting with new technology approaches and value offerings.

In conclusion, digital transformation is a complex issue, consisting of different aspects such as adoption of new digital strategy (digital transformation vision), framework (operational backbone), ecosystem approach and adoption of open environment for experiments. While sophisticated technologies could not replace human labor, next-generation workers will have to cope with increasing social complexity. Only creativity, adaptability, knowledge discovery and expertise, flexibility and dreaming can make people prepared and aware how to turn technologies into business opportunities, successfully overcoming and minimizing the imposed social price.

REFERENCES

Agah, A., Cabibihan, J. J., Howard, A. M., Salichs, M. A., & He, H. (Eds.). (2016). *Social Robotics: 8th International Conference, ICSR 2016 Proceedings (Vol. 9979)*. Springer.

Almada-Lobo, F. (2016). The Industry 4.0 revolution and the future of manufacturing execution systems (MES). *Journal of Innovation Management*, *3*(4), 16–21.

Atzori, L., Iera, A., & Morabito, G. (2010). The internet of things: A survey. *Computer Networks*, *54*(15), 2787–2805. doi:10.1016/j.comnet.2010.05.010

Baesens, B., Bapna, R., Marsden, J. R., Vanthienen, J., & Zhao, J. L. (2014). Transformational issues of big data and analytics in networked business. *Management Information Systems Quarterly*, *38*(2), 629–631.

Barile, N., & Sugiyama, S. (2015). The automation of taste: A theoretical exploration of mobile ICTs and social robots in the context of music consumption. *International Journal of Social Robotics*, *7*(3), 407–416. doi:10.100712369-015-0283-1

Bartodziej, C. J. (2016). *The Concept Industry 4.0: An Empirical Analysis of Technologies and Applications in Production Logistics*. Springer.

Birtchnell, T., & Urry, J. (2013). Fabricating futures and the movement of objects. *Mobilities*, *8*(3), 388–405. doi:10.1080/17450101.2012.745697

Blanco-Novoa, Ó., Fernández-Caramés, T. M., Fraga-Lamas, P., & Vilar-Montesinos, M. A. (2018). A Practical Evaluation of Commercial Industrial Augmented Reality Systems in an Industry 4.0 Shipyard. *IEEE Access: Practical Innovations, Open Solutions*, *6*, 8201–8218. doi:10.1109/ACCESS.2018.2802699

Brettel, M., Friederichsen, N., Keller, M., & Rosenberg, M. (2014). How virtualization, decentralization and network building change the manufacturing landscape: An industry 4.0 perspective. International Journal of Mechanical. *Industrial Science and Engineering*, *8*(1), 37–44.

Brynjolfsson, E., McAfee, A., & Jurvetson, S. (2015). Open Letter on the Digital Economy. *MIT Technology Review*. Available on: http://openletteronthedigitaleconomy.org/

Choi, S., Jung, K., & Noh, S. D. (2015). Virtual reality applications in manufacturing industries: Past research, present findings, and future directions. *Concurrent Engineering*, *23*(1), 40–63. doi:10.1177/1063293X14568814

Christensen, C. (1997). *The Innovator's Dilemma: When New Technologies Cause Great Firms to Fail.* Boston, MA: Harvard Business School Press.

Coccia, M. (2018). Disruptive Firms and Technological Change. *Journal of Economic and Social Thought*, *4*(4), 437–450.

Coleman, S., Göb, R., Manco, G., Pievatolo, A., Tort-Martorell, X., & Reis, M. S. (2016). How can SMEs benefit from big data? Challenges and a path forward. *Quality and Reliability Engineering International*, *32*(6), 2151–2164. doi:10.1002/qre.2008

Decker, M., Fischer, M., & Ott, I. (2017). Service robotics and human labor: A first technology assessment of substitution and cooperation. *Robotics and Autonomous Systems*, *87*, 348–354. doi:10.1016/j.robot.2016.09.017

EOP. (2016). *Artificial Intelligence, Automation and the Economy*. Accessed on https://obamawhitehouse.archives.gov/sites/whitehouse.gov/files/documents/Artificial-Intelligence-Automation-Economy.PDF

Fraga-Lamas, P., Fernández-Caramés, T. M., Blanco-Novoa, Ó., & Vilar-Montesinos, M. (2018). A Review on Industrial Augmented Reality Systems for the Industry 4.0 Shipyard. *IEEE Access*.

Gawer, A., & Cusumano, M. A. (2014). Industry platforms and ecosystem innovation. *Journal of Product Innovation Management, 31*(3), 417–433. doi:10.1111/jpim.12105

Gershenfeld, N. (2012). How to make almost anything: The digital fabrication revolution. *Foreign Affairs*, 43–57.

Gilchrist, A. (2016). *Industry 4.0: the industrial internet of things*. Apress. doi:10.1007/978-1-4842-2047-4

Gladden, M. E. (2015). Cryptocurrency with a conscience: Using artificial intelligence to develop money that advances human ethical values. Annales. *Ethics in Economic Life, 18*(4), 85–98

Graetz, G., & Michaels, G. (2015). *Robots at Work*. IZA Discussion Paper No. 8938. Available at SSRN: https://ssrn.com/abstract=2589780

Guo, B., Yu, Z., Zhou, X., & Zhang, D. (2012, May). Opportunistic IoT: Exploring the social side of the internet of things. In *Computer Supported Cooperative Work in Design (CSCWD), 2012 IEEE 16th International Conference on* (pp. 925-929). IEEE.

Hayes, A. S. (2017). Cryptocurrency value formation: An empirical study leading to a cost of production model for valuing bitcoin. *Telematics and Informatics, 34*(7), 1308–1321. doi:10.1016/j.tele.2016.05.005

Hermann, M., Pentek, T., & Otto, B. (2016, January). Design principles for industrie 4.0 scenarios. In *System Sciences (HICSS), 2016 49th Hawaii International Conference on* (pp. 3928-3937). IEEE.

IFR. (2016). *The World Robotics Report 2016*. Available on https://ifr.org/ifr-press-releases/news/world-robotics-report-2016

Ivanov, S. (2016). Will robots substitute teachers? Conference proceedings, 29 June 2016, Varna, University of Management, Bulgaria. *Yearbook of Varna University of Management, 9*, 42-47.

Ivanov, S. H., & Webster, C. (2017). The robot as a consumer: a research agenda. In *Conference proceedings June 2017*. University of Economics.

Kagermann, H., Helbig, J., Hellinger, A., & Wahlster, W. (2013). *Recommendations for implementing the strategic initiative INDUSTRIE 4.0: Securing the future of German manufacturing industry; final report of the Industrie 4.0 Working Group*. Forschungsunion.

Katz, R., Koutroumpis, P., & Martin Callorda, F. (2014). Using a digitization index to measure the economic and social impact of digital agendas. *Info, 16*(1), 32-44.

Korpela, K., Hallikas, J., & Dahlberg, T. (2017, January). Digital Supply Chain Transformation toward Blockchain Integration. *Proceedings of the 50th Hawaii International Conference on System Sciences*. 10.24251/HICSS.2017.506

LaGrandeur, K., & Hughes, J. J. (Eds.). (2017). *Surviving the Machine Age: Intelligent Technology and the Transformation of Human Work*. Springer. doi:10.1007/978-3-319-51165-8

Lansky, J. (2018). Possible State Approaches to Cryptocurrencies. *Journal of Systems Integration, 9*(1), 19–31. doi:10.20470/jsi.v9i1.335

Lee, J., Bagheri, B., & Kao, H. A. (2015). A cyber-physical systems architecture for industry 4.0-based manufacturing systems. *Manufacturing Letters, 3*, 18–23. doi:10.1016/j.mfglet.2014.12.001

Leonhard, G. (2016). *Technology vs Humanity*. Fast Future Publishing Ltd.

Luthra, S., Garg, D., Mangla, S. K., & Berwal, Y. P. S. (2018). Analyzing challenges to Internet of Things (IoT) adoption and diffusion: An Indian context. *Procedia Computer Science, 125*, 733–739. doi:10.1016/j.procs.2017.12.094

Majeed, A. A., & Rupasinghe, T. D. (2017). Internet of things (IoT) embedded future supply chains for industry 4.0: An assessment from an ERP-based fashion apparel and footwear industry. *International Journal of Supply Chain Management, 6*(1), 25–40.

Maurer, M., Gerdes, J. C., Lenz, B., & Winner, H. (2016). *Autonomous driving*. Berlin, Germany: Springer Berlin Heidelberg. doi:10.1007/978-3-662-48847-8

Monostori, L. (2014). Cyber-physical production systems: Roots, expectations and R&D challenges. *Procedia CIRP, 17*, 9–13. doi:10.1016/j.procir.2014.03.115

Mosterman, P. J., & Zander, J. (2016). Industry 4.0 as a Cyber-Physical System study. *Software & Systems Modeling, 15*(1), 17–29. doi:10.100710270-015-0493-x

Müller, J. R., Panarotto, M., Malmqvist, J., & Isaksson, O. (2018). Lifecycle design and management of additive manufacturing technologies. *Procedia Manufacturing*, *19*, 135–142. doi:10.1016/j.promfg.2018.01.019

Nam, T., & Pardo, T. A. (2012, October). Transforming city government: a case study of Philly311. In *Proceedings of the 6th International Conference on Theory and Practice of Electronic Governance* (pp. 310-319). ACM. 10.1145/2463728.2463787

Neapolitan, R. E., & Jiang, X. (2012). *Contemporary artificial intelligence*. CRC Press.

Otto, B., Juerjens, J., Schon, J., Auer, S., Menz, N., Wenzel, S., & Cirullis, J. (2016). *Industrial Data Spaces*. Fraunhofer Institute whitepaper. Available on: https://www.fraunhofer.de/content/dam/zv/en/fields-of-research/industrial-data-space/whitepaper-industrial-data-space-eng.pdf

Pfeiffer, S. (2016). Robots, Industry 4.0 and humans, or why assembly work is more than routine work. *Societies (Basel, Switzerland)*, *6*(2), 16. doi:10.3390oc6020016

Reed, B. (2014). *Bill Gates: Yes, robots really are about to take your jobs, in media, BGR.* Accessed on 2018 on http://bgr.com/2014/03/14/bill-gates-interview-robots/

Reich, A., Gleich, R., & Sauter, R. (2017). *Study report, Technology Trends for Industry 4.0.* Available on https://cn.bcsoa.it/wp-content/uploads/sites/114/2017/08/170713_Study-report-Tech-Trends-Industrie40_eng.pdf

Rose. (Ed.). (2016). The Fourth Industrial Revolution: A Davos Reader. *Foreign Affairs.*

Rüßmann, M., Lorenz, M., Gerbert, P., Waldner, M., Justus, J., Engel, P., & Harnisch, M. (2015). Industry 4.0: The future of productivity and growth in manufacturing industries. Boston Consulting Group, 9.

Saldivar, A. A. F., Li, Y., Chen, W. N., Zhan, Z. H., Zhang, J., & Chen, L. Y. (2015, September). Industry 4.0 with cyber-physical integration: A design and manufacture perspective. In *Automation and computing (icac), 2015 21st international conference on* (pp. 1-6). IEEE.

Schwab, K. (2016). *The Fourth Industrial Revolution.* Crown Business.

Sirkin, H. L., Zinser, M., & Rose, J. (2015). Why advanced manufacturing will boost productivity. Boston Consulting Group, 2.

Smith, I. G. (2012). *The Internet of Things 2012 New Horizons*. Halifax: IERC.

Sommer, L. (2015). Industrial revolution-industry 4.0: Are German manufacturing SMEs the first victims of this revolution? *Journal of Industrial Engineering and Management*, *8*(5), 1512. doi:10.3926/jiem.1470

Sovbetov, Y. (2018). Factors Influencing Cryptocurrency Prices: Evidence from Bitcoin, Ethereum, Dash, Litcoin, and Monero. *Journal of Economics and Financial Analysis*, *2*(2), 1–27.

Strange, R., & Zucchella, A. (2017). Industry 4.0, global value chains and international business. *Multinational Business Review*, *25*(3), 174–184. doi:10.1108/MBR-05-2017-0028

Tiihonen, J., & Felfernig, A. (2017). An introduction to personalization and mass customization. *Journal of Intelligent Information Systems*, *49*(1), 1–7. doi:10.100710844-017-0465-4

Trautman, L. J. (2014). *Virtual currencies; Bitcoin & what now after Liberty Reserve, Silk Road, and Mt. Gox?* Retrieved from http://jolt.richmond.edu/v20i4/article13.pdf

Wang, S., Wan, J., Li, D., & Zhang, C. (2016). Implementing smart factory of industrie 4.0: An outlook. *International Journal of Distributed Sensor Networks*, *12*(1), 3159805. doi:10.1155/2016/3159805

Williams, J. (n.d.). *Will robots take our children' jobs*. Available on https://www.nytimes.com/2017/12/11/style/robots-jobs-children.html

Ylijoki, O., & Porras, J. (2016). Perspectives to definition of big data: A mapping study and discussion. *Journal of Innovation Management*, *4*(1), 69–91.

Chapter 2
Why Institutions Matter

ABSTRACT

Institutions play a crucial role both on an individual and on a societal level. Many of the personal life choices as well as the decision making on an organizational level and the development of the society as a whole are functions of various institutional arrangements. In the second chapter, the author defines institutions and their characteristics, elements, and functions. By analyzing the complex framework of institutional settings and rules, the author further points out what makes institutions a unique human achievement and why understanding of their functions will be crucial for the defining path ahead. Further, an overview of the rules and regulations sum up their functions as main ingredients of the social interactions. The last part proposes an in-depth study and analysis of the mechanisms by which new technologies influence institutional settings.

INTRODUCTION

Institutions matter. Individuals are social creatures. Every person is born in a specific social context, predefining a large part of his personal choices and social standings. Family, nationality, religion, language and culture take important role for building stereotypes and mind models, affecting later individual choices and life-arrangements. Even more, individual' life often reproduce specific patterns, cultural traditions and norms, embedded deeper in his personal cognitive schemata. Recent authors as Thibaut (2017), Triandis (2018) come again to study social psychology in the groups, highlighting

DOI: 10.4018/978-1-5225-6270-2.ch002

how social groups and its norms determine specific social reality, influencing individuals' actions, decisions and social standings. Social psychology and group dynamic processes determine not only personal, but also organizational success (Katz & Kahn, 1978). That is how institutional settings define many of the social rules and enable individuals to live together in a complex social network of relationships. All formal and informal rules and norms actually aim to facilitate human and organizational behavior, providing a degree of stability and predictability of social interactions. By determining the framework of social interactions, institutions enable individuals to reduce uncertainty and to work together in order to resolve many complex natural and social problems. Cooperation strategies allow social agents to combine their efforts, resources and competences in order to achieve specific goals and to transform the physical reality. By applying innovative solutions, instruments, technologies and knowledge individuals push constantly the limits of the physical constraints. However, how these achievements will influence social realms in the next years to come?

During the last century, institutions became subject of research from different perspectives, bringing contributions of hundreds of scholars. For example, from political perspective, Peters (2011) resumes the following institutional schools of thought, ranging from Old and New Institutionalism to Normative Institutionalism, Historical Institutionalism, Empirical Institutionalism, Discursive and Constructivist Institutionalism, Sociological Institutionalism and International Institutionalism. The economic perspective reveal the concepts of Old and New Institutional Economics (Mirowsky, 1988; Hodgson, 1988). The social perspective enrich understanding of institutional theories' implication in organizations (Meyer, 2008). All these insights show the various interdisciplinary aspects of institutional research, focusing on micro and macro dynamics of institutional frameworks and proposing complex models and methodologies for its improvement. However, the current level of institutional rules, norms and social agreements are far from optimal in its function to protect the social interest and to serve for communities' sustainable development (Olstrom, 2015). The world today suffers from multiple crisis and many social systems operate in discordance. There still lack a common understanding how to act together and to cooperate for achieving common global goals, like for example the UN Global Sustainable Goals (Sacks, 2012). Grave environmental crisis and climate change issues, raising social disintegration, populism, inequality and war prospects are again among the key topics of discussion. Uncertainty for the future accumulate and many scenarios in the popular culture nurture fears for machine invasion and utopia.

However, at the end of the day, it is upon us to figure out and design the next social realms. In this particular moment of fast changing technology *possibilities,* we need to reconsider what kind of institutions we need for the future.

The present chapter aims to introduce the basic definitions for institutions and to discuss their main characteristics and roles. By analyzing the framework of institutional settings, we will further point out what makes institutions unique human achievement and why understanding of their functions will be crucial for later survival. Further, it will provide an overview of the rules as the main ingredients of the social interactions. The last part will propose an in-depth study of the mechanisms by which new technologies influence institutional settings. The next two chapters will focus on institutional transformation. The incremental and evolutionary types of institutional change will be discussed in details in chapter three, and the revolutionary institutional transformations will be analyzed in chapter four.

Institutions are closely related to the human evolution and to the formation of complex human society. In the seminal works of the anthropologists Richardson and Boyd (1999; 2001; 2009) can be identified the processes of early social evolution and the emergence of complex institutions. The scholars trace the evolution of institutions back to the Pleistocene-Holocene transition and the development of the agricultural society (11 500 years – 8 000 years before J.C.). According to them, both biological and social factors - the *coevolution of genes and culture* allowed humans to adapt psychologically to live in social groups and social systems. Richardson and Boyd (2001) point out that institutions came as social innovation, following evolutionary trajectory from small-scale, egalitarian groups of hunters and gatherers to large-scale complex agrarian societies with stratification and hierarchical political systems, attaining large-scale cooperation and division of labor. Thus, emergence of agriculture as main economic source provoked the general need of division of labor, specialization and identification of more structured social roles. Making a detailed analysis of the main contemporary anthropologist, biological and social theories, the authors conclude that individual (and biological) instincts became the building blocks of the formed group culture. Moreover, sustainable institutions historically outperformed the pure forms of coercion, hierarchy nesting of social units of command and control and most often tried to combine acceptable social culture based on complex social symbolic systems.

DEFINING INSTITUTIONS

Institutions can be generally defined as *complex social structures or complex social systems*. Many scholars use the term *institutions* to designate both their evolution and functioning as complex socio-politico-economic and cultural phenomena. Institutions generally dominate the social interactions between the individual and the group (Commons, 1924). From a very small human group representing the family, to more complex social, political and economic groups, institutions shape the society and define individual choices, individual behavior and therefore individual life and individual fate. Thus, before defining in details the complex term "institution", we will analyze some more general concepts about institutions and the social aspects of economic relationships.

While researchers still try to find the best definition for the complex term "institution", the intersection point between them is that institutions in general determine "the rules for living together". Therefore institutions can be widely defined by the capacity of setting rules and designating the roles and functions of individuals and organizations within a social group. Stated differently, society represents "an agglomeration of institutions" (Berger & Luckmann, 1966).

Some of the popular definitions of institutions state that "it's collective action in control of individual action" (Commons, 1924). Thus, Commons underline that institutions represent a collective action exercised by different types of organization such as the family, the corporation, the trade union, and the state in control of individual action. Richardson and Boyd (2001) define institutions as *customary rules of behavior that have the effect of creating sociopolitical structures serving collective functions*. Other authors as Streek and Thalen (2004) define institutions as the "building blocks" of the social order: they represent socially sanctioned (or collectively enforced) expectations with respect to the behavior of specific categories of actors or to the performance of certain activities. Institutions provide *regulative, normative and cultural-cognitive elements that, together with associated activities and resources, provide stability and meaning to social life* (Scott, 2008). Further, institutions define standard solutions for collective problems. Institutions are *relatively widely diffused practices, technologies, or rules that have become entrenched in the sense that it is costly to choose other practices, technologies, or rules* (Lawrence, Hardy & Phillips 2002). Typically institutions involve mutually related rights and obligations for actors, distinguishing between appropriate and inappropriate, 'right' and 'wrong', 'possible' and 'impossible' actions and thereby organizing behavior into predictable and reliable patterns. North (1991) states that institutions are "humanly devised constraints that structure political, economic, and social interactions [consisting of] informal constraints (sanctions, taboos, customs, traditions, and codes of conduct), and formal rules (constitutions, laws, property rights)". Thus, institutions determine the "rules of the game in the society" (North, 1991).

The dominance of the social aspect of human institutions is supported as well by Polanyi (1957, 46p), who underline that human economy, as a rule, is submerged in human social relationships. Therefore, the main individual interest is not in the possession of material goods but in the individual's *social standing, his social claims, his social assets*. The social and not the economic origin of the *Homo Economicus* is confirmed as well in the empirical studies of the antropologists Henrich et al., (2001). Polanyi (1957) further insists that neither the process of production nor that of distribution is linked to specific economic interests attached to the possession of goods; but every single step in that process is geared to a number of social interests, which eventually ensure that the required step be taken. Therefore, individuals and individual choices are social and thus individual actions and behaviors mainly reflect the culture of the social realm. Thus, we can state that institutions determine social rules and orders that influence and shape the individual ones.

Generally, most of the human social processes are instituted process (Polanyi, 1957). For example, economic activities emerged over time as a function of social relations in a co-evolving cultural context. Moreover, he finds out, that previously to our time,

...no economy has ever existed that, even in principle, was controlled by markets. In spite of the chorus of academic incantations so persistent in the nineteenth century, gain and profit made on exchange never before played an important part in human economy. Though the institution of the market was fairly common since the later Stone Age, its role was no more than incidental to economic life...(Polanyi, 1957).

In his work, Parto (2005) makes a detailed overview of some other definitions of institutions. Institutions have regional and geographic aspects, as they are defined as *set of conventions and rules of action prevailing in the economy, which are embedded in the local social structure and show a marked regional differentiation* (Krätke, 1999). In a more general interpretation, Coriat and Dosi (1998) view institutions as being represented by formal organizations, patterns of behaviour, and negative norms and constraints. An institution is, rather, that actors are expected to conform to it, regardless of what they would want to do on their own. Moreover, such expectations are held, not just by actors directly affected by the expected behavior, but by 'society' as a whole (Streek & Thalen, 2004).

Parto (2005) makes a summary of Scott's findings (2001) that institutions collectively act as an integrated web running through different systems (e.g., social, economic), scales of governance and levels of inter-relations. In addition, institutions are at once persistent, resistant to change while capable of changing in evolutionary time, and are transmitted through various means to consecutive generations thus providing a certain degree of continuity, stability, and security.

UNDERSTANDING INSTITUTIONS

Figuring out the complexity and ambiguity of different definitions, we will outline some of its structural elements and characteristics. Focusing more specifically on social institutions, Martin (2004) provides a general framework to study and understand their main characteristics. Defining their features, he claims that, institutions can be both discussed by what they "are" (their eminent characteristics) or by what they "do" (their positions and capacity to act, to perform a course of action in specific situation); As Barley & Tolbert (1997) prove further, institutional main feature is connected with its activities and capacity to act. Therefore, by summarizing these main concepts, there are identified the following characteristics of the institutions as presented in Table 1.

INSTITUTIONAL ELEMENTS, TYPES AND FUNCTIONS

The main difficulties for analyzing institutions result from the fact that institutions include a large set of formal and informal social organizations, complex social groups, cultural traditions, social norms and expectations (Chavance, 2001). Therefore it's a challenging task to make a general model consisting of different rules, characteristics and interdependences that influence institutions on different levels. Moreover, as Castells (2011) resumes, all institutional systems reflect power relations negotiated through a long historical process of domination and counter-domination struggles. Thus dominating

Table 1. Summary of Institutional Characteristics, based on (Martin, 2004)

	Institutions as Social Entity	Institutions as Course of Action
Social dimensions	Institutions are constituted by collectivities of people who associate with each other and, through interaction, develop recursive practices and associated meanings.	Through acting or doing, individually and collectively, group members constitute institutions. Institutions entail distinct social practices that recur, recycle, or are repeated (over time) by group members. Social institutions are reproduced in practices and are patterns of social activity that shape collective and individual experiences.
Time/location	Institutions endure/persist across extensive time and geographic space. Social institutions have temporal and space dimensions.	Over time, old institutions die out and new ones are constituted.
Embeddedness	Institutions are constituted and reconstituted by embodied agents. Institutions exist because agents and societal members with material bodies enact practices to constitute them.	Institutions have social positions and relations that are characterized by particular expectations, rules/norms and procedures. An institution entails a set of social positions that are interrelated, "make sense" and are enacted relative to each other.
Personalization/ internalization	Group members as identities internalize institutions. Group members due their positions, the practices they enact, and the positions they occupy of the institutional phenomena, acquiring personal meaning and significance.	Institutions are inconsistent, contradictory, and rife with conflict. Despite their persistence, institutions are not coherent or integrated. They entail many diverse practices, some of which conflict with others. Institutions both constrain and facilitate behavior/actions by societal/group members.
Ideologies	Institutions have a legitimating ideology that proclaims the rightness and necessity of their arrangements, practices, and social relations. Elites use ideology to legitimate and justify institutional practices and social relations.	Institutions continuously change. The interdependence of institutions means that changes in one institution "unsettle" conditions and practices in other institutions, causing disruption.
Self-and-group	Institutions and individuals mutually constitute each other; they are not separable into macro and micro phenomena. Organization per se creates power. Wherever social practices and relations are "organized," as they are in institutions, power differences and social dynamics are at play.	Institutional positions and practices allocate power, privilege and advantages to incumbents of some social positions and subordination and disadvantages to others. Power differentials are manifest in the recursive practices that orient, constrain, and facilitate members' behavior. Social positions that are highly valorized provide incumbents with power over incumbents of less valorized positions.

institutional frameworks and its role in the society is a function of long and complex socio-political, historical and economic processes.

Institutions aim to reduce risks and uncertainties in social transactions by providing "social order", "rules" and "prescriptions". All these have to structure the chaos and to set a course of action and norms giving clarity and predictability. Assuming that social agents will prefer any solution to a problem than to remain in a state of uncertainty, scholars identify that institutions' main function is to deliver solutions to complex problems, independently of their further characteristics. In this aspect, the institutional functions to distribute power, status and decision-making come as subordinate processes to the main function – to solve complex problems. From this perspective, "uncertainty" is recognized as any level of risk beyond which the efforts of the social agents for planning the future become obsolete (Dequech, 2004).

In economic terms, Coase (1937) find out that institutions enable economic agents to reduce transaction costs. Institutions and social agreement are based on the trust of the social actors, in terms of competence, efficiency and access (Bachmann & Zaheer, 2006). This way, individuals expect institutions to provide appropriate solutions for specific problems. Furthermore, Denzau and North (1994) focus on the role of institutions to provide common and shared *mental models* and to ensure development and spread of ideas, shared cognitive systems, structuring models and ideologies that enable individuals to interpret the reality and the environment. Institutions should be able as well to ensure the social sources of power, including forms of coercion, to guarantee that social agents will follow the rules and prescriptions. Thus any institutional framework (formal and informal) should first prove to be able to set appropriate rules, that will help to reduce uncertainty and make social life predictable, and second – to ensure the compliance or the protection of these rules. Another approach is to set institutions as "sets of practices" rather than sequences of individual actions. This means that individual actions can happen in a specific context, location and time, whereas "practices" involve an "invisible" quality of rules or customs that goes unnoticed if one only observes one instance of it.

Scott (2001) grouped the institutions in five main classes, analyzing the types of interactions between the social group and the individual. Thus, institutional functions can be characterized as follows (Scott, 2001):

- **Regulative:** Where the state and the society act as "inscriptors" and "proscriptors" of written and non-written "rules of the game"; (state and society toward individuals and social groups);
- **Constitutive:** As institutions set the bonds and the consistence of social relations between individuals and social groups; (individual toward individual; social group toward social group);
- **Cognitive:** Where institutions acts as "prescriptors" of mental models and socially accepted constructs or definitions; (as culture, values and knowledge); (social group toward individual);

- **Behavioral:** Institutions as standardized (recognizable) social habits; (individual toward social group);
- **Associative:** Institutions as mechanisms facilitating privileged interaction (individual member toward individual member).

All these types of institutions constitute the fabric of the society and serve as a base to realize further individual, group and social interactions. Moreover, the four basic functions of institutions can be identified as shown on Figure 1, mainly serving to: regulate individuals' behavior and relations; to prepare individuals for the society; to determine the relations between individuals and institutions; to maintain the social continuity (Scott, 2001).

Characteristics of Institutions

Institutions largely differentiates by the way of their functioning and emergence. Based on that there can be identified formal (explicit) institutions and informal or implicit institutions.

- **Formal Institutions:** Are frameworks of regulations, rules, agreements and prescriptions, assigned by official social authority.

Figure 1. Institutional functions according to Scott (2001)

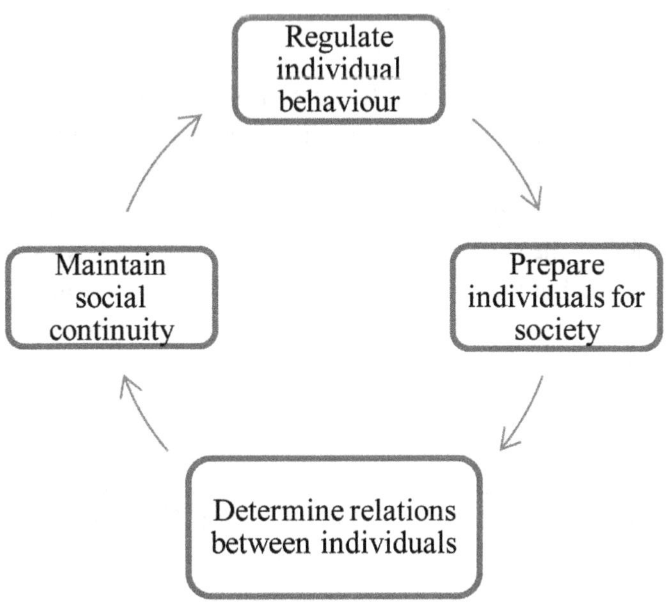

Formal institutions define both the formal rules and the mechanisms to enforce its compliance. These rules can be observable through written documents or through formal position, such as authority or ownership. Formal institutions can include explicit incentives, contractual terms, and firm boundaries as defined by equity positions (Helmke & Levitsky, 2004).

- **Informal Institutions:** Can be defined as rules, based on implicit understandings, being in most part socially derived and therefore not accessible through written documents. It is not necessarily that informal institutions are sanctioned through formal position, but they can be encouraged or protected through informal group sanctions. In general informal institutions include social norms, routines, traditions and political processes. Informal institutions are more sticky and embedded in social routines and thus they cannot be easily changed (Williamson, 2009).

Institutional Logic, Ideologies and Shared Cognitive Models

One of the key characteristics of institutions is their capacity to determine shared cognitive schemes or common institutional logic and ideologies among the social agents (Thornon & Occasio, 2008). 'Ideology' is widely discussed complex term, designating in general the main set of ideas, beliefs and concepts accepted and shared within a social group. On macro level, ideology reflects the structure of the shared beliefs and cognitive perceptions that hold together and unite one group. North (1988) defines ideology as "the societal arrangements of power and social order incorporated on a macro level". Van Djik (1998) considers ideologies as systems of ideas that are socially accepted and are associated with group interests, conflicts or struggles. Furthermore, the ideology forms the subjective perceptions that people have about what the world is like and what it ought to be (North, 1988). The ideology determines the choices and preferences of the social actors and constitutes the fabric of beliefs that justify the social order. Iyigun and Rubin (2017) state that ideologies are *shared cognitive rules that people use to interpret the world around them*. The complexity of the term "ideology" and how it relates to the "discourse" is further investigated (Purvis & Hunt, 1993; Van Dijk, 1998). Decomposing "ideology" characteristics, Gerring (1997) proposes a comprehensive definitional framework, consisting of seven elements and sub-elements (location, subject matter, subject, position, function, motivation, cognitive/affective structure). Analyzing its main characteristics, Gerring (1997) argues that the term ideology is context-dependent. Furthermore, he finds out that the core elements of the definition of ideology should include the ideas that are both "coherent" and "consistent" and that are bound together.

Historically the term "ideology" is politically loaded as it refers to various notions of power and dominance. As it determines the prevailing ideas and mental models of the specific age, it is associated with the dominance of specific ruling class (Soddart, 2007). Exploring the semantics and the origin of the term *Ideology*, the book of Van Dijk (1998) proposes an in-depth study, uncovering its historical roots and its development within sociology, philosophy and political schools. Thus, in popular culture ideologies are often used to create in-group – out-group differentiations, reflecting the "false" beliefs of the "others" (opposed to "our" truth). This shows how ideologies presuppose the socially and politically self-serving nature of the definitions of truth and falsity. Simply put, ideology is a way to publicly define what is fair or unfair. Lately, other phenomena such as social justice, group equality, moral choices and socially accepted types of behavior gain interest of the researchers. Ideology is a part of the superstructure and determines the economic or material base of the society. As the ruling class controls the means of production and reproduction of the dominant ideas in the politics, media, literature and education, it has the instruments to make their ideologies more or less accepted as undisputed knowledge (Van Djik, 1998). That is why, the contemporary approaches of studying ideologies stress on the link between the discourse and the cognition, which is a form of explicit ideology that is expressed and reproduced in the society.

Ideologies combine both individual and groups ideas and serve *as guiding principles for explaining the world (North, 2005).* The subjective perceptions (ideas, mental models, theories) that people use to explain the world, allow them to avoid rethinking the same situations and problems again. The shared beliefs and values in the group gradually evolve and converge (Rokeach, 2008). Later these shared values and beliefs spread to determine the norms, behaviors, boundaries, and subordinance between norms and regulations. That is how in the model of North (2005), individual and group *beliefs* are the founding elements of the ideologies and they precede the emergence of institutions. According to his model, the pattern of evolution follows the spiral "beliefs - institutions - organizations - politics - economic results". Furthermore, North (2005) concludes that disconnection of the ideologies and shared beliefs of the different social groups leads to the need to emergence of new formal institutions (rules) in order to structure and reconnect. This leads to additional costs for their observance and enforcement.

The emergence of ideologies is considered to be endogenous, reflecting technological, economic and institutional development of the society. However, it is important to highlight that ideologies are "sticky", they are difficult to transform and they need time to evolve and to allow social agents to adapt and to resume the changing social reality. In the same time, the shifts and changes of ideologies on macro level deeply influence the ideas and beliefs on interpersonal, intrapersonal and intergroup level (Nafstad, Blakar, Carlquist, Phelps, & Rand-Hendriksen, 2007). Further Iyigun and Rubin (2017) find out that ideologies slowly react on abrupt changes such as new technologies' wider implementation.

Institutional Rules

As institutions constitute the fabric of the society, they organize individual, group and social interactions through various set of rules, norms and regulations. The social rules can be generally defined as a prescription or ban for social action in certain circumstances, accompanied by sanctions or rewards (real or symbolic) (Chavance, 2001). Institutionalized rules are classifications built into society as "reciprocated typifications or interpretations" (Berger & Luckmann, 1966). Institutionalization involves the process by which social processes, obligations, or actualities come to take rule-like status in social thought and action (Meyer & Rowan, 1977). Institutional rules may be taken for granted or supported by public opinion or the force of law. That is how all institutions take part in defining some rules for expected social behavior and social norms.

Institutional rules differ from organizational rules, in that they subordinate them. Working rules guarantee that the group performs the actions as expected. Regulations determine what individuals can do and what they cannot do. The rules, norms and regulations rank in a specific hierarchy of rules, comprising four general levels – economic system, formal institutions, organizational rules and finally individual behavior (Chavance, 2001).

Analyzing the processes in the hierarchy of rules, Chavance (2001) set up that in stationary (stable situation), individual behavior is determined by organizational and institutional frameworks, organizations are formed and evolve within the institutional framework, and institutions are established and stabilized within the system, i.e. with a configuration of general rules. This means that when environment is stable and predictable, institutions largely influence the social development. On opposite, in the evolutionary process, the rules act on an opposite direction, as modification of individual and collective behavior leads to organizational or institutional change, further transforming organizational actions that lead to changes in the institutional framework, and institutional mutations cause the evolution, or the transformation of the economic system. Between the two polar representations of the stationary process and the reverse line, lie countless interactions, which constitute the real, historical evolutionary movement. The stationary levels hierarchy becomes a hierarchy tangled in the evolutionary process, and simple causality becomes a circular, complex and cumulative causation.

There can be identified three main functions of institutional rules (Chavance, 2001), as displayed on Figure 2: coordination function (giving instructions for coordinating activities of different agents), political function (providing regulations of power dimensions) and cognitive function (delivering instructions and limiting uncertainty).

First, institutional and organizational rules play a considerable role to coordinate complex relationships based on a division of labor (and therefore of knowledge), which is marked by both interdependence and relative autonomy of the actors (individuals and organizations). Coordination should be interpreted as a continuous and open, scalable and precarious process. Moreover, institutional rules have the function to regulate potential or existing

Figure 2. The main functions of institutional rules (Chavance, 2001)

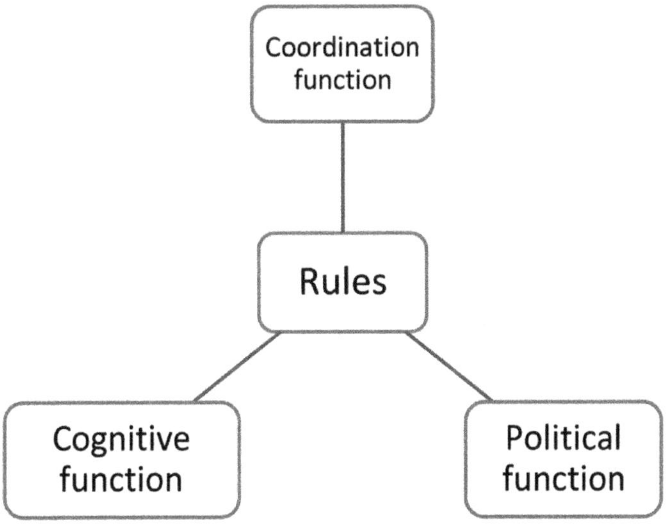

conflicts based on the existing power relationships and this explains its political functions. Finally, institutional rules help to reduce uncertainty and thus institutional rules serve to inform individuals and social agents about the expected and accepted social behavior and action.

On the other hand Scott (1995) distinguishes three rules' dimensions or three rule 'pillars': regulative rules (regulated by the state and by the legal framework), normative rules (as social values and social norms) and cognitive rules (or the way knowledge is codified and transferred in symbols or technologies). Further, rules do not exist as single autonomous entities, but they are linked together into rule systems. Rule systems may be purely private rule or 'personality system' or they may be collectively shared systems. Social rule systems, which structure and regulate social transactions and which are backed by social sanctions and networks of control, are referred to as rule regimes, as the sets of rules are linked together in a way that it is difficult to change one rule, without altering others. The alignment between rules gives a regime stability, and 'strength' to coordinate activities.

In summary, there are outlined the following statements for any institutional framework:

- Institutions are determined by rules and by systems of sanctions. Both the rules and the form of its control represent compulsory elements of any institution.
- Institutions determine processes, regulations and procedures to solve complex social problems and to set appropriate norms of behavior, reducing uncertainty and cognitive overload of the social agents. Institutions have instruments to encourage or to sanction specific behaviors, and to influence economic output.
- Institutions are stable structures, even subject to perpetual changes. While rules can evolve and change in order to respond better to the evolving needs of the environment, the authority of institutions remain stable under specific context.
- Both formal and informal institutions have to serve as instruments to decrease uncertainty in the social groups. Institutions provide instruments and models to reproduce the social order through different social mechanisms such as shared cognitive models for resuming the world (ideologies), commonly accepted rules (regulations) and socially accepted forms of coercion.
- Institutions are subject to different agency problems as any other social structures, such as lock-in factors, sink costs, and path dependence.

TECHNOLOGY INNOVATIONS AND INSTITUTIONAL SETTINGS

It is interesting to analyze how implementation of new technologies and innovations influence institutional settings and existing rules. Technologies are usually considered as exogenous factors to the socio-economic and political systems. In general, they influence economic performance as production efficiency, organizational competitiveness and wealth generation. However, it is important to recognize when technology innovations can lead not only to economic growth but as well to institutional transformation and social change. While institutional change will be discussed in details in chapters three and four, in the following sections we will focus more specifically on incremental technology changes. Analyzing how new technology factors influence institutional setting of rules, there will be discussed constitutive, regulative and cognitive perspectives.

Constitutive Perspective

Analyzing the constitutive role, or the functions of institutions to impose coordination and regulation actions among different actors, we can state that informal bottom-up institutions, such as associations, agents' network or formal cooperation such as clusters will lead the role when a new sector is formed. In order to constitute a new technology paradigm, social actors with substantial interests and up-front investments will mobilize appropriate economic, political and power resources to activate necessary support networks and alliances. Thus in many cases the political dominance, rather than economic or technology performance can determine further implementation and wider spreading of specific innovations, new technologies or new standards. Actually, new technologies create path dependences, lock-in and sunk costs. Thus constitutive function of institutions should on one hand support and encourage standardization, unification and new technology innovations, but on the other hand it should keep the potential for other actors to come later on in the sector, ensuring enough social mechanisms to protect competition and market dynamics.

Regulative Perspective

From regulative perspective, institutions need to constitute gradually the new "rules of the game", providing rules, regulations and prescription for the appropriate use of new technologies. With new technologies, there emerge new social, organizational and individual challenges, posing ethical questions and raising many problems concerning new rights and obligations and its further protection. Just to mention some examples, we can identify computer crimes and regulations, individual privacy (and the protection of individual rights), individual freedom and others. Laudon and Laudon (2014) identified five main groups of issues that have to be applied on individual, social and political level, that have to regulate new technologies. As showed on Figure 3, these include information rights and obligations (what can and cannot be done), property rights and obligations (IPR issues), accountability and control (who pays the costs of not functioning systems, computer crimes and attacks), system quality (social expectations of high-performing technologies), and quality of life (on individual, social and political level). Thus Laudon and Laudon (2014) define a complex set of problems, organized on these three main levels – ethical, social and political, that have to be constantly reviewed and focused when considering emergence of new technologies (Figure 3).

One of the biggest concerns with regulative function of institutions is that new technologies advances cannot be regulated on the up-front basis. For example, it is not possible to regulate the right action of using a drone, when technology issues and standards of operations are still under consideration and when technology norms still do not exists. Thus initially new technologies work in a regulation vacuum, imposing many ethical, social and political concerns. This allows companies and business organizations to profit from this regulative vacuum. Therefore, the regulative role of institutions becomes especially important both to encourage the economic progress and on the other hand to protect the public interest.

Some other problems related with the regulative function of institutions include geographical limitation of normative acts while new technologies will work in a global perspective, neglecting or outperforming some of the national rules and regulations. Thus as technology innovations accelerate, institutions will have to adapt in defining what is "right and wrong".

Figure 3. New technologies impact on ethical, social and political perspective (Laudon & Laudon, 2014)

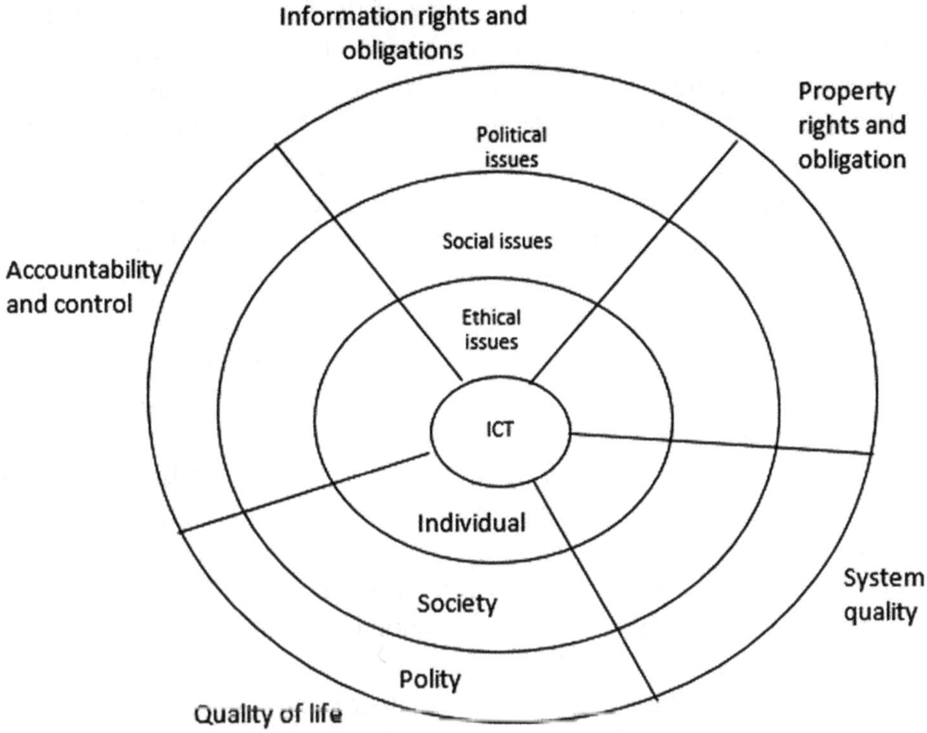

Cognitive and Behavioral Perspective

New technologies largely challenge the role of institutions to set cognitive and behavioral rules and perspectives. While traditional institutions as universities, research centers, government institutions, public systems and others still produce and distribute relevant information and knowledge, new trends and new technologies largely change their impact. First, new technologies usually decentralize knowledge processes, changing the opportunities to access, share and produce new information and knowledge. Second, from cognitive perspective, institutions lose their key instruments to impose "acceptable" mental models and to be the relevant source of "solutions" for raising uncertainties.

CONCLUSION

While institutions determine the capacity of the society to solve complex problems, their roles and positions are "pre-defined" and locked-in in the socio-technical context of the Industrial era. Human institutions on national and international level as a whole are far from reaching common agreement on different important problems of common interest such as climate change, raising waste, biodiversity conservation, natural ecosystem protection and others. Stuck to the dominant ideologies, the current institutional arrangements reproduce the same unsustainable systems, gradually eroding the grounds of sustainable development. In the same time, people expect new technologies to fix in a "magic" way the accumulating problems. Technologies are impersonal, insensitive, inhuman, but they cannot set how we apply them to "arrange our game".

In this perspective, it has to be clear, that science, innovation breakthroughs and smart technologies cannot provide magic solutions of the raising crucial issues. For example, the study of Chen et al, (2017) show that accumulating research in the field of food waste is not finding a model to solve unsustainability of the systems. In a similar way, many phenomena today are deeply political and the institutionalized. As discussed for example in Aghion et al. (1999) and Piketty (2015) the models of wealth distribution and inequality have been always political and institutionalized. Therefore, many of the current complex problems cannot be solved with better economic mechanisms or new technology solutions.

As ideologies reflect what economic, social, and political actors view as fair, just and efficient, we need new basis of the social contract. In plus, the late phenomena of "conservative revival" and rising populism emerge as an outcome or the lack of coherence and coordination between the dominating institutional ideology and the existing framework of rules. People feel unsecure in front of the new realms created by new technological and social progress. As new technologies can represent a fundamentally new way of producing or consuming at the expense of what one knows and is comfortable with, it increase the level of uncertainty, risks and opposition. In general, social agents are risk averse. That is why in this situation many of them will naturally oppose, turning back to the old paradigms, and closing to the external threats. Moreover, new technologies, especially those with foreign origins, may be defined as averse to the existing resource, institutional, or ideological bases. This further increase the inherent risk associated with how a society's cognitive rules evolve and "fit" with the new technology. Thus, the model of Lyigun and Rubin (2017) indicates that when uncertainty dominates, institutions and ideologies are unlikely to respond to occurring changes. Thus in the advent of the robotic era, we have to further reconsider what kind of institutions and social reality we need and how technologies will enable to achieve it.

Analyzing and understanding institutions and institutional settings is the first step toward the further research of institutional change in chapters three and four. Institutions are conservative and rigid social constructs, determining the main structures, mindsets and power relations within a social system. As institutions largely depend from different social interdependences, political and power mechanisms, they adapt slowly to changes, due to factors such as path dependence, lock-in and sunk costs. Recognizing the ability and the potential to transform institutional settings in the future is the key factor for imposing the patterns of the new Robotic era.

REFERENCES

Aghion, P., Caroli, E., & Garcia-Penalosa, C. (1999). Inequality and economic growth: The perspective of the new growth theories. *Journal of Economic Literature*, *37*(4), 1615–1660. doi:10.1257/jel.37.4.1615

Bachmann, R., & Zaheer, A. (Eds.). (2006). *Handbook of trust research.* Edward Elgar Publishing. doi:10.4337/9781847202819

Barley, S. R., & Tolbert, P. S. (1997). Institutionalization and structuration: Studying the links between action and institution. *Organization Studies*, *18*(1), 93–117. doi:10.1177/017084069701800106

Berger, P. L., & Luckmann, T. (1991). *The social construction of reality: A treatise in the sociology of knowledge (No. 10).* Penguin Uk.

Boyd, R., & Richerson, P. J. (2009). Culture and the evolution of human cooperation. *Philosophical Transactions of the Royal Society of London. Series B, Biological Sciences*, *364*(1533), 3281–3288. doi:10.1098/rstb.2009.0134 PMID:19805434

Castells, M. (2011). A network theory of power. *International Journal of Communication*, *5*, 773–787.

Chavance, B. (2001), Organisations, institutions, système: types et niveaux de règles. *Revue d'économie industrielle, 97*(4), 85-102. Retrieved from http://www.persee.fr/doc/rei_0154-3229_2001_num_97_1_1801

Chen, H., Jiang, W., Yang, Y., Yang, Y., & Man, X. (2017). State of the art on food waste research: A bibliometrics study from 1997 to 2014. *Journal of Cleaner Production, 140*, 840–846. doi:10.1016/j.jclepro.2015.11.085

Coase, R. H. (1937). The nature of the firm. *Economica, 4*(16), 386-405.

Commons, J. R. (1924). *The Legal Foundations of Capitalism*. New York: Macmillan.

Coriat, B., & Dosi, G. (1998). *Learning how to govern and learning how to solve problems. On the double nature of routines as problem solving and governance devices. In The Dynamic Firm. The Role of Technology, Strategy, Organization and Regions* (pp. 103–133). Oxford, UK: Oxford University Press.

Denzau, A. T., & North, D. C. (1994). Shared mental models: Ideologies and institutions. *Kyklos, 47*(1), 3–31. doi:10.1111/j.1467-6435.1994.tb02246.x

Dequech, D. (2004). Uncertainty: Individuals, institutions and technology. *cambridge. Journal of Economics, 28*(3), 365–378.

Gerring, J. (1997). Ideology: A definitional analysis. *Political Research Quarterly, 50*(4), 957–994. doi:10.1177/106591299705000412

Helmke, G., & Levitsky, S. (2004). Informal institutions and comparative politics: A research agenda. *Perspectives on Politics, 2*(4), 725–740. doi:10.1017/S1537592704040472

Henrich, J., Boyd, R., Bowles, S., Camerer, C., Fehr, E., Gintis, H., & McElreath, R. (2001). In search of homo economicus: Behavioral experiments in 15 small-scale societies. *The American Economic Review, 91*(2), 73–78. doi:10.1257/aer.91.2.73

Hodgson, G. M. (1988). *Economics and Institutions: A Manifesto for a Modern Institutional Economics*. Cambridge, UK: Polity Press.

Iyigun, M., & Rubin, J. (2017). *The Ideological Roots of Institutional Change*. IZA Discussion Papers, No. 10703.

Katz, D., & Kahn, R. L. (1978). *The social psychology of organizations* (Vol. 2). New York: Wiley.

Krätke, S. (1999). A regulationist approach to regional studies. *Environment & Planning, 31*(4), 683–704. doi:10.1068/a310683

Laudon, K., & Laudon, J. (2014). *Management Information Systems*. Prentice Hall.

Lawrence, T. B., Hardy, C., & Phillips, N. (2002). Institutional effects of interorganizational collaboration: The emergence of proto-institutions. *Academy of Management Journal, 45*(1), 281–290. doi:10.2307/3069297

Martin, P. Y. (2004). Gender as social institution. *Social Forces, 82*(4), 1249–1273. doi:10.1353of.2004.0081

Meyer, J. W. (2008). Reflections on institutional theories of organizations. The Sage handbook of organizational institutionalism, 790-811.

Meyer, J. W., & Rowan, B. (1977). Institutionalized organizations: Formal structure as myth and ceremony. *American Journal of Sociology, 83*(2), 340–363. doi:10.1086/226550

Nafstad, H. E., Blakar, R. M., Carlquist, E., Phelps, J. M., & Rand-Hendriksen, K. (2007). Ideology and power: The influence of current neo-liberalism in society. *Journal of Community & Applied Social Psychology, 17*(4), 313–327. doi:10.1002/casp.931

North, D. (1991). Institutions. *The Journal of Economic Perspectives, 5*(1), 97–112. doi:10.1257/jep.5.1.97

North, D. C. (1988). Ideology and political/economic institutions. *The Cato Journal, 8*, 15.

North, D. C. (2005). Institutions and the process of economic change. *Management International, 9*(3), 1.

Ostrom, E. (2015). *Governing the commons*. Cambridge University Press. doi:10.1017/CBO9781316423936

Parto, S. (2005). Economic activity and institutions: Taking stock. *Journal of Economic Issues, 39*(1), 21–52. doi:10.1080/00213624.2005.11506779

Peters, B. G. (2011). *Institutional theory in political science: The new institutionalism*. Bloomsbury Publishing USA.

Picketty, T. (2015). Putting Distribution Back at the Center of Economics: Reflections on Capital in the Twenty-First Century. *The Journal of Economic Perspectives, 29*(1), 67–88. doi:10.1257/jep.29.1.67

Polanyi, K. (1957). *The Great Transformation*. Boston: Beacon Press.

Purvis, T., & Hunt, A. (1993). Discourse, ideology, discourse, ideology, discourse, ideology.... *The British Journal of Sociology*, *44*(3), 473–499. doi:10.2307/591813

Richerson, P. J., & Boyd, R. (1999). Complex societies. *Human Nature (Hawthorne, N.Y.)*, *10*(3), 253–289. doi:10.100712110-999-1004-y PMID:26196336

Richerson, P. J., & Boyd, R. (2001, January). Institutional evolution in the Holocene: The rise of complex societies. *Proceedings of the British Academy*, *110*, 197–234.

Rokeach, M. (2008). *Understanding human values*. Simon and Schuster.

Sachs, J. D. (2012). From millennium development goals to sustainable development goals. *Lancet*, *379*(9832), 2206–2211. doi:10.1016/S0140-6736(12)60685-0 PMID:22682467

Scott, W. R. (2001). *Institutions and Organizations* (2nd ed.). London: Sage Publications.

Stoddart, M. (2007). Ideology, hegemony, discourse: A critical review of theories of knowledge and power. *Social Thought & Research*, 191–225.

Streeck, W., & Thelen, K. A. (Eds.). (2005). *Beyond continuity: Institutional change in advanced political economies*. Oxford University Press.

Thelen, K. (1999). Historical institutionalism in comparative politics. *Annual Review of Political Science*, *2*(1), 369–404. doi:10.1146/annurev.polisci.2.1.369

Thibaut, J. W. (2017). *The social psychology of groups*. Routledge.

Thornton, P. H., & Ocasio, W. (2008). Institutional logics. The Sage handbook of organizational institutionalism, 840, 99-128.

Triandis, H. C. (2018). *Individualism and collectivism*. Routledge.

Van Dijk, T. (1998). Ideology: A multidisciplinary approach. *Sage (Atlanta, Ga.)*.

Williamson, C. R. (2009). Informal institutions rule: Institutional arrangements and economic performance. *Public Choice*, *139*(3-4), 371–387. doi:10.100711127-009-9399-x

Chapter 3
Understanding Mechanics of Smooth Institutional Transformation

ABSTRACT

Institutions, similar to other human and social undertakings, emerge and evolve following different social dynamics. The third chapter aims to discover some of the mechanisms behind smooth institutional transformations and the main elements and characteristics of institutional change. The first part makes an overview of the neo-institutional schools and their considerations for institutional change. The second part defines the basic elements of institutional change, including the analysis of exogenous and endogenous processes and characteristics. The third part outlines the agency view of institutional change and proposes an analysis of theoretical concepts of institutional entrepreneurship, institutional work and proto-institutions, the types, processes, and stages of institutional transformation. Based on that, in the discussion part, there is presented a model defining how new technology can affect institutional change combining micro and macro perspective and social actors. Finally, there are analyzed the main criteria for successful transformation of the institutionalization process.

DOI: 10.4018/978-1-5225-6270-2.ch003

INTRODUCTION

Institutions, as presented in the previous chapter, provide a balanced and stable framework of rules and norms that make social interactions predictable. However, in the same time, institutions are not fixed constructs and as such, they represent a form of social agreement that is subject to dynamic social process. In order to cope with the emerging challenges, social institutions constantly rearrange and evolve (Dacin, Goodstein, & Scott, 2002). In fact, the "rules of the game" are formed and exist in a network of interdependent external and internal interests, complex social arrangements. They are a function of power distribution, leadership, culture, traditions and group dynamics. Furthermore, any change in the "rules" affects immediately the positions, investments and strategies of the actors in the game, challenging their plans and influencing their outcomes. In a highly dynamic and complex global environment of fast spreading crisis, technology breakthroughs and political instability, mastering institutional change is crucial to ensure adaptability, plasticity and smooth social progress. That is why exploring and explaining the mechanisms of institutional change represents a critical moment in all institutional theories. However, there still miss a common understanding and a single framework about how institutions transform (Campbell, 2004). Moreover, due to the complex nature of institutions, the accumulated body of literature on institutional changes is substantial, exploring it through sophisticated models, case studies and interdisciplinary methodologies from various fields such as economics and socio-political sciences, psychology, sociology, historical and organizational studies, group dynamics and others (Bush, 1987; Kingston & Caballero, 2009). Recognizing the mechanisms, actors and factors that influence institutional change is a crucial step to understand processes behind any social transformation. As Hodgson (1988) find out, institutional theories have to thrive to explain how institutions emerge, grow and change and not how institutions stabilize themselves in a static state. In this perspective, this is an in-depth analysis of how institutions form and emerge (or the birth of a new logic or governance structure), disappear - deinstitutionalization or dissolution of the existing logic or governance structure or transform - reinstitutionalization or replacement of the existing logic or governance structure by new one (Scott, 2001).

The present chapter aims to discuss some of the main concepts of institutional change that can be characterized as a smooth process of generating and renovating the norms and social agreements in the ecosystem. Understanding the basic mechanics and forces of incremental institutional transformations is necessary in the process of evaluating stages of institutional changes, and the micro-institutional trends for adopting new technologies, leading to new and redefined social rules. Thus, the focus is put to identify the main elements, factors, social actors and stages of evolutionary institutional change. Further analyzes of the dynamic revolutionary changes will be made in the next chapter, where revolutions in institutional development will be investigated, in order to explore the dynamics and processes of industrial and scientific revolutions.

It is important to stress that institutions inevitably determine resource allocation and invariably have distributional consequences (Mahoney & Thelen, 2010). As the theory of new institutional economics proves, economic institutions influence the growth potential, performance and distribution of the resources. Thus, distribution of the resources is a function of the real political power (Acemoglu, Johnson, & Robinson, 2005). That is why institutional change is not a simple form of social agreement, but a political negotiation process, actually reflecting deeper and more complex social and political ideologies and arrangements between centers of power. As institutions represent formal and informal set of rules and expectations, any institutional change will have unequal implication on resource allocation. More specifically many formal institutions are designed to distribute resources to particular kinds of actors and not to others. Therefore, any transformation of rules, social order, institutional practices and habits will provoke on one side resistance, but on the other side speculations, expectations and hidden opportunities for "free riders". This is true precisely to those institutions that mobilize significant and highly valued resources (like political and political-economic institutions). Thus, changes in formal and informal institutions are not an automatic process and should reflect the level of risk, the parties involved and the social price for accepting and implementing it.

The present chapter has the following structure. In the first part, an overview of different neo-institutional schools and their considerations for institutional change is discussed, summarizing the main theoretical concepts in the field. The second part defines the basic elements of institutional change, including the analysis of exogenous and endogenous processes and characteristics. The third part outlines the agency view of institutional change and on the theoretical concepts of institutional entrepreneurship, institutional work and proto-institutions. Then the types, processes and stages of institutional transformation are presented. Based on that, in the discussion part a model will be presented that will analyze how new technology affect institutional change combining micro and macro perspective, social actors. Finally there will be analyzed the criteria for successful transformation of the institutionalization process.

BACKGROUND

Institutional change and institutional transformation are widely discussed within institutional theories. Generally, institutional change can be defined as a situation where an existing set of beliefs, norms, and practices comes under attack, undergoes delegitimation, or falls into disuse and needs to be replaced by new rules, forms, and scripts (Scott, 2001). Institutional change is considered the recombination of old institutional elements and sometimes the introduction of new ones (Campbell, 2004). This is a complex process as institutions are relatively enduring features of political and social life (rules, norms, procedures) that cannot be changed easily or instantaneously. As the idea of persistence is virtually built into the very definition of an institution, the internal contradiction of the concept "institutional change" provoke various theoretical views for interpreting and resuming it. Path-dependence and the dominant logic in the field play a key role for institutional stability. Thus, the paradox of embedded agency or "fundamental paradox in new institutional theories" needs further explanations about how actors can "envision and enact changes in institutions if their actions, intentions, and rationality are all conditioned by the very institutions they wish to change" (Holm, 1995).

In order to investigate institutional transformation as a smooth and incremental social process, we will outline how different institutional theories explain institutional change. The main neo-institutionalism theories commonly identify institutions as given, static and constraining equilibrium of optimal cost-benefit arrangements between rational agents. Therefore, institutional change is generally explained as a rearrangement of the rules in response to external, exogenous shock. However the neo-institutionalism schools of rational-choice, historical and sociological institutionalisms (Hall & Taylor, 1996), discursive institutionalism (Schmidt, 2008) and critical institutionalism (Cleaver & De Koning, 2015) differ mainly in explaining the reasons and processes of institutional change. The Campbell' (2004) analysis of institutional change further underline motivation, complexity and multi-level perspective of different old and new institutional theories. In Table 1, there are summarized the main factors and elements for institutional change

Table 1. Analysis of institutional change according to main neo-institutionalism schools

Neo-Institutionalism	Main Elements	Explaining Change Factors
Rational Choice Institutionalism	Rational actors pursue their preferences following a 'logic of calculation' within political institutions defined as optimal structures of incentives;	Exogenous factors transform social equilibrium and lead rational agents to rearrange their preferences.
Historical Institutionalism	Institutions are regularized patterns and functions of historically distributed power, subject to a 'logic of path-dependence';	Only exogenous factors such as political junctures can open up opportunities for historical agents to change the trajectory of development and overcome path-dependency;
Sociological Institutionalism	Social agents act according to the 'logic of appropriateness' within political institutions, defined as socially constituted and culturally framed rules and norms.	Social actors - 'challengers' engage in strategic collective action to jockey with incumbents for change, particularly relying on the 'social skill' of particular actors to manipulate both material and existential concerns in the shadow of exogenous shocks that create destabilizing openings (e.g. uncertainty, crisis).
Discursive Institutionalism	Institutions are simultaneous structures and constructs internal to agents, who form ideas and then negotiate them within a given "meaningful context".	Based on the shared ideas, social agents by the "logic of communication" determine how institutions change or persist.
Critical Institutionalism	Critical institutionalism explores how institutions dynamically mediate relationships between people, natural resources and society.	In institutional bricolage social agents assembles or reshapes institutional arrangements and the change is happening at the "messy middle".
Neo-Institutional Economy	Optimization of institutional arrangement or equilibrium between social agents leads to decrease of transaction costs and therefore to economic growth.	Institutional change is a function of changes in "relative prices or in the tastes and preferences" based on (North, 1991);

according to the neo-institutional schools and a short overview is provided in the following paragraphs.

In the following paragraphs, there will be discussed the principle concepts of institutional change according to the main neo-institutional theories. We need to underline that the present chapter does not aim to propose an exhaustive list of references in the theoretical schools and findings of institutional change, but to serve as a basis for further analysis of its characteristics and elements.

1. Rational-Choice Institutionalism (RI)

The rational choice theory considers institutions as stable structures negotiated and formed by rational agents. The equilibrium in the social ecosystem and environment is ensured by the game theory. As institutional rules serve to optimize the interests of all rational agents, institutions are self-enforcing and provide internal coordinating mechanisms. Here the rational agents have fixed behavioral preferences. Thus, rational-choice school explains institutional change as exogenous factors: *changes in self-enforcing institutions must have an exogenous origin* (Greif & Laitin, 2004).

2. Historical Institutionalism (HI)

Historical institutionalism acknowledges institutions as function of the political distribution of power. Historical institutionalism traditionally stress on continuity over change (path-dependence), considering discontinuous model of institutional change in which enduring historical pathways are periodically punctuated by moments of agency and choice. The political costs of change increase over time due to the challenges of building collective action for an alternative, the interdependence of multiple elements in an institutional 'web', the incumbent political authority that can reinforce asymmetric power relations, and the 'intrinsic complexity and opacity' of political systems (Pierson 2000). Only critical junctures can open up opportunities for historic agents to alter the trajectory of development (Katznelson, 2003). The "critical junctures" are specific periods of contingency during which the usual constraints on action are lifted or eased (Capoccia & Kelemen, 2007).

3. Sociological Institutionalism (SI)

Sociological institutionalism aims to explain institutions as non-codified, informal conventions and collective scripts that regulate human behavior. Here institutions are defined by their self-reproductive properties, which are mostly cognitive and social in nature. Thus institutions are routine and "taken for granted". Actors often reproduce the same institutional logic across various domains and transfer the existing scripts forward when building new institutions even when it is not "efficient." In this theory, institutional change particularly depends on the 'social skill' of actors, who can master the exogenous shocks, created by destabilizing openings (uncertainty, crisis). Thus actors, who possess specific social skills to influence the interests, meanings and identities of the others on micro level, provoke institutional change. They influence the institutional dynamic on meso-level and provoke strategic (political) collective action that form patterns of social order and change on macro-level.

4. Discursive Institutionalism (DI)

The discursive institutionalism comes from political sciences and explains institutions as simultaneous structures, internal to agents with "background ideational abilities" and 'foreground discursive abilities' who negotiate the institutions within a given "meaning context". Ideas are the substantive content of discourse. Ideas exist at three levels—policies, programs, and philosophies. Norms are dynamic inter subjective constructs rather than static structures. Institutions are not external-rule-following structures but here agents, following the "logic of communication," determine how institutions change or persist. Within DI a more dynamic, agent-centered approach to institutional change is proposed than in the three other new institutionalisms (Schmidt, 2008).

5. Critical Institutionalism (CI)

Critical institutionalism (CI) explores how institutions dynamically mediate relationships between people, natural resources and society. It focuses on the complexity of institutions entwined in everyday social life, their historical formation, the interplay between formal and informal, traditional and modern arrangements, and the power relations that animate them. Critical institutionalists recognize that the governance of resources occurs through a variety of scales with no very clear boundary between the domains of the local and the global. From this perspective rules, boundaries and processes are 'fuzzy'; people's complex social identities, unequal power relationships and wider political and geographical factors shape resource management arrangements and outcomes. Institutions are not necessarily designed for a particular purpose, but they can be borrowed or adapted from other working arrangements. People's motivations to cooperate in collective arrangements are a mix of economic, emotional, moral and social rationalities informed by differing logics and world-views. Institutional bricolage is a process through which people, consciously and non-consciously, assembles or reshapes institutional arrangements, drawing on whatever materials and resources are available, regardless of their original purpose. In this process, old arrangements are modified and new ones invented. Institutional components from different origins are continuously reused, reworked, or refashioned to perform new functions. Adapted configurations of rules, practices, norms and relationships are attributed meaning and authority.

6. New Institutional Economy

According to the theory of new institutional economy, the main aim of institutions is to decrease transaction costs within the paradigm of rational agents (Coase, 1937). In this context, the new institutional economy investigates institutional change as a process for maximizing the effectiveness and growth potential of the economy. Focusing on economic aspects, institutions' efficiency is a factor for regulating the balancing strategies of the individual's rational choice within the game theory (Rational choice). Thus, institutional change is a three-stage process of assertion of rules and norms for limiting the transaction costs (Commons, 1934). Within a rational choice paradigm, institutional change can be an outcome of two main processes (North, 1990): *institutional change is mainly due to changes in the relative prices ... or changes in the tastes or preferences*. In this perspective, new institutional theory claims that institutions may emerge endogenously, from within the community, or, alternatively, are imposed from outside, for instance from organizations (Egbert, 2018).

ELEMENTS AND CHARACTERISTICS OF INSTITUTIONAL CHANGE

In general, institutional change can be classified as radical (revolutionary) or as incremental (evolutionary). This means that institutional change can be explored either as evolutionary pattern characterized by gradual accumulation of small, incremental changes over long periods of time, or revolutionary change with patterns of punctuated equilibrium followed by punctuated evolution (Gersick, 1991). Pierson (2004) emphasizes that in general as institutional settings are social processes they incorporate multiple kinds of overlapping temporal processes, including sequencing and conjunctures of events, slow-moving long-term processes, positive feedback processes, cumulative incremental changes and threshold effects. Thus, institutional change should be discussed not as an isolated event but rather as a dynamic process embedded into a dynamic reconfiguration of other long-term or short-term parallel practices. Time-horizon is substantial barrier to implement a completely encompassing framework for recognizing the patterns of institutional change as many interlinked processes overlap and thus some evolutionary developments can be confused with more revolutionary shifts

(Campbell, 2004). Munshi and Myaux, (2006) explain institutional change as a learning process, accumulating new knowledge in the process of transition from old arrangements to new social norms. Dorado (2005) point out that the main factors inducing institutional change are: agency (depending on temporal orientation of the actors), resources (cognitive, social and material) and opportunity (objective condition of organizational field). Kingston and Caballero (2009) differentiate two main factors for institutional transformation – centralization, where new institutions are purposefully designed and implemented by governing authority or evolutionary change, where institutions emerge spontaneously through uncoordinated choices of many actors.

Analyzing institutional change and institutional stability, we need to highlight that both of them are functions of human endeavor and social efforts. The elements of institutional stability often hinges on issues like path-dependence, social norm reproduction, and inertia. That is how Mahoney (2000) formulates the following four elements of institutional stability:

- Functional (institutions have useful societal function),
- Utilitarian (institutions support rational cost-benefit assessment),
- Power (institutions are supported from elite actors),
- Legitimating (institutions are perceived as legitimate and morally just).

However, we have to underline that not all forces are equal. In this model, the power and support from elite factors dominate over the other elements and can alone ensure institutional continuity. Following this perspective, it is interesting to compare it with Olivier' (1992; 1997) findings about institutional stability. The author claims that the main pressures for deinstitutionalization and institutional change come from functional, political and social sources. Functional pressures for deinstitutionalization arise from perceived problems with the performance, efficiency and utility associated with institutionalized practices. These pressures may be tied to broad environmental changes, such as intensified competition for resources or technology innovations. The political pressures on institutions result from the shifts of the interests and the power distributions among elites. Finally, the social pressures are associated with group dynamics processes, heterogeneity and changes in social expectations (Olivier, 1997). In this context, Mahoney (2000) underline that path-dependence is one of the main reason for institutional reproduction and institutional stability. Path-dependence is theorized to be caused by a 'dynamic of increasing returns' whereby positive feedback processes reinforce a particular path of institutional activity and rewards, which become increasingly difficult to change over time. There needs to be an extra effort to overcome path dependences. Thus, the summary of the main factors that can overcome the path-dependence, provoking further institutional change are displayed in Table 2, covering both exogenous and endogenous sources of institutional change (Mahoney, 2000). If institutions are changed not just in response to exogenous shocks or shifts, then their basic properties must be defined in a way that provide some dynamic elements that permits such change.

Exogenous Factors

The neo-institutional theories in the perspective of rational-choice theory and historical institutionalism, conceptualize that the main sources of institutional change can be only exogenous. Thus, exogenous factors are external to the existing social order and social arrangements, and can provoke the precipitating jolt - an external event that disrupts and alters the existing institutional order. Thus, institutional change comes as result of a reconfiguration process that takes rather unpredictable paths since no particular causal agent is involved. Further, the resulting institutional change can be considered as context-dependent. The main three types of exogenous factors that can provoke institutional transformation: exogenous shocks, crisis events or social pressures, technological progress and global diffusion.

Exogenous Shocks and Crisis Events

External exogenous shocks and crisis events are recognized as important source of distress (e.g. environmental, social, economic, and political) triggering institutional change and imposing the need of new rules and reconfiguration of the regulation framework. Usually, exogenous shocks are rare social events and incidents that discover inefficiency of institutional order and lack of rules for protecting the social interest. Therefore, the crisis comes as an evidence of institutional vacuum (overlooked or neglected situations) raising the need for new rules and mobilizing social actors.

Table 2. Analysis of exogenous and endogenous factors, following classification of Mahoney (2000)

Exogenous Factors	Endogenous Factors
Exogenous shocks (functional view);	Competition and learning (utilitarian view); Altering power relations (power view); Changing values and beliefs (legitimation view);

Technological Progress

Technological progress is considered as an important exogenous factor for institutional change. For example, Ayres (1944) views exogenous technological progress as the main driver of institutional change: *technological development forces change upon the institutional structure by changing the material setting in which it operates*. The old institutionalism such as the Veblen's theory explains that *changes in population and technology* trigger institutional change by ensuring that current institutions and habits of thought, inherited from the past are never ideally suited to the requirements of the present.

Technological progress leads to three-level evolutionary process in the institutional settings (Scott, 2001). First, the introduction of new technology disrupts the established institutional arrangements governing behavior of key organizational actors at subsystem (micro) level. Then the changes in practices and patterns at the organizational form reflect (ideological) changes in core values and beliefs at the societal level at (meso) level. Third, at the macro, societal level, changes in institutional logics (e.g., focus on effectiveness versus efficiency or vice versa) as well as associated changes in governance systems, have been found to affect the types and relative numbers of certain types of organization.

Endogenous Factors

The endogenous explanations of institutional change provoke many scholars, especially in the rational-choice theory to state that this is a "contradiction in term" (Scott, 1981), further emphasizing the paradox of embedded agency. The endogenous factors for institutional transformation suggest that most of the institutional changes in fact lie in human interactions, in social dynamics and in power-relations. As Thelen (2000) point out, institution's role can change over time as new interests come into power or as the environment, facing old interests is altered. Thus, institutional change occurs when problems of rule interpretation and enforcement open up space for actors to implement existing rules in new ways. The incremental change emerges in the "gaps" or "soft spots" between the rule and its interpretation or the rule and its enforcement. The change is explained by the distribution of power and changed interests of the social actors. Then the basic properties of institutions contain within them possibilities for change. Therefore, endogenous factors of institutional change come as function of social factors such as competition and learning, altering power relations and changing values and beliefs (Mahoney, 2000). Mahoney and Thelen (2010) propose a 'middle ground' approach, focusing on gradual and ongoing forms of institutional change. They argue that institutional rules are rarely unambiguous and, indeed, this ambiguity affords space for flexibility by actors that can give rise to gradual change over time as the meanings of rules are reinterpreted, re-cast under new circumstances, or otherwise contested. Their model explores endogenous institutional change driven by ongoing political-distributional struggles between actors seeking to influence the meaning, interpretation, and enforcement of institutional rules, which are inherently indeterminate and contestable. Gradual change may nevertheless lead to broader transformative change over time (Streeck & Thelen, 2005). They propose a framework based on analysis of various case studies to identify endogenous factors and change agents that generate change in institutions with positive-feedback effects. Holm (1995) considers that institutions should be analyzed as nested systems, or interconnected, multilevel systems in which each action simultaneously is a framework for action and a product of action.

SOCIAL AGENTS AND INSTITUTIONAL CHANGE

Institutions are social constructs and social actors play a crucial role for realizing new institutional rules and for changing the existing institutional frameworks. The models of micro-dynamics of institutional change analyzes how different configurations bringing together social actors, institutions and precipitating jolts interact to bring institutional change (Boxenbaum, 2004). The agency theory emphasizes on the role of the social actors to induce institutional change, but individuals are not acting alone. The individual role in this social process is defined by its ability to form and lead social alliances and coalitions. As Hall (2010) notes, the relative power of various actors is enormously important in affecting their ability to assemble the coalition they need to change (or defend) existing social arrangements. The rational choice approach holds that actors will agree to institutional reforms only when those reforms make them better off. Thus, scholars identify institutional losers and institutional winners to designate change agents positions and motivations. However, the ultimate impact of adopting new institutional rules is often hard to predict and thus differentiating between institutional losers or winners can be blurry. Therefore the actors behind institutional change should have both the rational interest to implement new reforms and second - the ability to mobilize social coalitions. Further the emergence and evolution of institutional structures is itself dependent on human behavior and human action (Lawrence & Suddaby, 2006), and thus it should be researched as complex power related socio-political process.

Making an overview of the social dynamics, Cleaver and De Koning (2015) sum up that power-relations are crucial for emerging social coalitions. The ability to form social coalitions is linked to the power or capacity of individuals to deploy material (allocative) and non-material (authoritative) resources. Individual power to exercise agency through institutions and to challenge boundaries is highly dependent on the possession of resources (land, knowledge, networks). Therefore, social power is exercised both in rule formation but also in the power to control the public agenda (what is discussed, who is represented) and the more invisible power to shape meaning and ideas about what is acceptable. Further Cleaver and De Koning (2015) find out that poor or marginalized people often are not represented in shaping the formal rules, the rules in use or in negotiation of social norms. Generally poor people experience costs and benefits of institutional functioning differently to more powerful people, and they are often more dependent on fewer institutions for their resource access and livelihoods (Cleaver & De Koning, 2015). This comes to show that social dynamics and change agents' behavior and motivation will largely depend on the access of individuals to resources and on their ability to form social coalitions.

Typology of Change Agents

Discussing in details the complexity of the change agents who can be intentional or unintentional and can pursuit different short-term and long-term strategies, Streeck and Thelen (2005) propose a framework to summarize the main change agents' characteristics and behavioral patterns. Identifying the roles of change agents is useful for explanatory purposes, as institutional change should not always emerge from actors with transformational motives. Rather it can be an unintended by-product that grows out of distributional struggles in which no party explicitly sought the changes. The model of Streeck and Thelen (2005), visualized on Table 3, includes four basic change agents: insurrectionaries, symbionts (either parasitic or mutualistic), subversives, and opportunists. These four types of behavior and motivation of the change agents are associated with a particular mode of institutional change. Further it leads to particular strategy for effecting such change, emerging in different institutional contexts.

Table 3. Classification of the change agents based on the model of Streeck and Thelen (2005)

Do change agents follow the rules of the institutions?	Do change agents seek to preserve institution? YES	Do change agents seek to preserve institution? NO
YES	**Opportunitists** Exploit whatever possibilities exist within the prevailing institutional system to achieve their ends.	**Subversives** Seek to displace an institution, but following the rules and the regulations of institutions.
NO	**Symbionts** Rely and exploit institutions for their own gain. They can be parasitic or mutualistic actors.	**Insurrectionaries** Actively reject the institutional status quo, institutional rules and regulations.

Insurrectionaries

Insurrectionaries are the most dynamic change agents who consciously and actively seek to eliminate and rapidly displace the existing institutions and rules. Insurrectionaries may be especially likely to emerge when a social groups or individual is disadvantaged by multiple institutions. This way, opposing to the rules become a basis for subjective identification and can lead to coordinated collective action. Insurrectionaries may lead to critical-juncture periods and rapid overturning of the institutional status quo in favor of radically new rules.

Symbionts

Symbionts can be parasitic or mutualistic actors that rely and exploit institutions for their own gain.

- **The Parasitic Actors:** Exploit an institution by carrying out actions that contradict the "spirit" or purpose of the institution, thus undermining it over the longer run. Parasites can flourish in settings where expectations about institutional conformity are high, but the actual capacity to enforce those expectations is limited. Indeed, parasites will not persist if institutional supporters are able to maintain and shore up institutions to address these gaps. As a result, parasites are especially associated with the neglect of institutional maintenance in the face of slippage between rule and practices on the ground.

- **Mutualistic Actors:** Thrive on and derive benefit from the existing rules, but using them in novel ways to advance their interests. In this case, they do not compromise the efficiency of the rules or the survival of the institution. Rather, they violate the letter of the rule to support and sustain its spirit – in contrast to parasites, who exploit the letter of the rule while violating its spirit. Mutualists ordinarily contribute to the robustness of institutions, expanding the support coalition on which the institution rests. In cases like this, parasitic behavior (as in the natural world) can compromise the stability of the system itself.

Subversives

Subversives actors seek to displace an institution, but in pursuing this goal they do not break the rules of the institution. They instead effectively disguise the extent of their preference for institutional change by following institutional expectations and working within the system. From the outside, they may even appear to be supporters of the institutions. As they wait, they may encourage institutional changes by promoting new rules on the edges of old ones, thus siphoning off support for the previous arrangements.

Opportunists

Opportunist actors have ambiguous preferences about institutional continuity, passively waiting to take advantage of the situation. They do not actively seek to preserve institutions, and in the same time they do not try to change the rules. Opportunists instead exploit whatever possibilities exist within the prevailing system to achieve their ends. The weight of opportunists within an institution can be a major source of *institutional inertia.* Their preference for making use of existing possibilities over the riskier strategy of mobilizing for change makes opportunists through their inaction "natural" allies of an institution's supporters.

In sum, change agents can influence institutional transformation processes both directly and indirectly, following different complex intentional and non-intentional strategies. The model of Streeck and Thelen (2005) highlights that incremental institutional changes can result to complex group interests. Here, change agents should not necessarily seek to challenge institutional rules, but their actions and motivations can initiate further subversive impact. While insurrectionaries seek rapid displacement, most often they will settle for gradual displacement. Symbionts will try to preserve the formal institutional status quo, but their parasitic variety carries out actions that cause institutional drift. Subversives seek displacement but often work in the short run on behalf of layering. Opportunists adopt a wait-and-see approach and eventually will pursue conversion when it suits their interests. That is how these types of agents can influence the type of institutional change.

Dorado (2005) proposes another model to define how leaders and social actors can take the position of change agents based on their time-orientation. Classifying social actors as change agents according to their dominant temporal type, the author determines how they can induce to temporally embedded engagement. Based on its model, the temporal function of any social actors reproduce and transform institutions through the interplay of their habits, imagination and judgment. This way, the actors with dominant "routine" temporal dimension have orientation towards past, reactivating past patterns of action. They will activate gradual institutional change by striving for institutional continuity and stability. The actors with "sense-making" behavior will outline present orientation. They will make practical and normative judgments in response to the emerging demands and ambiguities of the situations. These actors have to work in the situation of uncertainty, making sense of the situation, facts and context, in order to limit the uncertainty and identify space for action. The "strategic" behavior outlines the future temporal orientation of actors. These change agents will generate possible future trajectories of actions and strategies for the future, defined by their further visions, hopes, fears and desires.

Institutional Entrepreneurs

Institutional entrepreneurs purposefully and actively seek to initiate or change social rules and institutions. They are opposed to the unintentional social actors, discussed in Streeck and Thelen (2005) who thread and influence institutional stability by chance. Institutional entrepreneurs are the ones who make institutional formation and transformation, as they create, maintain or disrupt institutions in accordance with their values or interests (Garud, Hardy, & Maguire, 2007; Pacheco, York, Dean, & Sarasvathy, 2010). Research on the creation of institutions is mainly grounded on DiMaggio's work (1988) quoted in Greenword and Suddaby (2006), emphasizing that organized actors with sufficient resources (institutional entrepreneurs) contribute to the genesis of new institutions in which they see an opportunity to realize "interests that they value highly". Therefore, institutional entrepreneurs are individuals and organizations, serving as catalysts of new institutions, or actors who actively and purposefully invest in development of new institutions.

Institutional enterpreneurs, their characteristics and the processes of institutional enterpreneurship including institutional creation and transformation are investigated further in (Leca & Naccache, 2006), and Leca et al. (2008). Institutional entrepreneurs rarely act alone and they must typically mobilize supporters by forming alliances, founding cooperations and social coalitions. Beckert (1999), Battilana (2006) and others considers the importance of the personal social position and agency models in the entrepreneurship process. Therefore, institutional entrepreneurship focuses on agency issues or the manner in which interested actors can work together to influence institutional contexts through various strategies. Leca et al. (2008), define two main types of enabling conditions that activate institutional entrepreneurs and in the same time overcome the paradox of embedded agency. They name them field-level conditions and actors' social position in organizational field (Leca, Battilana, & Boxenbaum, 2008). In Table 4 there are displayed the main characteristics and enabling conditions, pointing out the role of environmental factors (the situation) and the "call" to act and the personal position – the ability of the agent to undertake the necessary changes.

Table 4. Summary of institutional entrepreneurs' enabling conditions based on Leca et al., (2008)

Field-Level Conditions	Actors' Social Position in Organizational Field
- Precipitating jolts, crisis, technological disruption, regulatory changes, competitive discontinuities;	- Position at the margins (periphery)/intersection of organizational fields; - Central position in various social networks;
- Presence of acute, field-level problems such as environmental issues or scarcity of resources;	- Access to organizational resources or sources of power such as economic, social, cultural, or symbolic capital;
- Favorable organizational arrangements such as high level of heterogeneity in the field and low level of institutionalization.	- Actors personality characteristics - social skills, empathy, ability to lead cooperative strategies and to undertake institutional projects.

The process of institutional entrepreneurship incorporates few common phases for imposing institutional change, including mobilization (of allies, of tangible and intangible resources), formulation of discursive strategies (that both blame the existing social arrangements and justify the superiority of the proposed changes) and design of new institutional arrangements (Leca, Battilana, & Boxenbaum, 2008). Institutional entrepreneurship attempts to overcome the paradox of neo-institutional theories by assuming that social actors can be both embedded in institutional arrangements and in the same time they can purposefully initiate the change by mobilizing its institutional knowledge and organizational resources.

Institutional Work

Institutional work emerged as another field of institutional research, recognizing the role of agency for institutional transformation (Lawrence, Suddaby, & Leca, 2009; 2011). The theory of institutional work takes his origin in organizational studies and thus is closely related to institutional entrepreneurship. Institutional work aims to analyze the role of actors to create, maintain or disrupt institutional structures and arrangements. Agency from this perspective is something often accomplished through the coordinated and uncoordinated efforts of a potentially large number of actors. Further institutional work should be considered as a complex social process as individuals may engage in it to attain emotional or symbolic goals rather than to pursue material needs (Voronov & Vince, 2012). Pawlak (2011) propose a typology of unintended consequences of institutional work comprised of the following: institutional failures, institutional compromises and constant re-institutionalization.

The fundamental objective of institutional work is to study both institutional stability and institutional change, trying to better explain the paradox of embedded agency (Zietsma & Lawrence, 2010). Thus, institutional work investigates how actors work to retranslate exogenous events and shocks into field-level practices by transposing, editing, and recombining institutions. Further, it notices how actions lead to unintended adaptations, mutations, and other institutional consequences. Zietsma and Lawrence (2010) find out that the interplay between boundaries/boundary work and practices/ practice work create a four-phase cycle of institutional stability, institutional conflict, institutional innovation and institutional restabilization. The move from institutional stability to conflict is related to the following conditions: disputed practices, intact boundaries and the existence of outsiders with capacity to challenge those practices and boundaries. On the other hand, institutional conflicts will shift to institutional innovation when practices are disrupted, the boundaries that protect those practices are compromised, and there is a motivated insider with the capacity to establish new boundaries to protect experiments from institutional discipline. Finally institutional innovation will shift to institutional restabilization when new practices are created that are broadly considered legitimate, previously legitimate boundaries are compromised, and a coalition of outsiders and insiders exists that has the capacity to cooperate to diffuse the new practices and legitimize a new boundary or re-legitimize the compromised boundary (Zietsma & Lawrence, 2010).

Institutional Bricolage

Institutional bricolage is another model applying to the agency theory and exploring how social actors, consciously and non-consciously, assemble or reshape institutional arrangements. The concept of institutional bricolage studies a transformational process where actors recombine locally available institutional principles and practices in ways that yield change (Campbell, 2004; 2006). Thus, institutions are considered as a patchwork of different new and inherited arrangements, including various models, habitual ways of doing things, common practices adapted to new conditions and organizational arrangements invented or borrowed from elsewhere. The meaning and relevance of institutions can be maintained, altered, contested, or even fundamentally rejected and replaced through the ongoing actions and interactions of actors within a governance system (Cleaver & Koning, 2015). It is important to state that institutional bricolage is a strategy for dealing with fragmented or weak governance arrangements. In the process of institutional bricolage, old arrangements are modified and new ones invented. In this context, when institutional logic of different rules can be easily combined, institutional change is likely to be incremental. On the contrary, when institutional logics conflict with one another, they are more likely to compete for dominance of the field. Thus, institutional bricolage has a good explanatory power in showing how norms are articulated, explaining both institutional endurance and change, enriching understanding of human agency and relations of authority and in questioning assumptions about institutional effectiveness. In this dynamic process, social actors modify the existing institutional arrangements, but they can do this within the limits of their own resources, social circumstances and what is perceived as legitimate. As Campbell (2004) finds out, the process of searching for solutions is path dependent because the range of actors' choices for innovation are more or less fixed by the set of institutional principles and practices at their disposal. Later on, the adapted configuration of rules, mix of practices, norms and relationships are attributed with new meaning and authority. When formalized institutions have to be localized and adapted to specific local context in order to fit to the existing arrangements (Cleaver & Koning, 2015).

Proto-Institutions

The theory of proto-institutions explores the main mechanisms for emergence and institutionalizations of the new practices and organizational routines. Therefore, proto-institutions are defined as new practices, rules and technologies that transcend a particular collaborative relationship and may become new institutions if they diffuse sufficiently (Lawrence, Hardy & Phillips, 2002). The transformation process from proto-institution to institution tends to be long and complex, and depends mainly if enough actors will adopt and diffuse the new framework. Thus, proto-institutions focus on the processes and mechanisms of transferring and imposing the new institutional logic. Transferring it to other fields is an effective solution.

The genesis of a proto-institution is about bringing into existence a new practice, rule or technology. It is interesting to note how an innovation, whether a practice or a technology becomes a proto-institution, including the micro-dynamics of the innovation process itself. Boxenbaum (2004) points out that many proto-institutions are non-intentional but are by-products of systemic processes. Thus according to the proposed model, the first stage is the emergence of a heterogeneous field with different competing logics (Boxenbaum, 2004). Then the field-level problem emerges and alternative solutions are developed. The process of institutionalization and adoption of new rules and institutional settings is finished when the selected innovation – practice, rule or technology is diffused through various networks. Thus, the transformation occurs when the dominant institutional logic loses its function and potential to be objective representation of the reality. Then if a new problem is specified, the innovative solution can become a new institutional logic if it is justified as appropriate and superior comparing to the others. Therefore, the transposed logics must appeal intuitive to members as superior solution to a specified problem. Therefore, the process of genesis of proto-institutions can be summarized as an intentional combination of divergent institutional logics (Boxenbaum, 2004).

THE MECHANICS OF INSTITUTIONAL CHANGE

Incremental institutional changes can follow different patterns depending on multiple factors such as characteristics of the dominant change agents and the general environment. In the model of Streeck and Thelen (2005) both political context and institutions determine what type of dominant change agents and how can provoke and influence specific type of institutional change (Figure 1).

Based on the model in Figure 1, both political context (power and political will for instutional change) and institutional form (the norms and regulations that will emerge or change) determine successful strategies for change. The ideology and the type of the dominant change agents define successful change strategies or behavior. Following this, Streeck and Thelen (2005) delineate four modal types and mechanisms of gradual institutional change: displacement, layering, drift, and conversion. They constitute the macro-scale outcomes of micro-scale interactions between change agents and institutional rules (Mahoney & Thelen, 2010).

Each type is defined by the locus of institutional transformation. The dimensions in the table generate four types of institutional change:

1. **Displacement:** The removal of existing rules and the introduction of new ones.
2. **Layering:** The introduction of new rules alongside with the existing ones.

Figure 1. Types of institutional change and the model of Streeck and Thelen (2005)

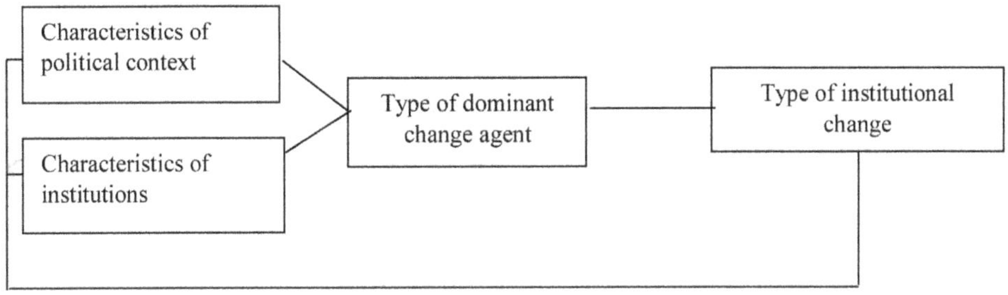

Table 5. Analysis of institutional change processes according to Streeck and Thelen (2005)

	Displacement	Layering	Drift	Conversion
	Rapid or slow-moving breakdown of old rules and their replacement with new ones.	New rules are attached to the existing ones and represent amendments, revisions, or additions to existing institutions.	Rules remain formally the same but shifts in external conditions change their impact and consequences.	Rules remain formally the same but they are interpreted and enacted in new ways by interested agents.
Removal of old rules	Yes	No	No	No
Neglect of old rules	-	No	Yes	No
Changed impact/ enactment of old rules	-	No	Yes	Yes
Introduction of new rules	Yes	Yes	No	No

3. **Drift:** The shifts in the environment lead to changed impact of the existing rules.
4. **Conversion:** The changed enactment of existing rules due to their strategic redeployment.

The type of institutional change reflects how institutional rules are transformed, intentionally or not. Furthermore, both change agents and factors from the environment can influence the outcomes, including modification of the rules', their emergence or final removal.

An alternative approach of institutional change is proposed in Dorado (2005). His model explains further, how dominant agent's behavior and position influence the development of institutional change. Therefore, based on his model, the three main profiles of institutional change are (Dorado, 2005):

- **Purposeful Institutional Entrepreneurship:** The transformational process is leaded by purposeful agents, possessing the power and to make the institutional change.
- **Partaking Institutional Change:** Where the change comes as result of uncoordinated and autonomous actions of countless agents.
- **Convening Institutional Change:** Where social agents convene other actors to define solution of institutional problem.

Additionally three other types of incremental institutional change are defined below:

1. **Deinstitutionalization:** Or endogenous institutional change, preceding the phase when a potential new institution is formulated (Greenwood, Suddaby & Hinings, 2002). Deinstitutionalization occurs because a precipitating jolt disturbs the established institutional order and actors make local innovations. Among these innovations, some will be subsequently theorized. Theorization is the formulation of new organizing principles in the field, defined as *the development and specification of abstract categories and the elaboration of chains of cause and effect* (Greenwood, Suddaby & Hinings, 2002).
2. **Global Diffusion:** Is explained by adoption and modification of institutions existing abroad. This model suggests that institutions diffuse across fields and become 'new' institutions in the focal field. For instance, human agency is evoked when actors 'transpose' an institution. Once an institution has diffused, it is modified to fit the local context.
3. **Incremental Modification:** Occurs when social actors develop new institutions by revising the scripts, where scripts are *observable, recurrent activities and patterns of interaction characteristic of a particular setting*. Here institutional change consists in revising scripts or changing behavioral patterns that are more effective in causing change than is unconscious or unintentional deviation from a script (Boisot & Child, 1988).

THE MAIN PROCESSES OF INSTITUTIONAL CHANGE

The analysis of the main processes of institutional transformation as discussed in the literature above provide many similarities and parallels between stages and phases (Greenwood, Suddaby & Hinings, 2002; Boxenbaum, 2004). In Table 6, there are identified the main stages of institutional change, following the cycle of deinstitutionalization and conversion, and varying from seven to four consecutive steps.

Table 6. Analysis of the main stages of incremental institutional change processes, based on Boxenbaum (2004)

Main Stages of Institutional Change				
Precipitating jolt	A precipitating jolt occurs	Institutional conflict		A precipitating jolt is a field-level event that unsettles an institutional order. A precipitating jolt unsettles the systemic equilibrium and result in a reconfiguration of components.
Deinstitutionalization	Intentional actors seek solutions. A collaborative network is formed.			Mobilization of social actors with intention to change institutions can influence the direction of institutional change. Collaborative networks are important for developing and diffusing new ideas, practices, and technologies
Preinstitutionalization	Institutional logic is transposed from other fields.	Institutional innovation	Encoding institutions into scripts	An institutional logic is transposed from one institutional field to another to solve the field-level problem.
Theorization	Transposed logic is justified.		Enacting scripts in practice	The new institutional logic should be justified, theoritized and approved to propose appropriate and innovative solution to the predefined problem.
Diffusion	Transposed logic is translated to local field.	Institutional restabilization	replicating or revising scripts	Through the process of translation, new institutional logic has to be recontextualized to fit into the new institutional context. Translation is necessary to convince the adopters to recognize that the transposed logic provides a superior solution for the existing problem.
Reinstitutionalization	Transposed logic is combined with local institutional logic.	Institutional stability	Externalizing and objectifying scripts	The new institutional logic is combined with the logics of pre-existing institutional frameworks. Once the new equilibrium is set, institutional change is complete.

The models and stages of Institutional change as identified in Table 6, further confirm that the main transformational processes have to follow the general cycle of change of the dominant institutional logic (Reay & Hinings, 2009). When new emerging problems provoke actors to find new solutions, they have to formulate ways to find a new issue and to assess alternatives solutions. Therefore, they need to identify different selection criteria in order to choose among different alternatives. When the solution is selected, analyzed and assessed, it becomes a "best practice" and diffuse as new norm, resolving the specified problem.

An in-depth view of the model in Table 6, find out that institutional change is decomposed on different steps and elements, but it is disregarding the cycle as a whole. Even more, it has to be highlighted that different social actors in different power configurations can intervene later in institutional transformation processes, in order to determine the outcomes of the new institutional settings. This way, the stages of "preinstitutionalization" and "theorization" as defined above can mix, as social actors can agree instead of looking for adopting the most appropriate institutional form and solution to come with some sort of institutional bricolage, combining a patchwork of old and new settings. Moreover, the motivation of institutional entrepreneurs to lead the change process across all the stages can reverse, due to competing and dynamic social processes. That is how path-dependence and dominant logic can prevail, even if it is recognized the need to impose new social rules. These processes usually remain hidden for the public, moreover as empirical data, case studies and field studies rarely display unsuccessful transformation processes or go into details how interested parties and social agents rearrange and reconfigure power relations in the later stages of institutionalization cycle.

Finally, the process of institutional change, intentional or not, will follow the transformation cycle until the new institutional logic is adopted. Actually, institutional change will close when the social agents accept the result of the social agreement and lose their interest and motivation to pursue further changes. That is why, in most of the cases, institutional work and change processes will resemble on institutional bricolage, combining old and new settings, existing and new, local and translated rules and agreements. Thus, social dynamics and power configurations have the main role determining the outcomes and the level of institutional change, as well as the cycle of successful institutional transformation process.

DISCUSSION

The present chapter aims to discuss the social actors and the mechanics of incremental institutional change. Following the analysis above, there are identified the main elements, types and characteristics, of institutional changes, including roles of the change agents and the stages of the transformation cycle. Based on that we will propose a model to further illustrate how new technologies lead to incremental institutional changes. On Figure 2 there are visualized the main process dynamics and forces.

According to the main institutional theories, new technologies represent an exogenous factor, external to the local ecosystem and to existing social arrangements. In this situation, the rational choice theory states that the main social actors are in equilibrium and their interests are stabilized. Furthermore, technology innovations will be implemented and will impose new institutional changes only if they propose new benefits to the social actors (improving their situation). In economic terms, the new technologies can increase the overall sum of the game by transforming the production functions. In this situation, it is important to note that the existing equilibrium among social agents is discontinue. As not all social actors will benefit from the new transformation of the social order, this automatically will change the distribution of sources of power.

Therefore the two main groups of social actors who will take the role for triggering institutional change are first the technology' "losers" and then - the technology' "winners". This is confirmed by the examples of the wider diffusion of Uber and AirBNB. In many countries around the world the same scenario was developed. The first social change agents, actively requiring

Figure 2. A model of technology implementation and institutional transformation

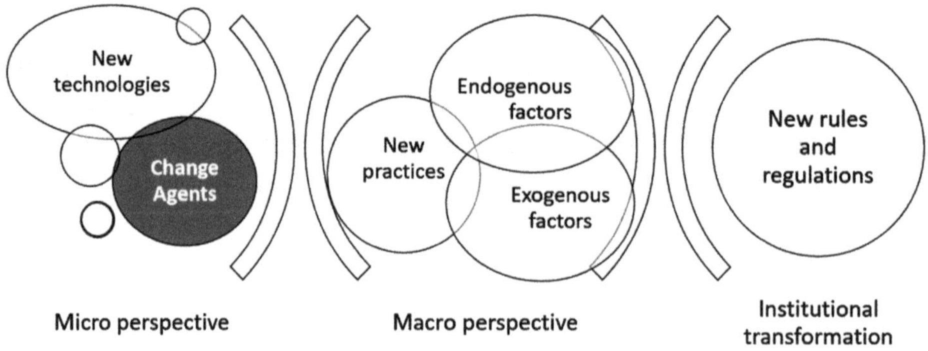

new institutional change were the taxi drivers and hotel owners, insisting for new regulations and better protection of their rights. On the other hand, the technology "winners" or individuals and businesses who benefit from the new opportunities, formed an opposition but gradually both social groups negotiate the form of the new equilibrium, usually based on the relative social power.

However, two main issues have to be considered. First not all innovations are created equal, and thus not all technology innovations will lead to institutional change. Second, the process of technology innovation is complex and not linear, usually triggering a number of incremental technological, social and economic innovations, before imposing as a new trend.

The change agents who can actually benefit from the new technologies - the "winners" need to further prepare and invest. It includes both investments as resources for developing, translating and diffusing the new technology and investments in time for learning, testing and new knowledge development. Furthermore, as technology innovations usually are not problem-driven but technology-driven, a good combination of external factors needs to be present in order to diffuse and succeed.

The change agents behind new technologies include not only entrepreneurs, inventors, researchers or high-tech organizations, inventing and implementing new technologies into daily life. They consist of the larger ecosystem including customers, investors, logistic chain network and competitors. Active networking and collaboration are substantial factor for developing and diffusing new ideas, practices, and technologies. Gaining fast the interest of the end-users is substantial and that is why innovations often are couched in familiar design to appeal to potential adopters. Competitors can be identified as change agents as well, as new technologies lead to path dependences and lock-in costs. Challenging the sources of power and power distribution, the process of imposing new technological change is a subject to careful planning and strategic alliances.

Usually the emergence of new fundamental technologies lead to many new incremental innovations such as technology modifications, organizational innovations, adoption of new practices and prescriptions, habits, customs and cultural settings. That is how most of the social agents will follow some strategies (insurrectionaries, symbionts, parasitic or mutualistic, subversives, and opportunists) as discussed above, actively or passively supporting or rejecting the new social rearrangements. In this moment, several institutional entrepreneurs can emerge, recognizing the needs to institutionalize the new rules, practices or routines. It is interesting that this process will happen simultaneously on micro-perspective - inside organization but as well in macro-perspective - inside the social ecosystem. Thus, several parallel processes can be initiated on different levels, challenging in the same time different aspects of the dominant institutional logic.

The process of institutional transformation will cover three main stages. First - new technology development and implementation, second- its wider implementation and diffusion in social fabrics and third, its widely adoption and formal institutionalization. The social dynamics of these three phases are different; and institutional changes will affect first the informal and then the formal institutions.

During the first phase, the leading role will be in the hands of the entrepreneurs and change agents. The risk is substantial and the returns of investments are scarce. The new institutional logic emerge as trial-and-error effort and informal agreements stay at the core of entrepreneurial process. On the first place, technology innovations emerge as exogenous factors. In this phase change agents can adopt three main positions – either to assume the changes, rearranging their social positions under pressure in order to get some benefits later on, either to oppose it, subversively working to mine it, or adopt "wait and see" behavior, waiting to see the others. Campbell (2004) makes a point arguing that *the more entrepreneurs can demonstrate that their innovations fit the prevailing institutional situation, the greater will be their capacity for innovation and the greater will be the likelihood that their innovations will stick.* During the first phase, the main institutional entrepreneurs take the main risks by mobilizing resources and making arrangements to attract larger social and investments' support and cooperation. By generating good practices, best use cases, successful implementations and returns on investments, they develop new institutional logic, challenging the existing institutional arrangements.

Second, the process of transformation from proto-institutions to institutions requires further diffusion and transposition of new-emerging institutional logic to different fields. Usually this process is related to scaling-up of organizations and requires a new set of skills and social positions. Thus, institutional entrepreneurs transfer the leading role to more professional actors, involving power mechanisms and social dynamics to impose and to outperform the competition. Institutionalization process is then codified as rules that are formal, norms, social expectations and demands are related with the functioning of the new technology. During this phase, the process is based on the social dynamics of the environment, attracting more diverse groups of change agents and followers. As endogenous factor prevail, the social dynamics and power distribution of the change agents will determine the new institutional logic. Thus in most of the cases, the new imposed institutional logic will combine to the dominant institutional logic, and the process of incremental institutional change will resemble on institutional bricolage.

The third phase is about wider adoption and further implementation of the new technologies. In macro-perspectives, the new institutional norms are imposed and social actors have to comply and adapt accordingly. The new formalized institutions define standards, procedures and unified rules. Even more, they make specific sanctions and regulations in the case of breaking the rules. As technology regulations determine service or technology providers, at the end of the process they aim to create barriers of entry for new comers, assuring its leading or monopolistic position, additionally to path-dependences and lock in factors. By imposing new regulations, formal institutions ensure path-dependence and customer lock-in that is later imposed to the end-users as a new norm. It is interesting that most of the social processes in the society will happen afterwards as only when accepted on general level, the new technologies will come back and impose a new transformational micro-level process. This means that the majority of social agents – individuals and organizations will adopt new changes only after the social environment accept them and impose them as new fixed agreements through formal and informal institutions. New technologies are on one side path-dependent and on the other hand need to diffuse faster than the competition. That is why the dominant model for technology innovations will be based on a larger network of social actors including an overall ecosystem of users, suppliers, investors, supply chain and others.

CONCLUSION

New technologies are expected to create a substantial impact and to lead to fundamental shifts in the dominant socio-economic processes. While the processes of digitalization play a substantial role in the dynamic social networks, new institutions will be required to reformulate new social agreements and social dynamics. That is why it is important to discuss the models of incremental institutional changes. Different change agents will determine how social framework of norms, rules and agreements can be affected by technology innovations. Then, the new formal and informal institutions created by the introduction of new technologies transform additionally both the macro perspective of the general framework of rules as well as the micro-perspective.

The main conclusions from the analysis of the present chapter can be summarized as:

- Different groups of change agents will lead the transformational processes, taking several courses of actions regarding the new coming technologies;
- The technology innovations will impose at least three phases of institutional change:
  - Exogenous dynamics, managed by the entrepreneurs, inventors and early-stage investors;
  - Endogenous dynamics, managed by institutional entrepreneurs and professional agents;
  - Social transformation dynamics, managed by formal institution, identifying how most of the social actors will join on a later stage institutional transformation.

It is important to notice that due to the new technologies, power dynamics in the ecosystem will change, as new technologies will transform dominating institutional settings. In the same time, it should be noted that the main institutional processes enabling implementation of new technologies and practices would not influence the dominating models of the redistribution of the resources. On opposite, new institutional arrangements will mainly serve to protect the interests of the power-dominant agents, enhancing the elements such as path-dependence, lock-in and entry barriers. The proposed model help us to identify that this will happen through the processes of diffusion and formalization, when professional officers will take the leading role and will involve more powerful actors on the board. This means that new technologies can further increase social divide. New technologies will enable more powerful social actors to accumulate additional resources and even if the economic performance increase, it brings larger level of inequality and social disintegration.

REFERENCES

Acemoglu, D., Johnson, S., & Robinson, J. A. (2005). Institutions as a fundamental cause of long-run growth. Handbook of economic growth, 1, 385-472.

Ayres, C. E. (1944). The Theory of Economic Progress. Chapel Hill, NC: Academic Press.

Battilana, J. (2006). Agency and institutions: The enabling role of individuals' social position. *Organization, 13*(5), 653–676. doi:10.1177/1350508406067008

Beckert, J. (1999). Agency, entrepreneurs, and institutional change. The role of strategic choice and institutionalized practices in organizations. *Organization Studies, 20*(5), 777–799. doi:10.1177/0170840699205004

Boxenbaum, E. (2004). *The emergence of a proto-institution.* Working Paper. Copenhagen Business School.

Bush, P. D. (1987). The theory of institutional change. *Journal of Economic Issues, 21*(3), 1075–1116. doi:10.1080/00213624.1987.11504697

Campbell, J. L. (1998). Institutional analysis and the role of ideas in political economy. *Theory and Society, 27*(3), 377–409. doi:10.1023/A:1006871114987

Campbell, J. L. (2004). *Institutional change and globalization.* Princeton University Press.

Capoccia, G., & Kelemen, R. D. (2007). The study of critical junctures: Theory, narrative, and counterfactuals in historical institutionalism. *World Politics, 59*(3), 341–369. doi:10.1017/S0043887100020852

Cleaver, F., & De Koning, J. (2015). Furthering Critical Institutionalism. *The International Journal of the Commons, 9*(1), 1–18. doi:10.18352/ijc.605

Commons, J. (1924). *The Legal Foundations of Capitalism.* New York: Macmillan.

Dacin, M. T., Goodstein, J., & Scott, W. R. (2002). Institutional theory and institutional change: Introduction to the special research forum. *Academy of Management Journal, 45*(1), 45–56. doi:10.5465/AMJ.2002.6283388

Dorado, S. (2005). Institutional entrepreneurship, partaking, and convening. *Organization Studies, 26*(3), 385–414. doi:10.1177/0170840605050873

Egbert, H. (2018). *The Gift and Open Science (No. bep-2018-04). St Kliment Ohridski University of Sofia, WP.* Center for Economic Theories and Policies.

Garud, R., Hardy, C., & Maguire, S. (2007). *Institutional entrepreneurship as embedded agency: An introduction to the special issue.* Academic Press.

Gawer, A., & Phillips, N. (2013). Institutional work as logics shift: The case of Intel's transformation to platform leader. *Organization Studies*, *34*(8), 1035–1071. doi:10.1177/0170840613492071

Greenwood, R., Suddaby, R., & Hinings, C. R. (2002). Theorizing change: The role of professional associations in the transformation of institutionalized fields. *Academy of Management Journal*, *45*(1), 58–80. doi:10.2307/3069285

Greif, A., & Laitin, D. D. (2004). A theory of endogenous institutional change. *The American Political Science Review*, *98*(4), 633–652. doi:10.1017/S0003055404041395

Hall, P.A. (2010). *Historical Institutionalism in Rationalist and Sociological Perspective*. Academic Press.

Hall, P. A., & Taylor, R. C. (1996). Political Science and the Three New Institutionalisms. *Political Studies*, *44*(5), 936–957. doi:10.1111/j.1467-9248.1996.tb00343.x

Hodgson, G. M. (1988). Economics and institutions. Journal of Economic Issues.

Holm, P. (1995). The dynamics of institutionalization: Transformation processes in Norwegian fisheries. *Administrative Science Quarterly*, *40*(3), 398–422. doi:10.2307/2393791

Kingston, C., & Caballero, G. (2009). Comparing theories of institutional change. *Journal of Institutional Economics*, *5*(2), 151–180. doi:10.1017/S1744137409001283

Lawrence, T., Suddaby, R., & Leca, B. (2011). Institutional work: Refocusing institutional studies of organization. *Journal of Management Inquiry*, *20*(1), 52–58. doi:10.1177/1056492610387222

Lawrence, T. B., & Suddaby, R. (2006). Institutions and institutional work. In S. R. Clegg, C. Hardy, T. Lawrence, & W. R. Nord (Eds.), *Handbook of Organization Studies* (2nd ed.; pp. 215–254). London: SAGE Publications. doi:10.4135/9781848608030.n7

Lawrence, T. B., Suddaby, R., & Leca, B. (Eds.). (2009). *Institutional work: Actors and agency in institutional studies of organizations*. Cambridge University Press. doi:10.1017/CBO9780511596605

Leca, B., Battilana, J., & Boxenbaum, E. (2008). Agency and institutions: A review of institutional entrepreneurship. Cambridge, MA: Harvard Business School.

Leca, B., & Naccache, P. (2006). A critical realist approach to institutional entrepreneurship. *Organization*, *13*(5), 627–651. doi:10.1177/1350508406067007

Mahoney, J. (2000). Path Dependence in Historical Sociology. *Theory and Society*, *29*(4), 507–548. doi:10.1023/A:1007113830879

Mahoney, J., & Thelen, K. (Eds.). (2010). *Explaining Institutional Change: Ambiguity, Agency, and Power*. New York: Cambridge University Press.

Munshi, K., & Myaux, J. (2006). Social norms and the fertility transition. *Journal of Development Economics*, *80*(1), 1–38. doi:10.1016/j.jdeveco.2005.01.002

North, D. (1990). *Institutions*. Cambridge: Institutional Change, and Economic Performance.

Oliver, C. (1997). Sustainable competitive advantage: Combining institutional and resource-based views. *Strategic Management Journal*, *18*(9), 697–713. doi:10.1002/(SICI)1097-0266(199710)18:9<697::AID-SMJ9093.0.CO;2-C

Ostrom, E. (2010). Beyond markets and states: Polycentric governance of complex economic systems. *Transnational Corporations Review*, *2*(2), 1–12. doi:10.1080/19186444.2010.11658229

Pacheco, D. F., York, J. G., Dean, T. J., & Sarasvathy, S. D. (2010). The coevolution of institutional entrepreneurship: A tale of two theories. *Journal of Management*, *36*(4), 974–1010. doi:10.1177/0149206309360280

Pawlak, M. (2011). *Unintended consequences of institutional work*. Academic Press.

Pierson, P. (2000). Increasing Returns, Path Dependence, and the Study of Politics. *The American Political Science Review*, *94*(02), 251–267. doi:10.2307/2586011

Reay, T., & Hinings, C. R. (2009). Managing the rivalry of competing institutional logics. *Organization Studies*, *30*(6), 629–652. doi:10.1177/0170840609104803

Schmidt, V. A. (2008). Discursive Institutionalism: The Explanatory Power of Ideas and Discourse. *Political Science (Wellington, N.Z.)*, *11*(1), 303–326. doi:10.1146/annurev.polisci.11.060606.135342

Scott, W. (2001). *Institutions and Organizations* (2nd ed.). London: Sage Publications.

Streeck, W., & Thalen, K. (2005). Introduction: Institutional Change in Advanced Political Economies. In Beyond continuity: Institutional change in advanced political economies (pp. p. 1-39). Oxford Univ. Press.

Van Dijk, S., Berends, H., Jelinek, M., Romme, A. G. L., & Weggeman, M. (2011). Micro-institutional affordances and strategies of radical innovation. *Organization Studies*, *32*(11), 1485–1513. doi:10.1177/0170840611421253

Voronov, M., & Vince, R. (2012). Integrating emotions into the analysis of institutional work. *Academy of Management Review*, *37*(1), 58–81.

Zietsma, C., & Lawrence, T. B. (2010). Institutional work in the transformation of an organizational field: The interplay of boundary work and practice work. *Administrative Science Quarterly*, *55*(2), 189–221. doi:10.2189/asqu.2010.55.2.189

Zucker, L. G. (1983). Organizations as institutions. *Research in the Sociology of Organizations*, *2*(1), 1–47.

Chapter 4
Institutions on the Move and Revolutionary Shifts

ABSTRACT

After the analysis of evolutionary institutional changes, the fourth chapter will define revolutionary transformations. Revolutions, conceptualized as abrupt processes of social transformation, follow specific life-cycle and result from two main reasons: lack of efficiency and social justice. The chapter is structured as follows. In the first part, the author will provide a general overview of revolutions and revolutionary processes, discussing in detail its main classifications, characteristics and causes, leading actors, overall phases, and outcomes. The second part will outline different revolutionary processes, zooming on scientific revolutions, technology revolutions, and industrial revolutions. There, industrial revolutions and its main elements are investigated in detail, showing how technological innovations lead to dramatic changes of the social reality. By comparing characteristics of the first, second, and third industrial revolutions, there is proposed a model defining the elements of the Fourth Industrial Revolution. Finally, there is discussed a model outlining how of industrial revolutions can change and transform the social institutions.

DOI: 10.4018/978-1-5225-6270-2.ch004

INTRODUCTION

New technologies such as robots and cognitive computing along with cyber-physical systems and IoT have the potential to disrupt fundamentally existing social order and to open the floor to new disruptive and revolutionary changes. As Schwab (2016) formulates it *...in its scale, scope and complexity, the (new coming) transformation will be unlike anything the humankind has experienced before.*

However, what is a revolutionary process? How can we recognize the characteristics, the dynamics and the deployment of an industrial revolution? Can we prepare, individually or as a group, by adopting appropriate policies and measures to protect our socio-economic realms? Should we take the lead or oppose to transformational processes? The revolutionary movements in a whole and the abrupt transformations in institutional settings attract scholars since Antiquity (Goldstone, 2015). Looking for new understanding of these phenomena, the present chapter will further present and investigate revolutionary movements and radical institutional changes, giving insights into its main characteristics, stages and outcomes. Following the analysis of institutions and their main characteristics in the second chapter, and after discovering the processes of incremental institutional changes and the role of agency in the third chapter, the present chapter will go further by making an in-depth analysis of the causes and outcomes of radical, fundamental and revolutionary institutional changes. As earlier discussed, institutions represent complex socio-political and economic structures that serve to guarantee continuity and reproduction of the existing social arrangements, preserving the established order and stability. Furthermore, designed to sustain the existing social realms, institutions usually have instruments to endure the crisis. That is why, revolutionary transformations in the dominant institutional logic, rules set and social ideologies are rare events in human history (Beck, 2013). Factors as path-dependence, historical distribution and standings of power, lock-in costs, socially embedded mental models, dominant ideologies and shared cultural beliefs impede institutions to react on more dramatic, dynamic and abrupt social demands for new rules. Furthermore, fundamental transformations of rules (and institutions) are possible only through disruptive social processes or "revolutions". That is why, further analysis of the "revolutionary" processes and how they emerge, erupt and lead to profound transformations of the existing rules and institutional frameworks can help us to recognize the common patterns for redefining, accepting and adopting new disruptive social order.

Generally, revolutions confront both the current situation and the mechanisms of the evolutionary processes to resolve it. Many evidences prove that only abrupt revolutionary transformations can change the dominant social order. The studies about substantial transformative changes, as for example for abolishing slavery (Lane & McDonald, 2011), adoption of human rights codes (Donnelly, 2013; Iriye, Goedde & Hitchcock, 2012), and ban of the child labor (Humphreis, 2010) prove that revolutionary institutional transformation cannot be undertook as side projects. Stick to the paradox of institutional embeddedness (Coriat & Dosi, 2000), neo-institutional theories search to interpret institutional transformations only as an evolutionary and incremental process of reconfiguration, bricolage and absorption of new institutions by social actors in the framework of the existing social order. However, we need to gain better understanding about radical changes processes in different fields. Many of the existing institutional settings became obsolete and working within the dominant institutional logic is not efficient. Therefore, it is important to comprehend deeper social and institutional transformations as response to dramatic and unpredicted social shocks, opening the floor to new waves of development and better social arrangements.

During the last few centuries, different political, social, economic and psychological theories emphasized different details of the revolutionary processes and its consequences for the social development. Revolutions are not just a way to reconfigure the existing power dynamics, but they provide mechanisms to overcome path dependences, leading to subversive shift in the dominant paradigms, ideologies and mental models. Therefore, the main aim of the present chapter is to identify the theoretical concepts and models behind revolutions and revolutionary processes. In order to gain better understanding and explanations of the characteristics, phases and processes of revolutionary transformations, we will propose a general overview of the revolutionary patterns, highlighting similarity, parallels and analogies of revolutionary processes, comparing institutional transformations by socio-political, industrial, scientific, productive and other revolutionary processes.

The structure of the chapter is as follows. In the first part, we will provide a general overview of revolutions and revolutionary processes, discussing in details its main classifications, characteristics and causes, leading actors, overall phases and outcomes. The second part will outline different revolutionary processes, zooming on scientific revolutions, technology revolutions and industrial revolutions. Here, we will emphasize on industrial revolutions and its main elements, investigating in details how technological innovations can lead to dramatic changes of the social reality. By comparing characteristics of the first, second and third industrial revolutions, we will derive to a model of the elements of the Fourth Industrial Revolution. Finally, analysis is proposed, discussing how industrial revolutions can change and transform the social institutions.

BACKGROUND

It is difficult to find a single definition of the term *revolution*, as it is widely used in political and social sciences to designate a "fundamental turnover of the social order" (Beck, 2013). Generally, in the strict sense, the term 'revolution' means *a rapid, fundamental transformation of the state and social structure, accompanied by mass uprising from below*[1]. Commonly, revolutions mark a process of social instability and violent unrest. In this context, Huntington states that revolution is a: *rapid, fundamental, and violent domestic change in the dominant values and myths of a society, in its political institutions, social structure, leadership and government activities and policies* (Huntigton, 1968; 2006). Skockpol (1976) transfer this definition to social revolutions, summing up that they are *rapid, basic transformations of socio-economic and political institutions*. Goldstone (2015) defines that on theory, revolutions can change everything:

it can create new states, produce new institutions of government, rearrange holdings of land and wealth, change the basis for social status and transform the dominant ideology in the society... In the same time, revolutions are not completely transformative events as they promise to be....

But as it is highlighted later on: *revolutions and revolutionary situations are those rare times where people challenge the very order of things, seeking to recreate the societies they live in.* (Goldstone, 2015).

In its general use, the term "revolution" is opposed to the concept of "evolution", and designates a radical break with the past. Revolutions mark a situation of "abrupt discontinuity" (Allen, 2011). This way the term "revolution" fast transfer to wider fields, such as "scientific revolution" (Kuhn, 1962), "agrarian revolution" (Paige, 1978), "industrial revolution" (Stearns, 1998; Labor, 1990), "technology revolution" (Perez, 2009), "information revolution" (Robertson, 1990) and even "domestic revolution" (Mintz &

Kellogg, 1989) in order to highlight the radical shift with the processes, practices and traditions in the past. Thus, revolutions designate a rapid, fundamental and irreversible conversion of the dominant logic, ideology and wide spread mental models, leading to radical change of the established social norms.

It is important to make a differentiation between the terms "revolution" and "war" comprising different forms of military actions and violence. On the first place, revolutionary processes are not automatically leading to violence and criminal social unrests. More recently, the studies of Stephan and Chenoweth (2008) prove that non-violent forms of revolutions and huge social protests can lead to efficient and abrupt institutional transformations. Other scholars classify mass social protests as forms of revolution as well (Goldstone, 2001; Gurr, 2015). On the second place, the term "war", even in its wide meaning such as "trade wars" do not mean transformation of institutional realms, but rather assume change in the power domination. Here, wars imply for violent and forceful taking over the dominance and the control on specific territory (market).

Thus, in terms of our research, we will define "revolution" as a bottom-up social process, disrupting the logic of the established institutional settings. The revolutionary movements in institutions do not necessarily have "ready proposals" and better offerings for new type of regulations and new social agreements. Rather they raise the need to overcome the existing "path dependences" and to define new ideologies that can better serve and organize the social order. In this specific role, revolutions come as a social act highlighting the need for more efficient social mechanisms to reduce uncertainty.

THE THEORIES OF REVOLUTIONS

Revolutionary theories evolve since centuries in the attempt to focus the efforts, to structure the scope, methodology and interests of the researchers to understand their complexity. During the last century, four primary generations of revolutionary schools developed, extending the used methods, subject and theories (Beck, 2013). In this perspective, most of the revolutionary theories that emphasize on the structural conditions of revolutions tend to focus on the revolutionary seizure of the state power, while theories outlining actors' motivation view revolutions as an open-ended process of social transformation. Psychological and functional theories aim to explain revolutionary movements while structural theories focus on revolutionary outcomes. Political theories look to study and research revolutionary situations. Based on the fourth generational study (Goldstone, 2001; Lawson, 2016), we will make a general overview of revolutions in an attempt to structure a general framework and interplay between factors and elements behind any revolution movement. Thus making a summary of the main theoretical approaches, Goldstone (2001) find out that revolutions are classified sometimes by its outcomes, sometimes by its leading actors. On Table 1 there are presented the main types of revolutions following his approach.

Reasons and Causes of Revolutionary Movements

Institutional stability is not an inertial state but it implies an ongoing, successful process of reproducing social institutions and the cultural expectations of the social actors across the time (Thelen, 1999).

Making an overview of the social theories, Beck (2013) discovers that revolutions evolve due to three main reasons: when state structures are under increasing strains (due to economic pressure or international influence); in the case of brittle governing regimes (mainly due to political unrepresentation of powerful social groups); and finally following the structuring of larger revolutionary social coalitions, formed by powerful social groups and elites. This is confirmed as well in Goldstone (2001) who outlines the main two factors for political and institutional stability. On one side, the internal stability is ensured by effective interplay between the state (the rulers), the elites and the popular groups. On the other side, a big impact has the international configuration of forces and the stability of the positions of external influencers.

Table 1. Classification of revolutions and revolutionary types based on Goldstone (2001)

Outcomes	Actors	Non-Political Revolutions
Great revolutions (as French revolution of 1789)	Elite revolutions (elites initiate mass mobilization to reverse the power)	Scientific revolution
Political revolutions (Changes in government institutions)	Rebellions (oppositional movements, that do not aim to take power - like worker protests, strikes, regional rebellions and others)	Industrial revolution
Social revolutions (autonomous lower-class revolts)	Protests (peaceful social movements) Color revolutions Non-violent forms of revolutions, strikes, social movements	Production/ Technology revolution

In this complex configuration, the stability of the rulers and institutional framework of the ruling regime depends mainly on how "effective" and "just" they are perceived by the elites and by the popular groups.

Institutional framework is stable, when the ruler - the government, the ruling class, the established social order, is perceived both as effective in terms of "competent" and "able to tackle with the rising challenges" and "just", or fair, loyal and equitable according to the expected standards. Only in this situation, rulers can get support and sustain among different complex configurations of the social dynamics. Otherwise, in case that the rulers (and its institutions) appears both "ineffective" and "unjust", this will undermine the support from the elites and the popular groups, and this will lead to social protests, subversive tensions and unrest. However, the revolutionary movement is not an automatic response, as there should be present some further prerequisites. Thus in order to raise an organized revolutionary opposition, there should be in place such elements as plasticity of the elites and popular groups alignments, the processes of revolutionary mobilization and leadership, clear goals and outcomes set by the revolutionary actors (Goldstone, 2001).

In the border cases, when the rulers are perceived to be ineffective, but just, they can still gain the elite support for reforms, by restructuring institutional settings. On the other case, when rulers are considered unjust, they may be tolerated as long as they are perceived to be effective in pursuing economic or nationalist goals. Therefore, in order that a situation emerge as a revolutionary, it is necessary that the state and the popular groups are in a configuration where the elites are largely united or deeply divided or polarized and where opposition elites link up the protest with popular groups.

The bottom-up support of the social groups play a crucial role (Mann, 2012). If population is distressed by government actions (or inaction in the face of the crisis and hardships), and express their anger through riots, revolts, workers' strikes, demonstrations, acts of protest and disorder, it is the elite's responses that determine whether these actions will spread and grow into a revolutionary process or not. History proves that social protests only rarely give rise to political or social revolutions. (Goldstone, 2001). To overturn the ruling regime and the dominant institutional framework, an organized opposition must exist. Furthermore, it should be capable to persuade the military to desert the regime or to raise an alternative force capable of engaging the military. Thus, the potential for a truly revolutionary process arises only when skilled and influential members of society start criticizing the regime, calling for change, and seeking followers who will help them promote their new vision for the society and social order. This inevitably requires the skills of elites who can formulate a persuasive vision of a better society and better institutions, undermine the credibility of the existing rulers, and organize sufficiently large-scale popular protests or sufficiently strong armed forces of their own, that then can challenge the regime.

The revolutionary processes can be checked as well with the recently emerged mathematical and stochastic models (Howlett & Rayner, 2006). One of the findings of Goldstone (2001) proves that historical data of political upheavals and institutional change correlate with three main variables: regime type, international trade, and infant mortality (Goldstone, 2001). As the empirical data suggest, regime type has a U-shaped relationship to political unrest: democracies and autocracies are both stable, but partial democracies are at higher risk. National stability is linked as well with international trade, explaining that larger portion of the gross national product (GNP) is tied to international trade. Finally, national stability correlates with lower infant mortality. Goldstone (2001) find out that partial democracies are precisely those states in which elites and rulers have begun the process of conflict, reform, and concessions and rulers are at a highly unstable juncture. As an example, Machiavelli in his seminal book *The Prince*, advised rulers to undertake reforms only from the position of strength; if undertaken from a position of weakness, they will further undermine the support for the regime.

The intensive international trade can mean both manageable levels of corruption and restrained elite competition. Conversely, countries that have below-expected involvement in international trade for the size of their economy are likely to have elite factions that are distorting trade or economic activity for their benefit, heightening intra-elite conflicts. Finally, infant mortality is a summary indicator for standard of living. It can addresses popular perceptions of the effectiveness of the regime in providing for the popular welfare and nationalist programs of economic development. In all the major studies, regardless of methods, it is those factors that affect the strength of the state, competition among elites, and popular living standards that determine the stability or instability of the ruling regime (Goldstone 2001).

The findings about regime stability are supported by the study of Skockpol (1976) who analyzed social revolutions in France, Russia and China. The author concludes that the three big social revolutions are remarkably similar in the basic causes. Thus the lack of the ability of the old regime officials, the ruling dynasty or generally the rulers to mobilize resources in order to meet credibly the challenges posed by involvement in the modernizing world. The three emblematic social revolutions came as a response of the crises of modernization and technological challenges. The lack of national economic development and/or counter military competition or threats from more developed nations abroad and in its structural dynamics, undermined the national political institutions that failed to mobilize resources to guarantee order at home and to counter foreign threats (Skockpol, 1976).

The Social Movements and Institutional Change

Social movements are important motors of institution building, deinstitutionalization, and reinstitutionalization, taking substantial role for any institutional change (Rao, Monin, & Durand, 2003; Scott, 2010).

Social movements are collective challenges to authority in political and cultural domains (Jenkins, 1983). Scholars distinguish between instrumental movements and identity movements. Instrumental movements seek to redress injustices, challenge economic and political structures, and strive for policy impact in the form of new laws or governance structures. By contrast, identity movements arise in opposition to the dominant cultural codes, consist of a "we-feeling" sustained through interactions among movement participants, and are expressed through cultural materials such as names, narratives, symbols, and rituals (Taylor, Whittier, Morris, & Mueller, 1992; Allardt, 1971). Identity movements seek autonomy rather than justice, aspire to cultural change, and promote new institutional logics (Gamson, 1995; Polleta & Jasper, 2001). Unlike instrumental movements powered by bureaucratic social movement organizations, identity movements tend to be more informal, decentralized, and diffuse (Melucci, 1995).

Scott (2010) states that social movement scholars give particular emphasis to three general classes of variables: (1) political opportunities: the extent to which extant governance structure provide openings to insurgent groups seeking change; (2) the forms of organizing available to insurgents – vehicles such as informal networks, neighborhoods, unions, and churches, that allow individuals to mobilize and engage in collective action, and; (3) collective processes of interpretation, such as theorization, translation, and framing, that mediate between opportunities and action. When social movements are successful, it is usually because they are able to persuade established powers – employing organizations or governments to adopt their reform goals. When this happens movement actors 'hand-off' the responsibility for following through on programs of reform to others – executives or elected officials.

Identity movements arise when activists construct institutional gaps by showing how the existing logic cannot be an effective guide for action. In doing so, activists exploit the inherent mutability of an institutional logic or seize on its incompatibility with other master logics on the landscape. Identity movements create institutional gaps through framing activities that situate *relevant sets of actors in time and space and by attributing characteristics to them that suggest specifiable relationships and lines of action* (Rao, Monin, & Durand, 2003).

The Outcomes of Revolutions

Among the most interesting characteristics of any revolutionary process are the outcomes. Revolutions represent a structured social movement of protest, organized by goal-oriented leaders that mobilize popular groups, united behind specific ideology. Therefore, the leaders of the revolutionary movements are expected to strive for more just and efficient rules and institutions by restructuring the bases of the previous political power and reshaping the traditions of the societies. However, empirical results demonstrate that in general, revolutions lead to institutions and regimes that are more centralized and more bureaucratic than the ones they replace (Skocpol, 1976). The immediate goals of the leaders of revolutions are first to seize and expand their (state) authority, to change the rules for access to political power, and to restructure beliefs and institutions for cutting the opportunity for counter-revolution. Further it appears that the very effort to rebuild political institutions undermine the economic growth, and undermine the efficiency of the new regime. However, whatever their failings, revolutions are remarkably successful in mobilizing population and utilizing that mobilization for promoting values and ideologies as fairness, democratization, equality or prosperity along with political and military power (Skocpol, 1994).

Structure of Revolutions

Any revolutionary movement in general unfolds in 12 main phases (Goldstone, 2001), as visualized in Table 2. The first phase – instability, emerges with the decline of the general conditions and degeneration of institutional stability. The list of factors that may produce institutional degeneration is long, ranging from global transformations of the economy or political system to localized corruption or unsatisfactory reforms by the ruling clique. Any factors that overstrain the military or financial capacity of the regime can lead to ineffectiveness; any actions that traduce traditional or legal norms or inflict unexpected harms can undercut perceptions of justice. Both changes in macro-level and micro-level conditions can deteriorate current situation. For example, factors as deteriorating access to jobs, falling real incomes, or heightened elite competition for positions, can produce accusations of both injustice and ineffectiveness, leading to perceptions of regime vulnerability and solidarity within and across networks and persuading people to act against a regime. The precise combination of factors by which a particular state becomes "unhappy" maybe highly specific to that regime— in fact, even the cardinal cases of the revolutions in Russia, China, and France showed different combinations of factors with varying magnitudes (Goldstone, 2001; Mahoney & Snyder 1999).

Emerging opposition among elites occurs when the regime loses its grip on the essential conditions of stability. Then a process of opposition mobilization and struggle begins, which in turn affects perceptions and relationships among actors. In this struggle, opposition actors, rulers, and counter movements deploy ideologies, seek to link up with different groups and networks, and build a sense of the justice and inevitable triumph of their cause. In some cases, a long struggle is required for the opposition to build support and for the state to lose it; in other cases, perceptions and actions shift so quickly that the state collapses with startling rapidity.

Mobilization the actors include formation of leaders and factions, dominating the revolutionary coalition, intervention of foreign powers. Vanguard groups, interpersonal networks, and cross-class coalitions are clearly pivotal in these processes; without them, revolutions are unlikely to develop. In addition, the ideology and organizational position of key actors can help account for the variety of outcomes.

In most historical cases of revolution, the first three stages form a "suite" of changes that develop before the overthrow of the old regime, with all three going on at the same time and reinforcing one another. However, the intensity and character of these conditions can vary considerably. The initial regime change usually occurs before all the tensions and contradictions in the opposition coalition have been resolved. Then additional struggles can follow, explaining stages from five to nine that form another suite of connected events (counterrevolution), as these stages often occur together or in tight sequence as a cluster of events, again mutually reinforcing one another.

Only when radicalism, counterrevolution, civil and international wars end, the revolution reaches a stage of moderation and stability. However, even this stage is not the end, as many revolutions experience a further stage of renewed radicalism. The revolutionary process is over only after conservative

Table 2. Classification of four main revolutionary stages based on Goldstone (2001)

INITIATION PHASE	1.Economics deteriorate, undermining state authority; elite defection & formation of opposition;	2. Polarization and coalition building	3. Mass mobilization
CHANGE OF THE REGIME	4. Initial change of the regime	5. Further social polarization	
COUNTERREVOLUTION	6. Restauration of the old regime	7. Counterrevolution; 8. Civil war 9. International war	10. Radicalization of the changed regime and "terror"
RESTABILIZATION	11. Revolutionary moderation	12. Regime consolidation	

or stable consolidation, in which the main goals of the new regime are simply to prosper and to remain in power (Goldstein, 2001).

SCIENTIFIC REVOLUTION

In order to reveal more structural process of the abrupt revolutionary movements, we will further structure the theory of non-violent revolutions. In this context, scientific revolutions are another illustration of the complex social process, showing the abrupt and radical shift with the past. Since the Enlightenment and the formulation of the modern scientific method (Hall & Dunstan, 1954), scientific research develop as conservative and evolutionary process. In this framework, Kuhn defines the concepts of scientific revolution. In summary, he finds out how new scientific theories replace the old ones in a revolutionary manner rather than incrementally building on them. Thus, Kuhn defines the term "scientific revolution" to designate the radical change of the new theory in science and makes it analogous to social and political revolutions (Kuhn, 1962; 2006). The main building block of the Kuhn's theory is the life cycle of a scientific paradigm. The core cycle of scientific revolution deployment is illustrated in Table 3. Getting into details of the development of the scientific paradigm, he concludes that the process of

Table 3. Stages of scientific revolution –Life-cycle of scientific paradigm, based on Kuhn (1962)

Stage	Characteristics	Reason
Emergence	Absence of commonly accepted beliefs or standards governing scientific activity.	Needs for a new theory, explaining the real phenomena
Normal science	As a theory attracts nearly every scientist in the field—thereby becoming the dominant paradigm—normal science begins.	Emergence of a paradigm, studies, accumulation of data and case studies
Crisis	During normal science, clashes between theory and data are often resolved in favor of theory—it is often presumed that any anomalous observations are wrong, or the calculations erroneous, so that further puzzle-solving effort will resolve the anomaly. A paradigm can enter crisis when enough unsolved puzzles become recognized by practitioners as important anomalies, persuading them that the theory must, after all, be questioned. As persistent anomalies accumulate, increasing numbers of scientists will devote their time to solving them rather than addressing new puzzles, and some may propose radical solutions. Normal science continues until a crisis arises.	Accumulation of anomalies, lack of explanations;
Revolution - emergence of a new paradigm	A revolution occurs when a new paradigm based on such a radical reconceptualization gains wide acceptance, and science is reconstructed from new fundamentals.	New paradigm better explaining the accumulated examples;

replacing the dominant paradigm may be quick, or the crisis may deepen for decades as new theories may fail to sprout or flower.

It is important to stress that scientific revolutions are social and institutional revolutions, as they aim to challenge the socially accepted dominant institutional logics and "mental model" by imposing a new "truth", new knowledge that extend understanding of the reality in a social environment (Corri,1993).

Scientific activity is highly embedded and structured in institutional arrangements. Scientist cannot work and validate their work alone. There exists many social levels of research communities, organized in a number of open collaboration networks, ranging from small group of researchers in a lab, to departments and universities, to the network of national and international funding agencies, journals' and conferences' boards, and professional societies. Thus, the dynamics of scientific revolution is closely related to a social process of radical institutional transformation in general. That is how Sterman and Wittenberg (1999) propose a new model to investigate what is more relevant – the new theory or its social acceptance. That is how they estimate the relative importance of the explanatory power of the new paradigm, or the "truth" of a new theory, versus contingencies external to science such as the social, political, and cultural context of emergence, or even chance factors. Based on a simulations, they find out that the fate of a particular new theory or paradigm is strongly conditioned by the circumstances surrounding its creation (social context), and only weakly influenced by its explanatory power or logical force (at least for theories above a minimum threshold of explanatory power).

Therefore, the environmental conditions at the time a new theory is created, such as the morale and confidence of practitioners in the old paradigm and the number of contending alternative new theories, powerfully determine whether a new theory will rise to dominance or quickly perish. Furthermore, weak competitive environments make it more likely that a new paradigm rise to dominance, but it can condemn even powerful paradigms to early deaths as it can be extended too far and too fast, generating anomalies and prematurely destroying confidence. On opposite, though competition reduces the likelihood of paradigm's survival, but gives those that do survive time to bootstrap themselves into normal science, insulating them against mere disconfirmation, and ensuring they persist until the anomalies ultimately cause a revolution.

TECHNOLOGY REVOLUTIONS

Following the methodology and the socio-technological innovations of Schumpeter, Perez (2010) proposes an in-depth investigation about the structures, main characteristics and elements of technology revolutions. In her model, presented below, she identifies six main technological revolutions, similar by their structure and development. Technology revolutions form a random collection of technology systems and justifies its conceptualization based on two main features (Perez, 2004):

- **Strong Interconnectedness and Interdependence of the Participating Systems in Their Technologies and Markets:** Sharing similar engineering principles, similar skills for design and operation, common network of suppliers of inputs, services, interdependent distribution outlets, very strong interlinkages, often being the main market for each other; diffusion generates coherent patterns of consumption and use, learning in one system facilitates the learning in the next and the installation of conditions for the use of one set of products becomes an externality for the next;

- **The Capacity to Transform Profoundly the Rest of the Economy (and Eventually Society).**

The core industries of each revolution respond on three main categories:

1. **The Motive Branches:** Produce cheap inputs with pervasive applicability.
2. **The Carrier Branches:** The most visible and active users of the inputs and represent the *paradigmatic products* of the revolution, carrying to the "world" the new opportunities: Computers, software and mobile phones, automobiles and electrical appliances in the fourth, steel steam ships in the third, iron steam engines in the second and textile machinery in the first.
3. **The Infrastructures:** Part of the revolution in terms of technology and whose impact is felt in shaping and extending the market boundaries for all industries: Internet today, roads and electricity in the fourth, the world transport network in the third (transcontinental railways and steamship routes and ports), national railways in the second and canals in the first.

Based on the Schumpeter's analysis of Technology revolutions, Perez (2004; 2009) derives a three-phase theory of the structure of technology revolutions. Based on her model (Table 4), she resumes that on average it takes about 50–60 years for the technologies of each revolution to fully deploy (and exhaust) their innovation and market potential. The cycle of the technology revolution is made of installation and deployment period, separated by a "turning point".

The installation period starts with a Big Bang and Irruption phase based on technology innovations, fast transforming to frenzy or gilded age. The technology investments create a large accumulation of capital and lead to

Table 4. Stages of technology revolutions (Perez, 2004; 2009)

Installation	Deployment
Creative destruction	Creative construction
New paradigm versus old paradigm	Widespread application of the new paradigm
Financial capital leads	Production capital leads
Bubble creation	Maturity

eruption of financial bubbles, followed by major crash. Perez (2009) thus explains this phenomenon with the high volatility of the financial capital. In this situation, technological innovation is swiftly followed by financial innovation. The world of finance itself is among the pioneers in adopting the new paradigm, especially in organization, equipment, transport and communications. It rapidly invents, learns and diffuses new ways of providing venture capital, of attracting new investors and new capital to the market and of leveraging, handling, hedging and spreading risk.

After the crucial turning point, institutional arrangements and adequate environment pave the way toward a deployment period or golden age, allowing wider diffusion and synergy and leading to maturity of the new technologies and creation of new technology shift. While the first phase is leaded by financial capital, it creates a big social and economic discrepancies, inequality raises, social price and crashed investments. This phase is characterized by development of basic infrastructure the second part is deployed by production capital.

INDUSTRIAL REVOLUTIONS

Industrial revolutions come as complex technology-triggered socio-economic shifts that attract the interest of researchers from various disciplines. Industrial revolutions provoke disruptive systematic changes, affecting every aspect of human and social life. In general, industrial revolution is a *massive set of changes that begin when radical innovations in technologies and organizational forms are extensively introduced in key manufacturing sectors* (Stearns, 1998). Industrial revolutions fuel the cycle theory of long waves, first observed by Kondratieff and Schumpeter (Lloyd-Jones, 1990; Wonglimpiyarat, 2005; Freeman, 2013). Kondratieff, based on statistical analysis of economic data from industrialized countries, observed for the first-time long-term growth cycles with a length of 40-60 years. Refining his long waves to comparatively shorter cyclical fluctuations, Schumpeter involved technical change and entrepreneurship at the root of the economic growth (Perez, 2009).

At the core of industrial revolutions are the basic scientific and engineering principles that opened a completely new universe of possibilities (Morkyr, 1997; 1998; 2017). The dynamism of innovation in those opportunity spaces is internally driven, and involved industries mutually reinforce. However, their evolution is constantly creating new spaces for innovation in the rest of the economy because of the generic technologies of ample applicability. Among the main all-pervasive generic technologies come new infrastructures and all others new sorts of materials and equipment that penetrate the operational context of every other industry (Morkyr, 1997).

However, the deployment of Industrial revolutions strongly depends from institutions and political factors (Labor, 1990). To put it differently, the decision-making institutions in each economy create an environment in which technological progress can either thrive or wither. It may seem trivial to state that society ought to be hospitable to new technology, which is a cheap way of increasing economic welfare, but the historical experiences indicates that few societies have followed this advice. The amount of resistance against technological progress that is observed through most of the history is such that *at times one wonders how new technologies emerged at all* (Morkyr, 1997). Thus, favorable institutional frameworks will induce triggers of progress to apply their efforts in the most remunerative and socially productive ways. In other words, institutions determine whether those efforts will result in the creation of wealth or primarily in the wealth redistribution.

The industrial revolutions are distinguished by a shift to capital-intensive production, rapid growth in productivity and living standards, the formation of large corporate hierarchies, overcapacity, and, eventually, closure of facilities (Stearns, 1998). Therefore, industrial revolutions are both technologically and organizationally driven and integrate both intellectual and manual power. Furthermore, innovations largely spread in all economy sectors, and in all facets – marketing, finance, industry and others (Morkyr, 1998). New technologies lead to changing attitudes and practices, encouraging formation of new culture of entrepreneurship, innovations and risk-taking. The result is a radical shift in the economy structure, including the general composition of total output, raw material and energy inputs, distribution of the employment. Finally, all economic changes are considered as part of general process rather than part of specific events.

By going deeper into analysis of the previous industrial revolutions, we will try to identify its main characteristics, processes, factors, and changes. However, it has to be outlined that they lead to complex systematic shifts. Therefore, spreading over different geographical locations and industries, they involve different institutional contexts and broad transformations that cannot be easily measured. Additionally, Solow defined the productivity paradox, claiming that *changes can be observed everywhere but not in the performance data* (Craft, 2002; David, 1990). Furthermore, industrial revolution boot aggregate welfare on the social price and lead to large costs from obsolete human and physical capital, generating substantial hardship, misunderstanding, and bitterness (Labor, 1990).

Different authors analyze and measure the models of industrial and technology revolutions and their impact differently. While Schwab (2016) and Economic World Forum defined the coming of the fourth industrial revolution in 2016, other scholars have difficulty to investigate the third industrial revolution. On the other turn, Perez (2009) claimed that based on the methodology of Schumpeter there can be clearly identified five technology revolution. The blurry differences between the revolutions and the intersection of complex political and economic curves make it difficult to identify strictly the moment of start and the deployment of every phase.

Characteristics of an Industrial Revolution

It is ambiguous to define the main elements of an industrial revolution. As Morkyr (1997) states neither the number of major technology breakthroughs, neither their impact could be an adequate criterion for defining one social process as Industrial Revolution. At the end of the date, he concludes that the main factors are technological advances that affect the economy. Based on that, Morkyr (1997) defines the following main characteristics and features of Industrial revolutions:

- **General Purpose Technology:** GPT, or cluster of macro-inventions and technologies (defined both as door-opening or gap-filling inventions).
- **Productivity Paradox:** The major impact of GPT on productivity may be very long-delayed, because it still needed to be refined and improved, and in part because good alternatives are still available (David, 1990).
- **Network Dependencies:** A number of compatibility conditions have to be satisfied, as innovation is a coordination game since the development of railroads and the telegraph in the 1830s.
- **Research and Development:** Or improving our understanding for the underlying scientific principles, allowing adapting techniques to changing circumstances. Technological progress is quite different, as serendipity still plays a bigger role in the process.
- **Organizational Structure:** A real Industrial Revolution consists not just of technological innovations but also of such innovations that make an impact at the level of industrial organization.

The Causes of Industrial Revolutions

Morkyr (1994) observes one important fact, that not "inventions" but their "practical implementations" are the main triggers of complex social disruptive processes. Thus, in his analysis he found out that British were leading not in innovative ideas, but in their practical implementation in further innovative technologies and applications.

Further, Jehnsen (1993) makes an overview of the main causes of industrial revolutions, deriving to the following statements:

- **Increase in the Rate of Capital Formation (RoI):** Low interest rate encourage investments, triggering profits and capital gains);
- **Increase in the World Trade (Natural Result of Expanding Geographical Frontier):** Stimulating export industries;
- **Technology Revolution:** Autonomous increase in knowledge both in technology and in organization of the industry (business optimizations), making it more productive, the knowledge is practically transformed into machinery;
- **Growth of Laissez-Faire Ideology and Rational Ethic Towards Wealth:** The results of the changes both in philosophic and religious convictions,
- **Agricultural Change:** Supporting the raise of non-agricultural workforce (human capital)
- **Population Growth:** Both increased demand (for goods and services), supply (cheap labor costs);
- **Shifts in Internal Consumption:** Not only extension of traditional demands but new products generate increased demand for products and services.

It is interesting to mention the research of Dudley (2010). In order to explain the preconditions for rise of General Purpose Technologies that fuel Industrial revolutions and potential growth, the author investigate about 116 GPT. He makes a correlation analysis for the dates 1700-1850 and he finds out that innovation required favorable institutions and high factor prices. According to his findings, the key factors having favorable impact on the development of GPTs seems to have been cultural and connected to informal norms. For example, he claims that GPT flourished due to patterns of collaboration and altruism, supportive religion norms and level of education and not last – appropriate size of the language area.

Table 5. Factors and elements of the industrial revolutions, based on Morkyr (1998) and Jensen (1993)

Factors	Evidences	Reasons
Emerge new technologies	Cluster of technologies GPT	Increase the rate of capital formation
New organizational principles	Economy of scale and decease of the transaction costs	Formation of large corporate hierarchies
Growth	Increased aggregate welfare	Rapid growth in productivity
Capital	Large capital investments	Capital intensive production
Obsolescence of human and physical capital	Inequality	Overcapacity Closure of facilities
Infrastructure standardization	Coordination and standarization	Stimulate the trade and export

First Industrial Revolution (1760-1880)

Among the main findings behind the First Industrial Revolution is that it emerged in Britain from large implementation of new practices and routines, combining different technology and organizational innovations (Allen, 2011; Humphries, 2010; Lloyd-Jones, 1990; Stearns, 1998; Voigtländer & Voth, 2006). The First Industrial Revolution and the technological progress in the 18th century was essentially empirical and non-science based. Most of the technological developments preceding it had little or no scientific base. Further, it created a chemical industry with no chemistry, an iron industry without metallurgy, power machinery without thermodynamics. Engineering, medical technology, and agriculture until 1850 were pragmatic bodies of applied knowledge in which things worked, but rarely people understood why they worked (Stearns, 1998). In 1750 was born the model of the manufacturing firm, or the idea of placing all workers together in a single site. Economies of scale at the plant level become prominent with a centralized power supply, with a decline in transportation costs, and with the appearance of such novelties as gas lighting. Some further factors that can be added to that analysis is the information costs, the growing need for standardized products and quality control in larger and anonymous markets, the need to retrain workers in an age of rapidly changing technology and others.

Second Industrial Revolution (1870 - 1914)

Some main differences are observed between the first and the second industrial revolutions. Morkyr (1998) sum up his findings for the Second Industrial Revolution, outlining its main characteristics such as:

- **Rise in Scientific Knowledge and the Mutual Feedbacks:** Between the two main forms of knowledge, or between science (very broadly defined) and technology (practical know-how);
- **Organization of Production Processes and Economy of Scale:** Changed organizational practices in production, leaded to growth in the industries with huge economies of scale, especially manufacturing.
- **Standardization:** Unified measuring systems and industry standards demanded for a great deal of coordination and institutionalization, including for example: determining railroad gauges, electricity voltages, the layout of typewriter keyboards, rules of the road, and other forms of standardization.

Third Industrial Revolution

While there is a consensus about the emergence of the First and the Second Industrial Revolutions, the Third industrial revolution remain a subject of discussions. Based on general economic indicators, Greenword (1996) marked 1974 as the date of the start of the Third industrial revolution. His finding is based on a complex correlation between technology progress, income inequality and productivity growth. Troxler (2014) put another vision for the Third Industrial Revolution, invoked by the authors such as Neil Gershenfeld (2005), who wrote about '*Fab. The Coming Revolution on Your Desktop*' and Jeremy Rifkin (2011) describing '*The Third Industrial Revolution -How Lateral Power is Transforming Energy, the Economy, and the World*'.

Recognizing the importance of ideas and values, Mokyr (2017) underline that among the key factors triggering the first three Industrial revolutions in Europe is the significant shift of the values of the ruling elites, putting science and technologies high in the hierarchy of social prestige in the centuries before and during the industrial revolutions. Thus, even if "Industrial revolutions are not made by superstars", Mokyr (2017) identifies the importance of small groups of savants who define the new theoretical concepts and knowledge and then the role of the larger group of fabricants, who adopt them and through incremental modifications and innovations replicate them in a larger scale. Further by outlining the main characteristics of the industrial revolutions, Mokyr (1988) mentioned that formation of knowledge and institutional arrangements (such as ideologies, shared concepts and beliefs), play a significant role for emergence of new technologies and the subsequent economic growth (in parallel to the findings of North (1988) and Inglehart (2015).

In the same time, according to the model of Perez (2002), each techno-economic paradigm evolves and diffuses on three inter-related levels:

1. Any real new technology systems first grow and diffuses in the productive sphere.
2. Accumulation of empirical observations lead to "best practice" models, and it is adapted to the new technologies, taking the best advantage of them. This model diffuses across all industries, modernizing them and establishing new emerging managerial "common sense" for further investments and innovations.
3. The changed general set of "common sense" principles in organizations spread wider in the society and require new forms of institutions and new institutional design.

Based on the overview of the theoretical findings from the previous industrial revolutions, we will outline how the trends of Industry 4.0 surpass the level of simple technology innovations and define more important transformational processes. Even if the historical analogies with the past may be misleading and dangerous, our approach aims to highlight the new coming social changes. Thus, more specifically, the factors that determine an Industrial revolution are explored following the model of Mokyr (1988) and are synthesized in Table 6.

DISCUSSION

It is important to stress that revolutions provoke paradigm shift and transformation of the complete socio-economic systems, changing the gravity and influencing the existing equilibrium between the power and control in the social system. Actually revolutionary changes in institutions (or changes of dominant social rules) try to reestablish a new network of rules and to stabilize a new social order. It will succeed only if it provides more efficient

Table 6. Analysis of the characteristics of Industry revolutions based on Mokyr (1988) and adopting the model to Fourth Industrial Revolution

Characteristics of an Industry Revolution	Fourth Industrial Revolution
The progress is not limited to a single sector but it is omnipresent	The new coming digital innovations disrupt all sectors such as manufacturing, transportations, city development, utilities, power generation, agriculture, logistics, healthcare and many others
General purpose technologies (GPT)	New technologies under the Industry 4.0 can be classified as GPT as they become universally adopted as new technology backbone
Emergence of new organizations and company forms	Emerging platform-based organizations outperform and challenge the process-based organizations, requiring new organizational forms
Networks and standardization	Innovations become a larger coordination game, depending on networks and standardization effects within innovation ecosystems
Knowledge formation	Considerable accumulation of new empirical knowledge is expected, based on the data provided by sensors; AI and machine learning will further contribute for the emerging data models and others
Skills, human capital and income distribution, technology unemployment	Increasing global inequality rates, raising debates about technology unemployment, raising needs for new digital skills and human capital up-grading
Globalization effect	Communication and information flows along with intensified movements of humans, capital and goods along the stage of industrial revolutions

and socially just models. In the same time, new technologies and innovations are not "neutral". First, they lead to changes in the "common sense" or the ideology settings and cognitive bases within the society. Second, they create path dependences and standardization, which in term determine power distribution and the emergence of new specific ideology mindset.

In order to outline the transformation processes in the framework of the "Fourth Industrial Revolution" we will come back to the *four main revolutionary stages* as defined in Figure 1: initiation, change of the regime, counterrevolution and restabilization.

Figure 1. Political phases of Institutional Radical Changes during Industrial revolution

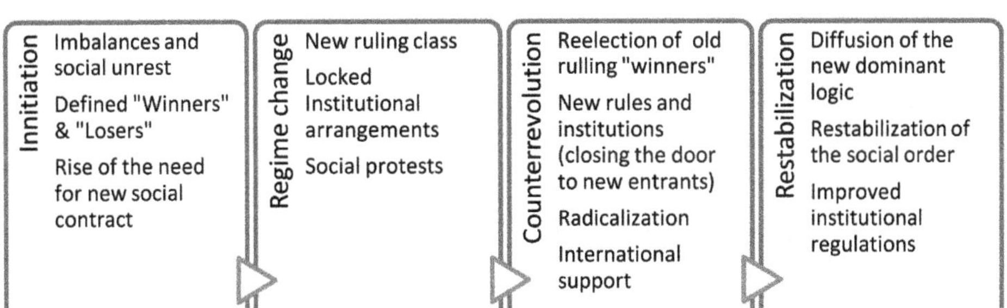

During the Initiation phase, the ruling class and the elites lose its authority to ensure socially fair and efficient institutional arrangements. As earlier discussed, any shift in the technology paradigm provoke economic uncertainties and nurture speculations, power abuse and inefficiencies. Therefore, as institutions determine the capacity of the economy to produce wealth, they influence both on the general regulations within the economy and affect further some basic costs and minimum prices. In this situation, elites and ruling class have the potential to obtain better economic, political and social returns from innovations and to profit from the lack of regulations and social arrangements in new emerging areas. This way, new technologies create a new class of "losers", or new social groups, directly or indirectly affected from transformation processes. The levels of inequality raises, leading to distortion of the perceptions for social justice.

The emergence of new social groups of "losers" challenge the capacity of institutions to provide efficient "rules of the game" and fair social mechanisms. It is formed an opposition to the ruling class, following different socially polarization processes, social protests and forms of social unrest.

During the second phase, the change of the regime determines a general change of the ruling class (through elections, social protests and other). However, these specific "revolts" rarely lead to improved regulations and better institutional settings. Usually path dependences and lock-in factors (such as predefined contracts, earlier adopted technologies, fixed regimes, already started public procurement processes and large international influence) limit the options of the new ruling elite to transform fundamentally the existing institutional frameworks. Therefore, even if the new elite initiates some institutional reforms, it rarely results in expected institutional transformations. During the second phase, additional struggles derive from the raising uncertainty and lack of confidence. Based on the lack of specific competences (constitutive function), new elected ruling class cannot reform institutional settings and models of power distribution. This radicalize the social groups and make them susceptible to populist, non-systematic and radical policy parties. Meanwhile, the old elites continue to monetize its primary economic and politic advantages and accumulate additional resources, profiting from the lack of institutional effectiveness.

As wealth concentration and social inequality extend, the social perceptions for institutional "efficiency" and social "fairness" does not improve. This leads to the next phase of counterrevolution. Here, the old regime is restored, usually bringing back the old ruling class, through populism claims, reelection, or by changing the rules (as for example restoring autocracies). This time the old ruling class, is restored, officially recognized as more efficient and more competent for dealing with new technology paradigm shifts.

In this situation, the wider spread of new unformal institutional logic will play crucial role. It will enable of larger transformation processes and development of new ideology, starting to transpose from production sphere to other cultural environment, by sharing new best practices and cultural norms, social values and common perceptions. New culture enriches the paradigm shift and further incremental innovations are initiated. In the restauration phase, the regulations and new institutional arrangements will largely emerge in order to limit the new entrants. During this phase, international processes intensify but they come mainly to the support the main actors and local elites. International coalitions and alliances among the main technology providers define the outcomes on any local scene, largely lobbying for further technology diffusion, implementation and adoption in a larger global scale. Finally, during the last restabilization phase, incremental innovations support more evenly distributed economic growth, reaffirming the new level of institutional settings and arrangements among the key players in the field.

In this model of revolutionary changes, the main question for stabilizing the new social order is to find efficient and socially acceptable and just model of wealth distribution. On one hand, the big "winners" of the recent technology boom - the highly volatile tech companies and their investors (ruling elites), continue to profit from "empty" institutional areas, globalizing their activities and minimizing their contribution to social public systems by exploiting tax havens, or dominating leading to new pressures, and lobbies over the policy makers. On the other hand, the group of "losers" largely spread among all social groups. In this complex situation, national institutions need to adopt new types of "rules" and new ways to finance the increased transaction sector and public services (education, healthcare, social security, etc.) that cannot automatically profit by digitalization shift.

As labor costs will lose its social function to distribute wealth, other types of social contracts need to be accepted in order to redistribute the new generated wealth, produced by new "smart factories". While replacing the work of people with work of machines, new forms of wealth has to find its way to reach a larger group of people. In this perspective, institutional regulations have to transform in order to protect better the social interests. Further, as restructuring of the economy will limit the labor needs, it will result in less employment and lower incomes from salaries and decreased level of social payments as social security, pensions, healthcare payments and others taxes from personal income.

In this situation, social institutions need to prepare for both reduced income from salaries and increased demand for social services and support. In the same time there have to be considered new regulations, allowing adoption of more flexible and temporary labor forms, combining different incomes from various sources (freelancers, micro-entrepreneurship, part-time working, non-for-profit working, temporary contracts and many others). Therefore, institutions need to prepare for better personalized services, for more efficient solutions for the social problems and for more open innovation patterns and processing, allowing more individuals to integrate and engage with the new economy potentials.

The further work on the theoretical model of radical institutional change proposed on Figure 1 can extend with more quantified indices and specific examples both from historical perspectives and from actual socio-political processes.

CONCLUSION

Considering that distribution of wealth is shaped by the way economic, social, and political actors view what is just and what is not, Picketty (2015) claims that inequality is a highly political concept. In a situation of reduced labor demand and shrinking social funds, the problem of wealth inequality will raise many new questions coming to wealth distribution. Therefore, even if new technologies can bring substantial growth for the global economy, this will not create automatically better social systems and better institutions. Even more, the existing economic developments further threatens not only social cohesion, but as well other pillars of the sustainable development (environmental, economic and social), leading to more serious problems for the next generations and the rise of cheap nature (Moore, 2016).

The social and institutional change during revolutionary processes is a political question and ideologies have a big role to determine its particular deployment. The level of political consensus, conflict or confusion strongly influences the speed and the ease or difficulty with which the new mode of growth is established (Perez, 2010). Therefore, network dependences and standardizations make the innovations in Industry 4.0 a much complex coordination game (Mokyr, 1988), in the way that new technologies and innovations should fit within the existing technology and institutional frameworks.

REFERENCES

Allardt, E. (1971). Culture, structure and revolutionary ideologies. *International Journal of Comparative Sociology*, *12*(1), 24–40. doi:10.1177/002071527101200102

Allen, R. C. (2011). Why the industrial revolution was British: Commerce, induced invention, and the scientific revolution. *The Economic History Review*, *64*(2), 357–384. doi:10.1111/j.1468-0289.2010.00532.x

Allen, R. C. (2015). The high wage economy and the industrial revolution: A restatement. *The Economic History Review*, *68*(1), 1–22. doi:10.1111/ehr.12079

Avgerou, C. (2003). The link between ICT and economic growth in the discourse of development. In Organizational information systems in the context of globalization (pp. 373-386). Springer US. doi:10.1007/978-0-387-35695-2_23

Beck, C. J. (2013). *Revolutions: Robust Findings, Persistent Problems, and Promising Frontiers*. Academic Press.

Coriat, B., & Dosi, G. (2000). *The Institutional Embeddedness of Economic Change. In An Appraisal of the 'Evolutionary' and 'Regulationist' Research Programmes* (pp. 347–376). Edward Elgar Publishing.

Corry, L. (1993). Kuhnian issues, scientific revolutions and the history of mathematics. *Studies in History and Philosophy of Science*, *24*(1), 95–117. doi:10.1016/0039-3681(93)90026-G

Crafts, N. (2002). *The Solow productivity paradox in historical perspective*. Academic Press.

David, P. A. (1990). The dynamo and the computer: An historical perspective on the modern productivity paradox. *The American Economic Review*, *80*(2), 355–361.

Donnelly, J. (2013). *Universal human rights in theory and practice*. Cornell University Press.

Dudley, L. (2010). *General purpose technologies and the industrial revolution* (No. 1011). Papers on economics and evolution.

Freeman, C. (2013). *Economics of industrial innovation*. Routledge.

Gamson, J. (1995). Must identity movements self-destruct? A queer dilemma. *Social Problems*, *42*(3), 390–407. doi:10.2307/3096854

Goldstone, J. A. (2001). Toward a fourth generation of revolutionary theory. *Annual Review of Political Science*, *4*(1), 139–187. doi:10.1146/annurev.polisci.4.1.139

Goldstone, J. A. (2015). *The encyclopedia of political revolutions*. Routledge.

Greenwood, J. (1996). *The third industrial revolution (No. 435). University of Rochester-Center for Economic Research*. RCER.

Gurr, T. R. (2015). *Why men rebel*. Routledge.

Hall, A. R., & Dunstan, G. (1954). *The Scientific Revolution, 1500-1800: The Formation of the Modern Scientific Attitude (No. 29)*. London: Longmans, Green.

Howlett, M., & Rayner, J. (2006). Understanding the historical turn in the policy sciences: A critique of stochastic, narrative, path dependency and process-sequencing models of policy-making over time. *Policy Sciences*, *39*(1), 1–18. doi:10.100711077-005-9004-1

Humphries, J. (2010). *Childhood and child labour in the British industrial revolution*. Cambridge University Press. doi:10.1017/CBO9780511780455

Huntington, S. P. (1968, 2006). Political order in changing socictics. Yale University Press.

Inglehart, R. (2015). *The silent revolution: Changing values and political styles among Western publics*. Princeton University Press. doi:10.1515/9781400869589

Iriye, A., Goedde, P., & Hitchcock, W. I. (Eds.). (2012). *The human rights revolution: an international history* (Vol. 3). Oxford University Press.

Iyigun, M., & Rubin, J. (2017). *The Ideological Roots of Institutional Change*. IZA Discussion Papers, No. 10703.

Jenkins, J. C. (1983). Resource mobilization theory and the study of social movements. *Annual Review of Sociology*, *9*(1), 527–553. doi:10.1146/annurev.so.09.080183.002523

Jensen, M. C. (1993). The modern industrial revolution, exit, and the failure of internal control systems. *The Journal of Finance, 48*(3), 831-880.

Kuhn, T. S. (1962, 2012). The structure of scientific revolutions. University of Chicago Press.

Labor, C. (1990). *Industrial Revolution*. Bloomington, IN: Academic Press.

Lane, P. J., & MacDonald, K. C. (2011). *Introduction: slavery, social revolutions and enduring memories*. Oxford University Press.

Lawson, G. (2016). Within and Beyond the "Fourth Generation" of Revolutionary Theory. *Sociological Theory*, *34*(2), 106–127. doi:10.1177/0735275116649221

Lloyd-Jones, R. (1990). The first Kondratieff: The long wave and the British industrial revolution. *The Journal of Interdisciplinary History*, *20*(4), 581–605. doi:10.2307/204000

Mahoney, J., & Snyder, R. (1999). Rethinking agency and structure in the study of regime change. *Studies in Comparative International Development*, *34*(2), 3–32. doi:10.1007/BF02687620

Mann, M. (2012). The sources of social power: Volume 3, global empires and revolution, 1890-1945 (Vol. 3). Cambridge University Press.

Melucci, A. (1995). The process of collective identity. *Social Movements and Culture*, *4*, 41-63.

Mintz, S., & Kellogg, S. (1989). *Domestic revolutions: A social history of American family life*. Simon and Schuster.

Mokyr, J. (1997). Are we living in the middle of an industrial revolution? *Economic Review-Federal Reserve Bank of Kansas City*, *82*(2), 31.

Mokyr, J. (1998). The second industrial revolution, 1870-1914. *Storia dell'economia Mondiale*, 219-45.

Mokyr, J. (2017). Bottom-up or top-down? The origins of the Industrial Revolution. *Journal of Institutional Economics*, 1–22. doi:10.1017/S174413741700042X

Moore, J. W. (2016). The rise of cheap nature. *Sociology Faculty Scholarship, 2*.

Nanda, V. P. (2011). Revolution, Democracy and the Critical Role of Constitution-Making: Some Preliminary Thoughts. *Denv. UL Rev.*, *89*, 581.

North, D. C. (1988). Ideology and political/economic institutions. *The Cato Journal*.

Paige, J. M. (1978). *Agrarian revolution*. Simon and Schuster.

Perez, C. (2004). Technological revolutions, paradigm shifts and socio-institutional change. *Globalization, economic development and inequality: An alternative perspective*, 217-242.

Perez, C. (2009). The double bubble at the turn of the century: Technological roots and structural implications. *Cambridge Journal of Economics*, *33*(4), 779–805. doi:10.1093/cje/bep028

Perez, C. (2010). Technological revolutions and techno-economic paradigms. *Cambridge Journal of Economics*, *34*(1), 185–202. doi:10.1093/cje/bep051

Peters, M. (2016). Technological unemployment: Educating for the fourth industrial revolution. *Educational Philosophy and Theory*. doi:10.1080/00131857.2016.1177412

Phaal, R., Farrukh, C. J., & Probert, D. R. (2004). Technology roadmapping—a planning framework for evolution and revolution. *Technological Forecasting and Social Change*, *71*(1-2), 5–26. doi:10.1016/S0040-1625(03)00072-6

Picketty T., (2015) Putting Distribution Back at the Center of Economics: Reflections on Capital in the Twenty-First Century. *Journal of Economic Perspectives, 29*(1), 67–88.

Polletta, F., & Jasper, J. M. (2001). Collective identity and social movements. *Annual Review of Sociology*, *27*(1), 283–305. doi:10.1146/annurev.soc.27.1.283

Rao, H., Monin, P., & Durand, R. (2003). Institutional change in Toque Ville: Nouvelle cuisine as an identity movement in French gastronomy. *American Journal of Sociology*, *108*(4), 795–843. doi:10.1086/367917

Robertson, D. S. (1990). The information revolution. *Communication Research*, *17*(2), 235–254. doi:10.1177/009365090017002005

Schwab, K. (2016). *The Fourth Industrial Revolution*. Crown Business.

Scott, W. R. (2010). Reflections: The past and future of research on institutions and institutional change. *Journal of Change Management*, *10*(1), 5–21. doi:10.1080/14697010903549408

Skocpol, T. (1976). France, Russia, China: A structural analysis of social revolutions. *Comparative Studies in Society and History*, *18*(2), 175–210. doi:10.1017/S0010417500008197

Skocpol, T. (1994). *Social revolutions in the modern world.* Cambridge University Press. doi:10.1017/CBO9781139173834

Snow, D. A., & Trom, D. (2002). *The case study and the study of social movements* (Vol. 16). Minneapolis: University of Minnesota Press.

Stearns, P. N. (1998). The Industrial Revolution in the World History (2nd ed.). Boulder, CO: Westview.

Stephan, M. J., & Chenoweth, E. (2008). Why civil resistance works: The strategic logic of nonviolent conflict. *International Security, 33*(1), 7–44. doi:10.1162/isec.2008.33.1.7

Sterman, J. D., & Wittenberg, J. (1999). Path dependence, competition, and succession in the dynamics of scientific revolution. *Organization Science, 10*(3), 322–341. doi:10.1287/orsc.10.3.322

Taylor, V., Whittier, N., Morris, A. D., & Mueller, C. M. (1992). Collective identity in social movement communities: Lesbian feminist mobilization. *Social perspectives in lesbian and gay studies. A reader*, 349–365.

Thelen, K. (1999). Historical institutionalism in comparative politics. *Annual Review of Political Science, 2*(1), 369–404. doi:10.1146/annurev.polisci.2.1.369

Troxler, P. (2014). Making the third industrial revolution. *FabLab: Of Machines, Makers and Inventors*, 181.

Voigtländer, N., & Voth, H. J. (2006). Why England? Demographic factors, structural change and physical capital accumulation during the Industrial Revolution. *Journal of Economic Growth, 11*(4), 319–361. doi:10.100710887-006-9007-6

Webber, J. R. (2014). Revolution against 'progress': neo-extractivism, the compensatory state, and the TIPNIS conflict in Bolivia. *Crisis and contradiction: Marxist perspectives on Latin America in the global political economy, 79.*

Wonglimpiyarat, J. (2005). The nano-revolution of Schumpeter's Kondratieff cycle. *Technovation, 25*(11), 1349–1354. doi:10.1016/j.technovation.2004.07.002

ENDNOTE

1 Definition according to The International Encyclopaedia of the Social and Behavioural Sciences (Elsevier, 2001).

Chapter 5
Organizations Facing the Disruptive Change

ABSTRACT

Organizations take the lead of any innovation process and thus they pave the way for further social changes. Small companies and start-ups are in the avant-garde of innovations, proposing disruptive solutions on the market. In the present chapter the author will analyze the role of organizations in the framework of new digitalization shift. The first part of the chapter will discuss organizational development from institutional point of view. Then there will be outlined the main understanding of organizational change, organizational change management in the framework of the system theory. Further there will be assessed the mechanisms and methodologies for measuring maturity assessment models and its impact on organizational capacity to adopt new technologies. Finally, there will be analyzed some of the key findings of digitalization processes including business model innovations and organizational transformation. In the end, a general analysis will be made about digitalization shifts, company transformation, and the role of the institutions in this process.

DOI: 10.4018/978-1-5225-6270-2.ch005

INTRODUCTION

During the last few years, the terms as digitalization, digital disruption and digital transformation became part of the common business language (Dornberger Inglese, Korkut, & Zhong, 2018). Digital technologies provided a new battlefield for organizations, expanding their capacity to reach the global scale operations. Considered as a source of new efficiencies and innovations, digital transformation is highly prioritized in strategic business agendas (Schallmo, & Williams, 2018). However it is important to state that digitalization do not affect only business operations. Digitalization strategies aim not only to outperform company's operational processes, products or services. Actually today, digitalization is a new cultural mindset and reflects organizational attitude and capacity to innovate, its market positioning models and determine its future role in the new complex socio-economic and technological ecosystems. In the same time, the inherent technological risk for developing and implementing new business solutions based on artificial intelligence, blockchain or cyber-physical systems is still high. There still lack enough evidences, statistics and business cases, good and bad examples for digitalization models in practice. Digitalization is not about buying advanced operational robot or migrate to a cloud service for storing company data. Digital transformation stays for implementing new business models and building a new digital architecture merging digital and real-world processes, products and services in a complex ecosystem.

The complexity of the digital transformation is high, and the claims for "everything digitalization" should be carefully assessed by every organization (Andriole, 2017). This makes it difficult for the companies to justify investments and to plan next steps for further digital transformation. Furthermore, the returns, performance indicators and success rates within many innovative digital sectors do not provide sound statistical basis for making investments. On the other hand, there is no time for waiting as new disruptive businesses constantly evolve and take new market positions. Market dynamics is increasing but the dominant business logic is still stacked in the existing paradigms of consumerism, short-term growth, cost-based competition and resource exploitation (Holmlund, Strandvik, & Lähteenmäki, 2017). The pressure over the companies intensified also by the stakeholders' expectations. End-users and clients, other businesses, suppliers, shareholders, competitors, investors, media, policy makers and all other third parties further look for new digital success stories. Currently everybody anticipates that all businesses and organizations, big and small, local and international, should digitalize and reshape their main processes and models of operations in order to survive the next industrial shift. Furthermore, the promoters of the Fourth industrial revolution, industry gurus and tech giants assert the need for largely experimentation with new business models and value-creation mechanisms. Thus, digital transformation processes and adoption of innovative digital technologies nowadays induce an increasing stress for the companies.

All businesses operate in specific socio-political ecosystem, determining actually all of their factors of production, all of their possible action plans, future developments and growth perspectives. Formal organizations are generally understood to be systems of coordinated and controlled activities that arise when work is embedded in complex networks of technical relations and boundary-spanning exchanges. Institutionalized products, services, techniques, policies, and programs function as powerful myths, and many organizations adopt them ceremonially. In this perspective, Meyer and Rowan (1977) prove that the formal structures of many organizations dramatically reflect the myths of their institutional environments, instead of the demands of their work activities. Thus a considerable part of the company's strategies for success or survival largely depends from its specific business and cultural environment and external market conditions. In these settings, complex socio-economic and political institutional frameworks, formal and informal regulations and rules have a major impact on the business ecosystem.

Therefore, it is important to say that successful company digitalization will largely depend not only from its own efforts but also from institutional and environmental support. Thus companies need not only to provide proficient technological solution, able to solve problems and to deliver value to its customers. They have to survive the digital transformation processes following the general "rules of the game" defined by the established institutional framework.

On the other hand, ICT technologies largely enhanced companies' capacity to improve business efficiency and performance (Bandara, Syed, Ranathunga, & Kulathilaka, 2018; Yunis, Tarhini, & Kassar, 2017). Information technologies played a considerable economic role for reducing transaction costs (Cordella, 2006) and agency costs providing the backbone infrastructure for value formation (Laudon & Laudon, 2007). Thus, they allowed many new business models to emerge, bringing additional sources for value-creation for customers. Moreover, e-business applications have largely transformed companies to become more flat, boundary-less, entrepreneurial, process- and project-oriented, developing complex and innovative global business models.

Today, Internet is an essential and indispensable infrastructure for business transactions on many B2B and B2C levels, becoming a universal platform for services. Further business digitalization will bring new and unexpected dynamics of economic and social processes (Leimstoll, Dannecker, Knechtli, Quade, Tanner, & Wölfle, 2018).

The present chapter aims to analyze the role of organizations in the framework of new digitalization shift. As already discussed in the first chapter, the new technologies widely adoption promises to significantly transform current business realms. In the same time institutions and institutional support have a determining role for defining its company digitalization strategies.

The first part of the chapter will discuss organizational development from institutional point of view. Then there will be outlined the main understanding of organizational change, organizational change management and the system theory. Further there will be assessed the mechanisms and methodologies for measuring maturity assessment models and the company capacity to adopt new technologies. There will be analyzed some of the key findings of digitalization processes including business model innovations and organizational transformation. Finally a general analysis will be made about digitalization shifts, company transformation and institutional role in the process.

BACKGROUND

From institutional point of view, organizational change is a complex issue. Business organizations are generally defined as formal socio-economic agents, inaugurated following the law and operating within specific institutional context. By setting rules and designating the roles and functions of individuals and organizations within a social group institutions largely affect social environment. The institutional context represents a number of formal and informal regulations, set by the society, by the legal framework and the general environment. In the same time, business organizations have an active role in the society, and are able to contest some of the existing formal and informal rules and regulations. As Scott (1995) finds out, organizations are not just *passive pawns controlled by the demands of their environments, but active players, capable of responding strategically and innovatively to environmental pressures*. Thus they often are in position to define their own formal and informal norms, and to spread them through their own networks of influence, affecting different stakeholders. Furthermore, pursuing their own wealth and profit-maximization strategies, business organizations often use different opportunities to influence policy makers and institutions in their favor and to amend the rules that can positively affect their position. Therefore business organizations are complex agents within institutional theories and their transformation needs further analysis and attention.

Institutional theorists put a large accent on the institutional context or a set of values, norms, and organizational templates that exists outside of particular firms but that largely influences the way in which organizations are structured and managed (Newman, 2000). As institutions structure human action, organizations resemble each other and reflect little diversity (Meyer & Rowan 1977, DiMaggio & Powel, 1983). Moreover, organizations that adapt to institutional pressures are more likely to obtain scarce resources and to become more competitive in terms of survival capacity than those that do not (DiMaggio & Powell, 1991). Thus, organizations tend to become more similar over the time because of the normative social process that rewards similarity (Newman, 2000). Thus from institutional point, organizational change is a relatively continuous, converging process in which the drivers of change define extra organizational norms about what constitutes appropriate organizational goals, structures, and processes (Newman, 2000). Thus, organizational transformation has to overcome the dominating institutional context or the constraints, controls, and regulations enabling general economic activity (Harper, 2015). The dynamics of organizational change differ from institutional and social context, but economic aspects do not have a big role to play (Acs, Estrin, Mickiewicz, & Szerb, 2018). As stated further, tightly aligned to institutional context organizations are advantaged, which produces pressure on other firms to align, even if alignment is expected to have negative financial outcomes (Abrahamson & Rosenkopf, 1993).

The institutional impact on company digitalization and IT implementation is thoroughly discussed in the seminal paper of Orlikowski and Barley (2001). There the authors admit that various institutional settings both enable and constrain organizational actions. They point out that the rise of Internet technologies happen after 1991, when restrictions on commercialization of the Internet were eased, and firms have increasingly employed networking technologies to interact with customers, suppliers, and consumers (Orlikowski & Barley, 2001). Therefore, they insist that all socio-economic studies and implications should reflect the influence of institutions. Otherwise, it risks to provide a simplistic discourse which regularly treats "the digital economy" as if it were an independent, objective and inevitable phenomenon.

ORGANIZATIONAL CHANGE MANAGEMENT

Defining an organization as a social group of people working together in a coordinated and structured fashion to achieve one or more goals. Thus from structural point of view, organizational change can be defined as a transformation process of the firm characteristics between two points in the time (Barnett & Carroll, 1995). In this context, organizational change represents an action or a set of actions through which it seeks a partial or a total transformation. This way it enables the company transition from a current state to a future state that differs quantitatively and/or qualitatively from the first (Bradutanu, 2012).

Overcoming the practical and methodological challenges for companies, the organizational change management discipline recently emerged (Sturdy & Grey, 2003). It focuses on a wide set of academic and practitioner methods and models, enhancing company efforts to modify management structures and business processes, by constantly adapting to the fluid circumstances. It provides a structural and functional approach, defining the roles, the methods and the business elements affected by the change, including organizational design, roles and responsibilities, performance standards, workflow and processes. The goal of organizational change management is twofold (Hayes, 2014) On one side it enhances organizations to successfully transform to new circumstances (e.g., new market entry, new regulatory climate, new company goals, new technology, etc.); On the other side, it provides more flexible and adaptable processes in order to enable them to better control and respond to the future changes.

Furthermore, organizational change management methodologies provide the necessary procedures, functional steps and processes like checklist or tasks. In the same time it takes into account the social elements like organizational culture and personal resistance to change. Thus admitting the role of the social factors, it insist that pure top-down approach for organizational transformation is inefficient in technology adoption, new processes design or new rules implementations. Furthermore, employees who resist the change can negatively affect the success of any project. Thus, organizational change management focus to develop environment of supporting the change (Stadtmueller, 2014).

According to the vast research on organizational change, and namely in the last years, the main factors that have to be assessed include both the content of the change and the process of the change. Content analysis include all factors that should change in the organization. Process analysis refers to the adoption of specific organizational change models. Furthermore, analyzing organizational change the following threefold framework: why-what-how can be adopted as presented on Table 1 (Dainty & Kakabadse, 1990).

Furthermore, the literature identifies different characteristics and models of organizational change, including digital mergers and acquisitions, new technologies adoption, new products or processes or structural changes. Thus, organizations can further prepare and set clear criteria in order to properly measure organizational change, as presented on Table 2.

ORGANIZATIONAL CHANGE AS SOCIAL SYSTEM TRANSFORMATION

Organizational change is increasingly discussed and researched issue (Burke, 2017; Bolman & Deal, 2017). In the attempt to gain additional perspective on organizational change and to describe complex relationships between organizations and institutions, we will further apply the systematic approach. Recognizing that business organizations represent complex socio-economic

Table 1. An overview of the why-what-how model, adapted from (Dainty & Kakabadse, 1990)

The Reasons for Change	The Context of Change	The Methods of Change
- The general reason to change; - The need behind organizational change / transformation - The driving forces of change - The preconditions of change	- The elements that have to change - The type of organizational change	- The action plan of organizational change - Overall process management, style and methods used – stages, scale, timing and processes.

Table 2. Types of changes in an organization

Type of Change	Characteristic	Impact
Downsizing/ mergers/ acquisitions process change	Predictable managerial response in certain circumstances	Major/minor
Technology-driven innovation	New technology adoption;	Major/minor
New products or services	Renewal of the product range; a new service or performing in a better way the same service – performance, quality	Major/minor
Structural change	Restructuring/rearranging people/change in the relationships; adding/deleting knowledge and qualifications	Major/minor

systems, we will exploit the leading principles of the General system theory of Bertalanffy (1974) and the models of Open Social System analysis (Rice, 2013). Wester-Ebbinghaus et al., (2010) propose a reference model enhancing comprehension of complex system. They consider the organizational embeddedness in the institutional context by developing a "system-of-systems" approach. As they point out, an open system (like for instance an organization) relies on services and resources of other systems but at the same time constructs and continuously reconstructs its boundaries across which it relates to its environment. But more interestingly the environment does not only consist of other systems (that in turn view the first system as a part of their respective environments) but is itself a system. In this context, the market is considered as a complex system of systems, defining a common platform with rules and behaviors, adopted by the other companies.

Thus in the frameworks of the systematic approach, the following characteristics of the social system have to be taken in consideration. First, social systems consist of complex interdependent and evolving elements and sub-systems. In this respect, it is crucial to determine what are the elements and their respective dependencies. Second, the main factors of system change comes outside of the system borders, from the environment, via complex transformation and learning process. Third organizational systems tend to evolve into more complex socio-economic systems. Finally, the elements of organizations include: people; culture; business processes; technological level/applications; end users. All these elements in the system model can be transferred to: resources (input resources); environment (context), outputs (products and services), and transformation processes (information, data). In this perspective, digitization and business transformation consist of automation and information processes, improving the quality and level of value creation within the firm.

The main GST theory defines ten important principles (Bertalanfy, 1974). First it is needed a level of interconnection and interdependency between objects and their attributes, as independent elements cannot form a system. On the second place, social systems are holistic and should be studied as a whole, not divided or analyzed by its parts. Third, all social systems pursuit a purpose, and systems interdependencies have to be balanced in a stable situation. Then the system transform the input into output elements, and this is the main process for achieving the desired goals. Next, social systems are usually nested systems-of-systems and thus they follow specific hierarchies. Further, elements in the system differentiate by their functions, roles and specialized units. Eight, social systems have a capacity to regulate, including a feedback method, necessary for the system to function predictably. The two final principles include the entropy, or the random variables or chaos, inherent in every system and equifinality, or the alternative approaches for accomplishing the same goals. When analyzing organizational change, we need to take into account the social system approach, focusing on factors such as complexity of elements, dependences, and influences from the environment.

COMPANY DIGITALIZATION

As it was early discussed, company digitalization in the realms of the robotic era reflect more general business and organizational transformation processes. Therefore, in order to analyze company's capability to adopt new digital solutions, in the next sections we will discuss the following elements. On the first place an overview will be provided to outline the capability of the company to adopt new digital technologies. Then there will be analyzed its capacity to increase the flexibility of the production models and processes, through automation and extensive networks and mechanisms for decentralized management. Finally there will be outlined the new business models and how they can affect digital transformation.

Maturity Assessment Model

The maturity assessment models define how different organizations are digitally "mature" or how prepared they are for the digital transformation. In this respect there are developed different maturity assessment models and instruments, considering and evaluating different aspects of the company's ability to transform and its readiness for digitalization. "Maturity" reflects organizational processes, functional areas or people capacity to change.

Among the most used methodologies for measuring company capacity to transform are the so called "maturity models". More specifically maturity assessment models have been designed to assess a company's maturity (i.e. competency, capability, level of sophistication) in a specific domain based on comprehensive set of criteria. Therefore, maturity models aim to evaluate the organizational capacity in specific moment and its ability to adopt significant organizational shifts and changes. The adoption of maturity models imply different aspects as standardization, improves the ability to better understand, measure, and assess domain capabilities, enables benchmarking against a range of competitors, enables greater efficiency in the utilization of resources in improving domain capabilities and presents an opportunity for improved success in the domain. Thus the main elements of measuring maturity assessment include assessment of people/culture, processes/structures, and objects/technology (Mettler, 2011). The maturity model ideally contains the following components: a number of levels or stages, a denomination for each level, a description or summary of each level, a number of dimensions or process areas as well as specific elements or activities for those, and a description of relevant activities to be performed at each maturity level (Fraser, Moultrie, & Gregory, 2002).

In the research of de Bruin et al. (2005), there are outlined the main general 6 phases of any maturity assessment model. Thus, the main elements include: scope (defining the focus and the boundaries of the model application and use), design (architecture of the model, needs of the stakeholders), population (what has to be measured and how, methods and tools), test (for validity, reliability, generalizability), deployment (use and adoption by stakeholders) and maintenance (resources for its use and acceptance). In order to apply the methodology of the Maturity assessment models in the context of current company digitalization various researchers outline different aspects of Industry 4.0 adoption and company digitalization (de Carolis, Macchi, Negri, & Terzi, 2017; Boström & Celik; 2017, Klötzer & Pflaum, 2017). Some of the recently developed models like DREAMY - Digital REadiness Assessment MaturitY model (de Carolis, Macchi, Negri, & Terzi, 2017), or MMDS (Boström & Celik, 2017) aims to apply well known maturity models in current Industry 4.0 context. For example, the MMDS (Maturity assessment model for Digital Strategizing) of Boström and Celik (2017), is based on the Luftman (2004) model of business and IT alignment, and include the following dimensions: communication maturity, value measurement maturity, leadership maturity, ecosystem maturity, technology maturity and skills maturity, adapting it to the Industry 4.0 digital shift.

Assessing the digital transformation within companies from the German manufacturing industry, Klötzer and Pflaum (2017) propose another detailed manufacturing-oriented maturity assessment model. Applying the evolution from "product" to "service"-orientation and from "conventional" to "smart" manufacturing they identify the following nine elements, including: strategy development, offering to the customer, smart product, smart factory (CPS), complementary IT system, cooperation, structural organization, process organization, competencies and innovation culture. The main stages of Industry 4.0 adoption start with: digitalization awareness, smart networked products, service-oriented enterprise, thinking in service systems and data-driven enterprise. Based on Maturity assessment models, and following the detailed framework of this model, manufacturing companies can both assess their current stage of development and further design and adopt company digitalization roadmap. Resuming the main outcomes of the digital maturity assessment models, there can be defined the following main organizational structures that need to adopt digital transformation mindset: Strategic level, Leadership, Products, Operations, Culture, People, Governance and Technology.

More specifically addressing technological capability of a firm, Geribadze (1998) point out three areas of expertise that have to be mastered simultaneously:

1. The ability to understand new trends in science and technology, to manage R&D projects, and to generate useful new technologies.
2. The ability to design and manufacture products and to reconfigure products and services, which are useful and which generate a measurable competitive advantage.
3. A profound understanding of customer needs and requirements, of changing trends in the external system of demand articulation, and the ability to formulate new value propositions.

Business Model Transformation

Business models transformation is one of kcy clement of digitalization and organizational change strategy (Blaschke, Haki, Riss, & Aier, 2017). Business models are substantial part of any business and digital technologies plays non-linear but complex role in business model transformation (Hanelt, Hildebrandt & Polier, 2015). While traditional business models are simple and easy to understand, information technologies bring many new opportunities to organization including cost efficiency, better market positioning and value chain optimization.

Digital technologies and Internet are the main factors for business model differentiation and evolution (Ostenwalder, Pigneur & Tucci, 2005). New technologies largely contribute for the emergence of complex value-adding networks, resulting in adaptation and implementation of many evolving business models like the "long tail", "freemium", crowd-sourcing and crowd-funding, complex network business models and many others (Kahre, Hoffmann & Ahlemann, 2017).

Focusing more in details in one specific aspect of digital business models evolution, Van Alstyne, Parker and Sangeet (2016) highlight the substantial benefits of company transformation from pipeline business model to platform business model. Taking advantage on emerging technology platforms, many successful companies as Apple®, Amazon®, AIRBNB®, Facebook® and Google® constitute their businesses as platforms that bring together sellers and buyers, exploiting social networking and delivering value co-creation instruments. While more traditional pipeline businesses create value by controlling a linear series of activities, platform businesses can adopt more open (innovation) and value co-creation activities.

Thus, platform businesses lead to three main transformations: focus on resource orchestration (and not on resource control), focus on models of external interactions (and not on internal process optimization) and finally prioritize the value of the ecosystem (and not just the value of the customer). The platform model is characterized also by its architecture and rule system, defining the access to platform resources, governance and rewards mechanisms. As the authors further conclude, platform businesses are usually more competitive than pipeline models, outperforming them and directly menacing their existence (Van Alstyne, Parker & Sangeet, 2016). Investigating another aspect of digital companies, as continuous services (Kuula & Haapasalo, 2017) and data-exploitation, Roman et al. (2017) analyze that databased business models depend on data suppliers, (from simple data supplier to service provider), data sources (whether the data is internal or external) and what is done with the data (ranging from providing data for reuse, analyzing and aggregating existing data or even providing services). The revenue model for the different strategies are mostly subscription based but can also entail "freemium", pay-per-use or advertising. The more complex business models are also harder to execute, prompting open collaboration and co-creation (Roman, Liu, Nyberg, 2017). Further Zeleti et al., (2016) conclude that the main (open) data business models are Freemium, Premium, Cost Saving, Indirect Benefit and Parts of Tools. The main value proposition out of the open data can be Usefulness, Process Improvement, Performance and Customer Loyalty.

Evolution of Organizational Structures

Another interesting approach to analyze digitalization and organizational transformation is to further consider evolution of new organizational forms. Kapas (2008) proposes an in-depth overview, focusing on the fact that every industrial revolutions supported raising of specific organizational structure and organizational form. Since the First Industrial Revolution, when the form of the modern firm is firstly defined, organizational forms innovations followed the rising technologies requirements. Thus during the First Industrial Revolution, the "family firm" craft-shop were slowly replaced by the modern manufacturing firms or factory organizations. During the Second Industrial Revolution emerged the multidivisional form of organization and large enterprises, commonly adopting the mass production paradigm. During the ICT revolution another important shift in organizational structure is observed, as large vertically integrated firms become flatter, decentralized and organized in semi-autonomous project-based teams.

The technological inventions in the First Industrial Revolution were supported mainly by informal institutions, although there was a favorable congruence in all subsystems of the society and their positive mutual interconnection. The effect on institutions for the rise of multidivisional form of organization was the creation of a new set of rules, in accordance with the vertical integration of organizations, including antitrust law and other regulatory laws. The Third Industrial Revolution brings a new institutional change, supporting the markets globalization, the fall of the transaction costs and the reduction of market entry barriers. Thus, the Fourth Industrial revolution is expected to change the future of work and the structure of labor, leading to more self-employed, project-based work, focusing on human interaction and creativity, employing start-ups and freelancers.

DISCUSSION

Successful digital transformation of the companies and of the economy as a whole are among the key priorities today. Digital technologies in the framework of the Fourth Industrial Revolution have the potential to fundamentally reverse manufacturing logic, to improve company and resource efficiency, production costs and product life-cycle management. In the same time, digital transformation is a complex socio-economic and political shift and requires further efforts in order to adapt and to properly align with the new digital business realms. Sebastian et al., (2017) identified three main elements for digital success. The first is the adoption of digital strategy and technology-inspired value proposition. The main digital strategies can be either customer engagement (adopting technologies for increasing loyalty and trust) or development of digitized solutions (integrating combination of new products, services and data). The second element is to develop an operational backbone. Finally, the third element is to create digital service platform, enabling rapid innovation and responsiveness to the new market opportunities.

During the last few decades, information technologies and Internet already transformed economy structure, business realms and employment patterns. Company structure and business architecture simplified, there were reduced organizational hierarchical levels, and there were supported outsourcing and offshoring, business process reengineering, networking building and alliances. In the same time Internet technologies didn't reversed the business logic as companies still work in the "mass-production" paradigm, offering pre-defined products and services to the market and largely exploiting consumerism and short product uses. Thus, many efforts are needed not only to digitally disrupt businesses, but also to adapt new organizational development patterns, more responsible for the long-term economic development and global sustainability.

Defining the Roles of Institutions and Organizations

Economy digitalization is mainly a socio-economic and political process, leaded by both business organizations and institutions. Technologies play only a part in the process, as there already exists many digital solutions that wait for appropriate business model, legislation support or social acceptance. Furthermore, many digital start-ups fail to impose successful innovations on the market due to various social and economic issues. Thus, digitalization is not a technological but mainly organizational and social priority. Next, business organizations have the leading role for digital transformation. For many of them, conforming to the new technology paradigm is the only way to survive and to compete. Thus leading the digital change provide them with a chance to remain competitive on the global market producing more intelligent and smart, functional and complex products and services. Further, they have to reshape their business models, reorganizing value-offering, value co-creation, improving customization and user involvement, enhancing value-adding and self-service, increasing customer experiences and customer satisfaction. Besides, as thoroughly identified in the beginning, change management and maturity assessment models literature largely discuss the substantial role of the company culture in digital transformation. It include both efforts to deal with resistance to change and learning, encouraging employees, end users, and general communities and ecosystems to accept and apply the new digital paradigm. This way the digital transformation gradually spread across the overall economic ecosystem, submerging the dominant mental models and persistent beliefs.

However, it has to be stressed that institutions have an important role for shaping the companies' transformation success. First, company success is not global and universal, as it is often a function of specific conditions and circumstances from the local environment and ecosystem. Therefore, as institutions define "the rules of the game", they need to define and support specific values, shared beliefs and appropriate rules encouraging development of more efficient and socially responsible long-term development models. Furthermore, one of the main difficulties for analyzing institutions and institutional change comes from the fact that institutions include a large set of organizations, complex social groups, informal social norms and even expectations (Chavance, 2001). Therefore, it is a challenging task to make a general analysis how different rules, characteristics and interdependences evolve and lead to institutional transformation. In this perspective, digital technologies implementation first will affect business organizations and only indirectly can lead to formal or informal institutional change, requiring new rules and support. Applying the model of Chavance (2001) we can conclude that in stable and predictable environment, institutions have the main role for social and individual development. On the contrary, during fast evolutionary times, the processes act on the opposite direction. Then the modification of individual and collective behavior leads to organizational and then to institutional change. As institutions (formal and informal) are largely influenced by individuals - employees, end users, and communities, their changing preferences and beliefs will gradually affect their further development. Further North (1990) states that organizations and mainly "entrepreneurial undertakings" are among the main factors and agents provoking institutional change. Thus, it's the capacity of organizations to lead and undertake entrepreneurial projects that will make the digital disruption successful in larger sense. Following our analysis and in support of the claim of North (North, 1990), we can conclude that during technology transformation periods business organizations and business companies are the main triggers of social change and institutional transformation. On the one side, companies constantly supply more sophisticated disruption technologies and innovations, influencing preferences and personal beliefs of the end users. On the other side, companies are increasingly threatened from global competition and from even more disruptive technologies coming from other sectors. Thus they have to accumulate both power and resources to influence institutional change (following the cycle of Chavance 2001) and to influence individuals' behavior and cognitive mental models.

Analyzing the recent trends for digital transformation, we can conclude that companies still lack enough sources of practical knowledge for Industry 4.0 implementation and technology best practices. Even more, despite the fast- developing ICT sector, the vertical integration among industries is low and there is a lack of collaboration models among industries. Moreover, the regional aspects are important, as digital companies are highly concentrated in a few digital locations, while the rest of the country lacks human capital and infrastructure to boost digitalization. The lack of practical knowledge about digitalization and digital business models prevents SMEs' managers from understanding the opportunities for digital transformation. Furthermore, in general many SMEs owners miss an open mind-set (openness towards new digital technologies, new working styles, methods, new tasks for staff, new competences and processes, open network exchange), which is needed to implement new digitalization processes.

Secondly, as the CEOs or SMEs owners do not play a leading role in initiating a new digital strategy, it is more often outsourced to external consultants or to younger employees with no decision-making role. However, more importantly, the companies' management still does not see the competitive advantages of the digital transformation due to the constant profit margins and lack of strong market pressure. An appropriate ecosystem and common culture encouraging digital transformation knowledge formation and knowledge sharing is still missing. Thus the general readiness in SMEs to adopt Industry 4.0 and digital business models is low but more importantly, the practical knowledge of the digitalization projects is scarce and not freely shared. Moreover, the main sources of knowledge and good practices remain high-tech companies.

CONCLUSION

Digital transformation strategies can help companies to improve customer experiences, to facilitate adoption of Cyber-physical systems and to enhance data-driven decisions, providing complex business models integration in different sectors and application areas. Among the main recommendations for them are to start their digital transformation, focusing on performance management, developing customer touch points or starting new products digital business.

Technologies are gradually changing the society and its business patterns but most of the companies need to adjust to these trends. On one side, many products will change, becoming more intelligent and smart, upgraded and modernized. On the other side, companies have to reorganize all additional services. Thus new technologies propose many opportunities for company transformation as main center of value co-creation, improving customization and user involvement, enhancing value-adding and self-service, increasing customer experiences and customer satisfaction. Thus based on the new technology advances and digital transformation it can be expected another shift toward digital economy.

In this perspective the new knowledge, mental models and ideologies formed in the context of Industry 4.0 is slow. Most of the bottom-up social actors – individuals and small companies consider themselves to be end-users and not developers or value co-creators, looking for further integration among sectors and among countries. Industry 4.0 is not just about business automation and technologies adoption, as it will open the floor to new more dynamic value formation models, network business models and future path dependences. This means that if local businesses and more importantly the society as a whole miss the moment to adapt to the new waves of digital transformation, we can further expect waves of "conservative revival", as shown in the model of Iyigun and Rubin (2017).

REFERENCES

Abrahamson, E., & Rosenkopf, L. (1993). Institutional and competitive bandwagons: Using mathematical modeling as a tool to explore innovation diffusion. *Academy of Management Review*, *18*(3), 487–517.

Acs, Z. J., Estrin, S., Mickiewicz, T., & Szerb, L. (2018). Entrepreneurship, institutional economics, and economic growth: An ecosystem perspective. *Small Business Economics*, 1–14.

Andriole, S. J. (2017). Five Myths About Digital Transformation. *MIT Sloan Management Review*, *58*(3).

Autor, D., & Dorn, D. (2013). The growth of low skill service jobs and the polarization of the US labor market. *The American Economic Review*, *103*(5), 1553–1597. doi:10.1257/aer.103.5.1553

Bandara, W., Syed, R., Ranathunga, B., & Kulathilaka, K. S. (2018). People-centric, ICT-enabled process innovations via community, public and private sector partnership, and e-leadership: The case of the Dompe eHospital in Sri Lanka. In *Business Process Management Cases* (pp. 125–148). Cham: Springer. doi:10.1007/978-3-319-58307-5_8

Barnett, W. P., & Carroll, G. R. (1995). Modeling Internal Organizational Change. *Annual Review of Sociology*, *21*(1), 217–236. doi:10.1146/annurev.so.21.080195.001245

Bennet, A., & Bennet, D. (2004). *Organizational Survival in the new world, The Intelligent Complex Adaptive Systems*. Burlington: Elsevier.

Bertalanffy, L. v. (1974). *Perspectives on General System Theory*. New York: George Braziller.

Blaschke, M., Haki, M. K., Riss, U., & Aier, S. (2017, May). Design Principles for Business-Model-based Management Methods—A Service-dominant Logic Perspective. In *International Conference on Design Science Research in Information Systems* (pp. 179-198). Springer. 10.1007/978-3-319-59144-5_11

Bolman, L. G., & Deal, T. E. (2017). *Reframing organizations: Artistry, choice, and leadership*. John Wiley & Sons. doi:10.1002/9781119281856

Boström, E., & Celik, O. C. (2017). *Towards a Maturity Model for Digital Strategizing: A qualitative study of how an organization can analyze and assess their digital business strategy*. Academic Press.

Bouwman, H., Nikou, S., Molina-Castillo, F. J., & de Reuver, M. (2018). The Impact of Digitalization on Business Models. *Digital Policy, Regulation and Governance*. (accepted for publication)

Bradutanu, D. (2012). A Comparative Study of two Organizational Change Models. *Cross-Cultural Management Journal*, 29-34.

Burke, W. W. (2017). *Organization change: Theory and practice*. Sage Publications.

Chavance, B. (2001). Organisations, institutions, système: Types et niveaux de règles. *Revue d'Economie Industrielle*, *97*, 85–102. doi:10.3406/rei.2001.1801

Cordella, A. (2006). Transaction costs and information systems: Does IT add up? *Journal of Information Technology*, *21*(3), 195–202. doi:10.1057/palgrave.jit.2000066

Dainty, P., & Kakabadse, A. (1990). Organizational Change: A Strategy for Successful Implementation. *Journal of Business and Psychology*, 463–481.

De Bruin, T., Freeze, R., Kaulkarni, U., & Rosemann, M. (2005). *Understanding the main phases of developing a maturity assessment model*. Academic Press.

De Carolis, A., Macchi, M., Negri, E., & Terzi, S. (2017, September). A maturity model for assessing the digital readiness of manufacturing companies. In *IFIP International Conference on Advances in Production Management Systems* (pp. 13-20). Springer. 10.1007/978-3-319-66923-6_2

DiMaggio, P. J., & Powell, W. W. (1991). Introduction. *The new institutionalism in organizational analysis*, 1-38.

Dornberger, R., Inglese, T., Korkut, S., & Zhong, V. J. (2018). Digitalization: Yesterday, Today and Tomorrow. In *Business Information Systems and Technology 4.0* (pp. 1–11). Cham: Springer. doi:10.1007/978-3-319-74322-6_1

Fraser, P., Moultrie, J., & Gregory, M. (2002). The use of maturity models / grids as a tool assessing product development capability. *2002 IEEE International Engineering Management Conference*, 244-249. 10.1109/IEMC.2002.1038431

Gerybadze, A. (1998). *Technological competence assessment within the firm: applications of competence theory to managerial practice*. Forschungsstelle Internat. Management und Innovation.

Greenwood, R., Oliver, C., Lawrence, T. B., & Meyer, R. E. (Eds.). (2017). *The Sage handbook of organizational institutionalism*. Sage. doi:10.4135/9781526415066

Hanelt, A., Hildebrandt, B., & Polier, J. (2015, May). *Uncovering the Role of IS in Business Model Innovation-A Taxonomy-driven Approach to Structure the Field*. ECIS.

Harbi, S. E., & Anderson, A. R. (2010). Institutions and the shaping of different forms of entrepreneurship. *Journal of Socio-Economics*, *39*(3), 436–444. doi:10.1016/j.socec.2010.02.011

Harder, D. L., & Tokarski, K. O. (2018). The Power to Change a Social System. In *Organizational Behaviour and Human Resource Management* (pp. 49–72). Cham: Springer. doi:10.1007/978-3-319-66864-2_3

Harper, C. (2015). *Organizations: Structures, processes and outcomes*. Routledge.

Holmlund, M., Strandvik, T., & Lähteenmäki, I. (2017). Digitalization challenging institutional logics: Top executive sensemaking of service business change. *Journal of Service Theory and Practice*, *27*(1), 219–236. doi:10.1108/JSTP-12-2015-0256

Kahre, C., Hoffmann, D., & Ahlemann, F. (2017). *Beyond business-IT alignment-Digital business strategies as a paradigmatic shift: A review and research agenda*. Academic Press.

Kapás, J. (2008). Industrial revolutions and the evolution of the firm's organization: an historical perspective. *Journal of Innovation Economics & Management*, (2), 15-33.

Klötzer, C., & Pflaum, A. (2017). *Toward the development of a maturity model for digitalization within the manufacturing industry's supply chain*. Academic Press.

Kuula, S., & Haapasalo, H. (2017). Continuous and Co-creative Business Model Creation. In *Service Business Model Innovation in Healthcare and Hospital Management* (pp. 249–268). Cham: Springer. doi:10.1007/978-3-319-46412-1_14

Laudon, K., & Laudon, L. (2007). *Management Information Systems* (7th ed.). Prentice Hall.

Lee, J., Bagheri, B., & Kao, H. A. (2015). A cyber-physical systems architecture for industry 4.0-based manufacturing systems. *Manufacturing Letters*, *3*, 18–23. doi:10.1016/j.mfglet.2014.12.001

Leimstoll, U., Dannecker, A., Knechtli, H., Quade, M., Tanner, C., & Wölfle, R. (2018). E-Business in the Era of Digital Transformation. In *Business Information Systems and Technology 4.0* (pp. 81–101). Cham: Springer. doi:10.1007/978-3-319-74322-6_6

Lu, Y. (2017). Industry 4.0: A survey on technologies, applications and open research issues. *Journal of Industrial Information Integration*, *6*, 1–10. doi:10.1016/j.jii.2017.04.005

Masanell, R., & Ricart, J. (2007). *Competing through business models*. Working paper no 713, University of Navarra.

Metcalfe, M. (2005). Knowledge sharing, complex environments and small-worlds. *Human Systems Management*, *24*, 185–195.

Mettler, T. (2011). Maturity assessment models: A design science research approach. *International Journal of Society Systems Science*, *3*(1-2), 81–98. doi:10.1504/IJSSS.2011.038934

Meyer, J. W., & Rowan, B. (1977). Institutionalized organizations: Formal structure as myth and ceremony. *American Journal of Sociology*, *83*(2), 340–363. doi:10.1086/226550

Newman, K. L. (2000). Organizational transformation during institutional upheaval. *Academy of Management Review*, *25*(3), 602–619.

North, D. (1990). *Institutions*. Cambridge: Institutional Change, and Economic Performance.

O'Rourke, D., & Lollo, N. (2015). Transforming Consumption: From Decoupling, to Behavior Change, to System Changes for Sustainable Consumption. *Annual Review of Environment and Resources*, *40*(1), 233–259. doi:10.1146/annurev-environ-102014-021224

Orlikowski, W. J., & Barley, S. R. (2001). Technology and institutions: What can research on information technology and research on organizations learn from each other? *Management Information Systems Quarterly*, *25*(2), 145–165. doi:10.2307/3250927

Ostenwalder, A., Pigneur, P., & Tucci, C. L. (2005). *Clarifying Business Models: Origins, Present, and Future of the Concept Communications of AIS*. Springer.

Rice, A. L. (Ed.). (2013). *The enterprise and its environment: A system theory of management organization* (Vol. 10). Routledge.

Schallmo, D. R., & Williams, C. A. (2018). *Digital Transformation Now!: Guiding the Successful Digitalization of Your Business Model*. Springer. doi:10.1007/978-3-319-72844-5

Schwab, K. (2015, December 12). *The Fourth Industrial Revolution, What It Means and How to Respond*. Retrieved from Foreign Affairs: https://www.foreignaffairs.com/articles/2015-12-12/fourth-industrial-revolution

Scott, W. (2001). *Institutions and Organizations* (2nd ed.). London: Sage Publications.

Stadtmueller, L. (2014). *Helping IT Transform: The Rise of Organizational Change Management Services*. Stratecast.

Sturdy, A., & Grey, C. (2003). Beneath and beyond organizational change management: Exploring alternatives. *Organization*, *10*(4), 651–662. doi:10.1177/13505084030104006

Van Alstyne, M. W., Parker, G. G., & Choudary, S. P. (2016). Pipelines, platforms, and the new rules of strategy. *Harvard Business Review*, *94*(4), 54–62.

Weill, P., Malone, T. W., D'Urso, V. T., Herman, G., & Woerner, S. (2005). *Do some business models perform better than others? A study of the 1000 largest US firms*. MIT Center for Coordination Science Working Paper, 226.

Wester-Ebbinghaus, M., Moldt, D., & Köhler-Bußmeier, M. (2010). Modeling organizational units as modular components of systems of systems. *Transactions on Petri Nets and Other Models of Concurrency, 4*, 174-198.

Yunis, M., Tarhini, A., & Kassar, A. (2017). The role of ICT and innovation in enhancing organizational performance: The catalysing effect of corporate entrepreneurship. *Journal of Business Research*. doi:10.1016/j.jbusres.2017.12.030

Chapter 6
Institutions as Designers of Better Social Games

ABSTRACT

Institutions predefine and make possible development of many social processes. As already discussed, institutions define "the rules of the game," encouraging further social and organizational transformations. The aim of Chapter 6 is to propose an alternative approach for shaping the future institutions. By assuming institutions to be game-designers of complex social systems, there are explored the main mechanisms and elements of the game-design. Following this approach, the author discusses how institutions can transform to designers of new types of rules and social arrangements that will be more just and efficient for all. The structure of the chapter is as follows: In the first part there are identified the main elements of the game design, including game-mechanics, game-play, and game-word. The second part makes analysis of social ecosystems, where the new types of rules and regulations can stimulate creativity and innovations. Finally, an analysis is made about how institutions can figure out the gamification models and transform in order to promote new type of development and social cohesion. In this respect, Chapter 6 aims to propose an experiment of thought, discussing how to design more efficient and more socially just rules and regulations that can further ensure our sustainable development.

DOI: 10.4018/978-1-5225-6270-2.ch006

INTRODUCTION

The digital transformation processes under the paradigm of Industry 4.0 are expected to have a tremendous impact on the economic and social development. All stakeholders: businesses, private organizations, NGOs and public authorities have a role to play for shaping the next "robotic era". Even more, many new rules have to be defined and many new models for economic and social long-term development have to be discussed, taking into account the increased number of new machines on the job. Technologies cannot decide how our societies and how our personal life will change. Technologies provide us with tools and instruments, extending our abilities to cope more efficiently with the new coming challenges and future problems. Current digitalization trends focus to further improve human capacity to understand more complicated dynamic processes, switching the gap between virtual and real with sophisticated cyber-physical systems. The promise for better manufacturing processes can improve resource efficiency, customization, supply chain reorganization and product life-cycle management patterns. More advanced robots on the work can lead to increased service and production functions, confirming that digitalization processes come for more rational and data-based decision-making in order to better forecast, plan and implement the next models of development.

However, technologies cannot resolve our social and human problems and cannot make our societies more sustainable and future-oriented. The data all over the world continue to show accumulating waste, based on overproduction, neglected environmental and ecological balances, impermissible abuse of social and human rights and political oppression, short-focused and unsustainable global development movements. People increasingly feel excluded and unrepresented in main political and governance processes. Power distribution polarizes and inequalities intensify both internally in the countries and in the regions and internationally. New impactful Internet phenomena raise including fake news, social-network propaganda and intensified misinformation, using artificial intelligence applications to modify behavior patterns and social preferences. All this come to show that new technologies do not offer a "magic key" for the better future. Thus in the next robotic era there is a clear need for new social contract renegotiation. This means designing new institutions and defining new rules for making the "game" again more efficient and fair for all. Social exclusion, inequality, future of work and sustainable development are among the number of challenges that the new rules have to address.

Today is the moment to open the debate about the future of institutions. In order to "unlock" the potential of the next growth people should reach new common understanding for the next types of social arrangements and power distribution. Discussing the future of work and the new roles of humans in the labor force raise two main questions. On one side there should be redefined the new skillsets and new competences needed in the years to come. On the other side, much more attention should be paid on the issues of inclusive models of growth, encouraging and supporting people for cultivating and expressing talents and gifts in a socially enriching and responsible-for-the future way.

However, we have to admit that in the framework of the current institutionalized market-dominated, consumer-oriented and growth-based economic models, little attention is paid to many of the inherent human capacities. Due to the lack of monetization mechanisms and social support, many of the human gifts and dispositions remain undervalued and underestimated on the labor market, as for example the ability to take care, to protect, to persist, to share knowledge and competences, to artistically express, to encourage and motivate, to cooperate altruistically for a common cause. Thus, technically, human have the capacity and the potential to cope with the pressing problems of the future. However, in the current settings, many of the activities, ensuring sustainable development, environmental and social protection, crisis relief and poverty alleviation are just downsized to short-term campaigns, leaded by NGOs and volunteers. Thus in order to have much larger impact in the future, more efforts will be necessary to put all this hidden human capital to work. Meanwhile the existing institutional arrangements still widen the gap, measuring skills, personal success and organizational future perspectives only in economic terms.

All this come to show that the debates for the future of work can open the floor for the design and experimentation with new institutional arrangements. This way, by revising the main common principles, we can reevaluate the basic human rights and regulations, giving a chance for emerging more socially just and efficient institutions. Only adopting new forms of governance paradigms will help us to raise new informal institutions, ideologies (by North, 1990) and mental models, unlocking the potential for new types of personal and social development. In order to figure out on practice how institutions and organizations can further transform in the robotic era, we will analyze how rules and regulations can potentially evolve. Conceptualizing the models of (computer) games design, we will test the idea whether and how "rules of the game" can create enjoyable social interactions and fulfilling experiences.

The aim of the chapter six is to propose an alternative approach for shaping institutions in the future, discussing their role as game-designers of complex social systems. Exploring the game-design approach we will further investigate how institutions can design new types of rules and social arrangements that will be more just and efficient for all.

In the first part of the chapter there will be identified the main elements of the game design, including game-mechanics, game-play and game-word. By developing the main game design elements, there will be explored the elements of the social ecosystems that apply new types of rules and regulations in order to stimulate creativity and innovations. Finally, an analysis is made about how institutions can figure out the gamification models and transform, in order to promote new type of development and social cohesion. In this respect, chapter six aims to propose an experiment of thought, discussing how to design more efficient and more socially just rules and regulations, that can further ensure our sustainable development.

DEFINING THE GAME

The games design and game development started in antiquity and spread in a large continuum of ideas and directions, covering different aspects of the social subjects as philosophy, pedagogy, psychology, and others (Dixon, 2009). Based on the classification of Caillois (1961) play and games differentiate in a way that "ludus" represents a rule-based games and "paidia" is an anarchic playing. A game can be broadly defined *as a structured or rule-based social system in which players engage in a safe environment, resolving different challenges and leading to a quantifiable outcomes* (Huotari & Hamari, 2012). The game can be considered as a dynamic process and social activity rather than a simple object. Any game's primary objective and meaning is to motivate the player to perform well and to win. Therefore, he needs to have the ability and freedom to explore various strategies for success, experimenting with different techniques and analysing the feedback of the results. There are three main dimensions that characterize almost every game (Aerseth, 2003). The gameplay (the set of problems and challenges requiring the players' actions, strategies and motives); the game-structure (the rules of interaction in the game); the game-world or the game story (all plot and character fictional content, topology design and others). "Game mechanics" or the design of the rules and models of interactions within games, gained the researchers' interest in respect to the rise of the computer and video games. There game mechanics, game-structuring and the "rules of the game" include a general framework of rules that determine how a players can advance in a specific computer-generated game context. Without rules, the players' actions cannot be structured and there cannot be a gameplay (Aerseth, 2003). Thus game rules play a substantial role for the player's experiences. It is interesting to note as well that game mechanics are "second order designs", meaning that game designers can only indirectly design and influence the players' experiences by defining the rules of the game (Kultima, 2009).

GAME-STRUCTURE (RULES)

In order to identify the structure and the common characteristics and elements of the rules in the game-mechanics, there are identified two main approaches: studying casual games mechanics and investigating findings from gamification approaches.

Focusing to identify what triggers the casual games design, Kultima (2009) make an in-depth study of the main characteristics and common elements. It is important to stress that casual games are designed for heterogeneous groups of players with different backgrounds, skills, cultural settings and interests, and they are actually played by millions of people daily across different contexts and countries. The casual games are the most popular digital games and the current statistics prove that the overall playing time worldwide is gradually increasing at the expense of other media.

Casual games are designed mainly for entertainment and there is a huge Game industry, involved in its development and delivery. Casual games can play on different hardware platforms and devices. However, Kultima (2009) derived to main four common characteristics of the game mechanics that most of the casual games possess. They are: acceptability (of the content), accessibility (of the form), simplicity (of the use) and flexibility (in the context). Thus on Table 1 there are summarized the main aspects of these characteristics.

Gamification is a new rising phenomenon designating *the use of the game mechanics and applying them to other (web) properties to increase engagement*, or in general *the use of game design elements in non-game contexts* (Deterding, Dixon, Khaled, & Nacke, 2011). In the general aspect, gamification refers to a process of enhancing a service with affordances for game experiences in order to support user's overall value creation (Huotari & Hamari, 2012). Some other in-depth studies suggest that gamification is

Table 1. Analysis of Game mechanics characteristics in casual games adapted from Kultima (2009)

Acceptability	Accessibility	Simplicity	Flexibility
Content matches the norms of the players' social context.	Game is mentally or cognitively easy to access.	Player's cognitive load is alleviated by simplifying the design.	The game supports spatial, temporal and social pervasiveness and can be easily restarted.
Game avoids offensive topics.	Concise information is provided in the adoption phase, such as descriptive game title.	Functions are combined into one activity, as one-button interfaces.	Flexible intensity level.
Game uses abstract topics and game mechanics such as puzzles.	The design is simplified: players are not required to learn the rules before they start to play.	Some of the activities in the game are automated.	The game can be used for (many) different functions.
Game uses already accepted and established game designs, such as solitaire, chess etc.	Game is physically or materially easy to access.		Options for instrumental functions, for example, sports games.
Games are based thematically on topics with a universal appeal such as gardening, travelling, nature, cooking and other activities that a large population may already have as a common interest.	Game is accessible in environments that players use otherwise, for example, games in social media.		The game is error-forgiving: a player can make mistakes without punishment.
Game endorses positive emotions and values	Low price: the game is designed in a way to be accessible with low investments.		Options for user-created content: the player can adjust the functions of the game to his preferences.
Game uses mechanics, such as building, collecting, nurturing, exploration and collaboration instead of destruction, killing, fighting or survival.	Content of the game suits the norms of the players' social context.		Feedback can be provided, allowing users to decide what of the mistakes are decisive.
Investments of the game do not engage the player excessively and/or do not provide useful function outside the game			
Games can include instrumental functions, such as learning, mental exercise, measuring, losing weight, social interaction and physical prizes.			

a developing approach for encouraging user motivation, engagement and enjoyment in non-gaming, computer-mediated environments with an early collection of empirical work supporting its potential for beneficial effects in certain contexts (Seaborn & Fels, 2015).

Robinson and Belotti (2013) proposed a model of general gamification framework. It consists of six main categories of elements including: general framing (context and motivation for participation, back story or relevant information); general rules and performance framing (what is expected), social features (permit the user to interact with others), incentives (both intrinsic and extrinsic), resources and constraints, feedback and status information (allow user to understand what is going on). Making a review of different gamification applications, (Seaborn & Fels, 2015), find out that end-users mostly preferred strategies for collection (badges, points, and others), competition, status achievements, challenge and others.

In summary, among the main elements of the gamification approaches can be identified:

- Motivation (the ultimate reasons and conditions for taking certain actions and the observance of certain rules or behavior);
- Freedom of choice (the player must have the freedom to make decisions and to undertake his own strategies);
- Rules (The rules must be clear, honest, shared by the participants and easy to implement.);
- Risk-taking (ability to take risks and to make mistakes)

GAME-WORLD (INNOVATION ECOSYSTEMS)

The interest toward various forms of ecosystems raised in the recent years, based on their positive role for nurturing innovations and entrepreneurship and successful cultural mind-set transformation.

The term 'ecosystem' is built on biomimetic thinking, transposing it to economic development (Oh, Phillips, Park, & Lee, 2016). The ecosystem metaphor makes a parallel to the biological ecosystem, which can be defined as a complex set of relationships among people and animals, habitat and resources, whose function is to maintain an equilibrium (Frenkel & Meital, 2014). The ecosystem approach aims to explain and measure the ability of the local stakeholders to stimulate economic development and foster innovations. Jackson (2011) sets that *innovation ecosystem* is composed by *the complex relationships (intangibles) that are formed between actors or entities whose functional goal is to enable technology development and innovation.* Thus innovation ecosystem reflects the relationships between entities (such as firms, government bodies, universities) and individuals (such as researchers, entrepreneurs, consumers and investors), whose goal is to drive technology development and innovation. Recently the use of terms innovation/ business/ start-up or entrepreneurial ecosystem overlap, and de Vasconcelos Gomes et al. (2016) conclude that different labels, meanings and purposes combine: *digital innovation ecosystem, hub ecosystem, open innovation ecosystem, platform-based ecosystem.* It is important to mention, that *innovation ecosystems* differ from other networking constructs such as Science and technology parks, science cities, or innovation clusters, as innovation ecosystem is set for value co-creation. It is composed of interconnected and interdependent networked actors and include firms, customers, suppliers, complementary innovators and other agents as regulators both cooperating and competing de Vasconcelos Gomes et al. (2016). From practitioner's perspective, recently innovation ecosystems and creative hubs become a world-phenomena (Dovey, Pratt, Moreton, Virani, Merkel, & Lansdowne, 2016), defining "creative hubs" as various forms of platforms: *co-creation open (innovation) spaces, ecosystems, co-working spaces, accelerators and incubators, start-up or innovation spaces.*

The innovation ecosystem typology can cover the following models:

- **Geographic-Based:** Regional and national ecosystem, innovation districts and city-based innovation ecosystem, hyper-local innovation ecosystem (hosted and developed by specific incubators and accelerators) and others (Oh, Phillips, Park, & Lee, 2016).
- **Owner-Oriented:** Corporate-organized (open innovation) ecosystems, digital innovation ecosystem, high-tech ecosystems (consisting of digital platforms, apps, mobiles technologies etc.), university-based ecosystems, entrepreneurial ecosystems and others (Oh, Phillips, Park, & Lee, 2016).
- **Value-Based:** Focusing on innovation (value creation) ecosystem or business (value capturing) ecosystem (de Vasconcelos Gomes, Facin, Salerno, & Ikenami, 2016).

The successful innovation ecosystem leads to market innovations and increased economic activity: new jobs, new products and services, fuelling economic growth. Further impacts can include: start-up ventures, future investment (public and commercial), talent development, regional talent retention, informal education and engagement, training, urban regeneration, research and development, new networks, innovative models of organisation, quality of life enhancements and resilience (Dovey, Pratt, Moreton, Virani, Merkel, & Lansdowne, 2016). While public-funded ecosystem purposes are to encourage jobs creation, exports, environmental protection and local quality of life; privately funded focus on more efficient value chain and superior returns on investments (Luo, 2017). More generally Jackson (2011) states that the innovation ecosystem is successful when "intangibles" or the complex relationships between actors and entities can effectively influence the slope of the "valley of death" by decreasing the investor's risk, lowering the negative impact of entrepreneurial failure, decreasing the entry costs and increasing the success rate by increasing the number of attempts. Further, successful creative hubs are embedded in local cultural and economic ecosystems and are sustained by the respect of participants and audiences.

Some other studies show that the main success factors for the innovation ecosystems are: *talent; density of researchers, entrepreneurs and facilitating institutions; entrepreneurial culture, access to capital, and a supportive regulatory environment* (Oh, Phillips, Park, & Lee, 2016).

The main characteristics of the innovation ecosystem, as summarized by (de Vasconcelos Gomes, Facin, Salerno, & Ikenami, 2016) are identified as follows: *members' interconnectedness and interdependency; co-evolution; symbiosis, common platform, common set of goals and objectives and shared set of knowledge and skills*. The members play both cooperation and competition strategies; furthermore, the ecosystem follows a five-phase lifecycle model: emerging, diversifying, converging, consolidating and renewing.

The main actors can take the following role: keystone organizations, dominators and niche players; focal firms, customers, suppliers or complementary innovators (regulatory agencies and media). Thus ecosystem actors may be: bridge, hub or broker. Besides, the actors can have one of the following functional roles: initiators (who builds the ecosystem and set up the platform); specialists, (who add value to the central platform); or adopter, (who develops products following the initiator and co-designs the platform with the specialist) (de Vasconcelos Gomes, Facin, Salerno, & Ikenami, 2016).

The innovation ecosystems usually have an architecture, identified by the interfirm diversity, density and cyclicality. Its boundaries are porous and often nurture open innovations. The main four organizing problems in the ecosystem designs that commonly exist in innovation networks, innovation clusters, ecosystems and self-organizing groups, include four universal problems: task division, task allocation, reward distribution and information flow (Li, Du, & Yin, 2017). The management and operation of a hub is primarily about the careful selection and compatibility of tenants and the 'animation' of the interaction between the actors and activities based on a clear understanding of the values of the hub.

Further Li et al. (2017) identify that digital ecosystem is an organizational form or platform enabling individual actors to absorb (acquire) resources and knowledge. Unlike a traditional organization, an ecosystem lacks the formal authority that is needed for coordination. Thus a healthy and productive digital entrepreneurship ecosystem possesses a relatively stable organizing form whereby its stakeholders can effectively achieve a division of labor and integration of effort, without a hub or a central authority, while an ill organized digital entrepreneurship ecosystem is bound to fail. In this respect platforms help to aggregate various resources and facilitate collaboration. Because of the limited resources and knowledge available within individual firms, many firms seek to leverage external resources to generate innovations, and that is why digital innovation often takes place outside the boundary of firms through collective collaboration, which overcomes the resource limitations of a single firm (Adner & Kapoor, 2010).

In the report of (Dovey, Pratt, Moreton, Virani, Merkel, & Lansdowne, 2016) there are summarized the six possible innovation ecosystems/ creative hubs architectures:

- **Studio:** Small collective of individuals and/or small businesses in a co-working space.
- **Centre:** Large-scale building which may have other assets such as a cafe, bar, cinema, maker space, shop, exhibition space.
- **Network:** Dispersed group of individuals or businesses – tends to be sector or place specific.
- **Cluster:** Co-located creative individuals and businesses in a geographic area.
- **Online Platform:** Uses only online methods – website/social media to engage with a dispersed audience.
- **Alternative:** Focused on experimentation with new communities, sectors and financial models.

GAME-PLAY (MAIN CHALLENGES AND PROBLEMS)

As early discussed, in the framework of the game design, the game-play usually describes the set of the problems and challenges requiring the players' actions, strategies and motives. In order to design future-oriented and responsible institutions, focusing on the real humanity problems and outstepping the single market dynamics, we will discuss the approach of Ferraro et al. (2015).

In their work, the authors propose a pragmatic perspective, covering three robust strategies that can be applied for tackling with "grand challenges". Grand challenges are defined as complex, uncertain, evaluative events, difficult to predict and to address individually even by large organizations. Considering climate change and social inclusion as grand challenges, we can further mention digital transformation and institutional shift. The model of Ferrero et al. (2015) includes three main components: participatory architecture, multivocal inscriptions and distributed experimentations. The model claims to propose working pragmatic, distributed, and processual approach enhancing problem solving.

Thus on a structural level, it is needed a participatory architecture or a network of rules of engagement that allow diverse and heterogeneous actors to interact constructively over prolonged timespans. On interpretative level, multivocal inscription consists of defining common actions among various audiences with different evaluative criteria and different interpretations, in a manner that promotes coordination without requiring explicit consensus. There, the pragmatist approach is needed to facilitate the articulation, discussion, and negotiation of meaning across different actors, times and places. Finally, on the practice level, distributed experimentations can be planned by providing iterative action that will generate small wins, promoting evolutionary learning, and increasing engagement, while allowing unsuccessful efforts to be abandoned. By prolonging the ongoing local experimentation will encourage actors to solve not only one particular problem or another, but also improve their capacity for subsequent problem solving.

In summary, by putting together the three components: cooperating heterogeneous actors, common guidelines, shared inscriptions, and large-scale experimentations, Ferrero et al., (2015) expect to tackle the big challenges. One of the critical issues in the model is that usually "grand challenges" cover large scale and complex phenomena that can have be difficult to tackle by small-scale experimentations. However, this approach explore the design-thinking methodology, focusing on the fast and experienced based learning, reflections and experimentations.

PUTTING THE GAME TOGETHER: INSTITUTIONS AS GAME DESIGNERS

Since institutions define the rules of the game, their role as social "game designers" is substantial. Based on the elements and methods of the game design, as discussed above, we will analyse the role of institutions as "designers" and regulators of complex social systems and social relations. In order to model the processes in which institutions lay down the rules of the game, we will briefly look at the principles and patterns of gamification approaches and will attempt through the system approach to identify the key features that define

Gamification techniques, as thoroughly discussed, are gradually entering organizational practice, changing different organizational functions such as: marketing, customer relationships, career development and human resource management. Gamification and game playing recently became an important part of the culture of the modern society and its elements have been implemented in different directions. Furthermore, gamification techniques avoid the patterns of pure coercion and seek to achieve long-lasting results and more satisfying relationships that bring benefits (internal and external) both to the community and to individuals. Thus, different indications confirm that games improve social environment, lead to higher results, develop creativity, innovation, and improve players' competencies. That is why, by implying different gamification approaches methodologies, we will further discuss how institutions can shape relationships in the social environment through non-violent, internally motivating and satisfying way.

By summarizing the findings above, in Table 2 there are provided different elements and suggestions for performance indicators, that can help institutions to improve its processes of "setting the rules".

In this context, various elements of the "social game" can be measured by a set of quantitative and qualitative criteria and indicators. That is how, institutions can further lead social regulations setting processes, providing new models of games within holistic social system.

Table 2. Elements and indicators for evaluating game systems

	Elements	Performance Indicators
1. Motivation General factors	Goals Difficulty Feedback Challenges	Clarity of the goals Internal interest in the challenge Achievement level, level of success Internal motivation for taking part in the system
Motivation Internal factors	Autonomy Choosing own strategy Decision making	Degree of freedom in the system Alternative paths Options for implementing own strategies
Motivation External factors	Prize Competition Collaboration	Type of awards Competitive relations Cooperative relations
2. Content	Relevant content Adaptation to participants Internal motivation	System elements meet the objectives Level of adaptation and personalization Level of internal motivation to explore the content
3. Freedom, rules and feedback	Freedom to take decisions Level of control Clear feedback Acceptable rules Clear rules Relevant rules	Degree of freedom Control patterns Feedback models Socially acceptable rules Complexity of rules Linking rules to system goals
4. Errors, risks and emotional aspects	Recognition of errors A sense of security Identity Humor Attractive environment Friendly environment Presence of "fantasy" elements	Degree of freedom of error and risk taking Models for exploration and risk Opportunity for self-expression Creating a positive environment Stimulating creative thinking Collaboration Elements of Innovation
5. Integration of the game	Easy access and start of the game Easy way out of the game Awareness and reflection of experience	Intuitive and easy to use Easy way out of the game Analysis of experience and opportunities for reflection

DISCUSSION: DEMYSTIFYING THE ANATOMY OF INSTITUTIONAL CHANGE

When discussing institutions and institutional change, we have to admit that all social structures and all social transformations are subject of purposeful individuals' actions. Therefore, the main change agents inducing social and institutional change are individuals, who pursue their specific personal or group goals and objectives. In this respect, institutional entrepreneurs (or change agents) are individuals who can break the rules and practices associated with the dominant institutional logic and can develop and implement alternative rules and practices. Furthermore, a norm is not just an institutional paradigm, but this is the result of the purposive actions of discrete individuals. Both those who are particularly suited to providing new rule and those who are particularly eager to have it adopted play the role in the processes. Thus undertaking adoption or change of norms and rules is a human and social process.

In revolutionary times, the dominating institutional logic gradually loose its basic role to provide economic effectiveness and social coherence. Therefore, the new coming social rules follow the inherent logic of the emerging technologies and spontaneously transfer to new mental models. Starting to be promoted and admitted to be more effective, the new social logic gain further supporters, who gradually expand and become the new emerging social rules.

New technologies implementation is always a function of adaptation of the economic, cultural and institutional environment to the requirements of new technology systems. The social environment becomes a powerful selection mechanism for the inclusion or exclusion of particular innovations.

Furthermore, the deployment of each technology system involves several interconnected processes of change and adaptation. First, technologies and innovation require development of surrounding services (infrastructure, suppliers, distributors, maintenance services. Next, a "cultural" adaptation is needed, in order to transfer it with the logic of the interconnected technologies involved (among engineers, managers, service people, consumers, etc.). Finally, there should be set up institutional facilitators (rules and regulations, specialized training and education, etc.).

CONCLUSION

During the last years, it became clear that new disruptive technologies could not provide adequate response to the pressing social problems and larger institutional transformations have to be defined. Lack of efficiency and fairness are omnipresent. Rent-seeking became again a factor of success, as public institutions fail to impose appropriate rules to the fast changing environment. Moreover, the wealth accumulation in the top of the social pyramid accelerates. The social divide, inequality and disintegration intensify. It has to be underlined, that as previously discussed in chapters three and four, institutions strongly affect the socio-economic mechanisms and political models of wealth generation and wealth distribution. Furthermore, institutional arrangements reflect the social balance of power distribution, which is legalized, publicly recognized and protected by force within internal and international regulations. Therefore, any movement for revolutionary change in institutional arrangements should take in consideration the resources needed to oppose, the inherent reason behind the proposed change and the alternatives that can be proposed. As thoroughly discussed in chapter four, the successful revolutionary changes occur to oppose to rulers that are both inefficient and unjust. That is why, the main shifts in institutional settings that can overcome the social resistance need to address the changing dominant cultural mindset and the new coming shared mental models. This means that revolutions in institutional settings need to provide new set of alternative rules and regulations that provide more socially just, commonly acceptable and efficient rules, corresponding to the changed ideologies and mindsets.

REFERENCES

Aarseth, E. (2003, May). Playing Research: Methodological approaches to game analysis. In *Proceedings of the digital arts and culture conference* (pp. 28-29). Academic Press.

Adner, R., & Kapoor, R. (2010). Value creation in innovation ecosystems: How the structure of technological interdependence affects firm performance in new technology generations. *Strategic Management Journal*, *31*(3), 306–333. doi:10.1002mj.821

Caillois, R. (1961). *Man, play, and games*. University of Illinois Press.

de Vasconcelos Gomes, L. A., Facin, A. L. F., Salerno, M. S., & Ikenami, R. K. (2016). Unpacking the innovation ecosystem construct: Evolution, gaps and trends. *Technological Forecasting and Social Change*.

Deterding, S., Dixon, D., Khaled, R., & Nacke, L. (2011, September). From game design elements to gamefulness: defining gamification. In *Proceedings of the 15th international academic MindTrek conference: Envisioning future media environments* (pp. 9-15). ACM. 10.1145/2181037.2181040

Dixon, D. (2009). *Nietzsche contra Caillois: Beyond play and games*. Academic Press.

Dovey, J., Pratt, A., Moreton, S., Virani, T., & Merkel, J. L. (2016). *Creative Hubs, understanding the new economy*. Retrieved from https://creativeconomy.britishcouncil.org/media/uploads/files/HubsReport.pdf

Ferraro, F., Etzion, D., & Gehman, J. (2015). Tackling grand challenges pragmatically: Robust action revisited. *Organization Studies*, *36*(3), 363–390. doi:10.1177/0170840614563742

Frenkel, A., & Maital, S. (2014). *Mapping National Innovation Ecosystems: Foundations for Policy Consensus*. Edward Elgar Publishing. doi:10.4337/9781782546818

Huotari, K., & Hamari, J. (2012, October). Defining gamification: a service marketing perspective. In *Proceeding of the 16th International Academic MindTrek Conference* (pp. 17-22). ACM. 10.1145/2393132.2393137

Jackson, D. J. (2011). What is an innovation ecosystem. *National Science Foundation, 1*.

Kultima, A. (2009, September). Casual game design values. In *Proceedings of the 13th international MindTrek conference: Everyday life in the ubiquitous era* (pp. 58-65). ACM.

Li, W., Du, W., & Yin, J. (2017). Digital entrepreneurship ecosystem as a new form of organizing: The case of Zhongguancun. *Frontiers of Business Research in China*, *11*(1), 5. doi:10.118611782-017-0004-8

Luo, J. (2017). Architecture and evolvability of innovation ecosystems. *Technological Forecasting and Social Change*. doi:10.1016/j.techfore.2017.06.033

Oh, D. S., Phillips, F., Park, S., & Lee, E. (2016). Innovation ecosystems: A critical examination. *Technovation*, *54*, 1–6. doi:10.1016/j.technovation.2016.02.004

Robinson, D., & Bellotti, V. (2013, April). A preliminary taxonomy of gamification elements for varying anticipated commitment. *Proc. ACM CHI 2013 Workshop on Designing Gamification: Creating Gameful and Playful Experiences*.

Seaborn, K., & Fels, D. I. (2015). Gamification in theory and action: A survey. *International Journal of Human-Computer Studies*, *74*, 14–31. doi:10.1016/j.ijhcs.2014.09.006

Suseno, Y., & Standing, C. (2017). The Systems Perspective of National Innovation Ecosystems. *Systems Research and Behavioral Science*. doi:10.1002res.2494

Conclusion

CONCLUSION AND THE PATH AHEAD

When a flower doesn't bloom, you fix the environment in which it grows, not the flower. (Alexander Den Heijer)

In the present book, we used a multidisciplinary approach to prove that:

- **Institutions Matter:** Institutions constitute a multi-layered ecosystem of traditions, beliefs, social rules, norms, regulations, habits and routines. Institutions enable us to live together in complex social structures and allow us to cooperate, coordinate, to solve problems and to make plans for the future. Even more, institutions directly and indirectly influence every individual thought, decision, choice and action.
- **Institutions Are Social Constructs:** Institutions are enduring social agreements, but they are designed and adopted by our ancestors, by people like us. Institutions are not natural, they are not fixed and they can emerge, evolve, change, transform and adapt according to the needs of the social actors and their respective preferences and understandings.
- **Technologies Extend the Domain of the Possible:** New technologies, whether robots, artificial intelligence, cognitive computing, nanobots, automobiles or spaceships, just like any other tool or machine can serve as an instrument to extend the level of the possible and to provide more options to cope with the problems of the day. Robotic era will not differ substantially in terms of the place of technologies in peoples' life. Technologies in the robotic era would never make a person happy. Only social interaction with another person can bring joy and happiness.

- **Organizations Are the Triggers of Change:** Organizations play a crucial role for transferring new technologies into market-oriented offerings, adapting them into specific products and services. Furthermore, organizations enable people to collaborate, to cooperate and to innovate, experimenting with different approaches and building upon lessons learned.
- **Finally:** Finally, it is serious.

As formulated by Moore (2016):

Today we live at a crossroads in the history of our species – and of planetary life. What comes next is unknowable with any certainty. But it is not looking good. Environmentalist theory and research tells us, today, just how bad it is. Mass extinction. Climate Change. Ocean acidification. To these planetary shifts, one can add countless regional stories – runaway toxic disasters on land and at sea; cancer clusters; frequent and severe droughts.

The proofs that our institutions and organization are

UNSUSTAINABLE, INEFFICIENT, AND UNJUST

are everywhere.

And we have to fix.

Finally.

REFERENCES

Moore, J. W. (2006). *The rise of cheap nature.* Retrieved from http://www.academia.edu/27225850/The_Rise_of_Cheap_Nature

Related Readings

To continue IGI Global's long-standing tradition of advancing innovation through emerging research, please find below a compiled list of recommended IGI Global book chapters and journal articles in the areas of social enterprises, business models, and organizational development. These related readings will provide additional information and guidance to further enrich your knowledge and assist you with your own research.

Adams, S., Klobodu, E. K., & Lamptey, R. O. (2017). Electric Power Transmission, Distribution Losses, and Economic Growth in Ghana. In R. Das (Ed.), *Social, Health, and Environmental Infrastructures for Economic Growth* (pp. 216–233). Hershey, PA: IGI Global. doi:10.4018/978-1-5225-2364-2.ch011

Adams, S., Klobodu, E. K., & Lamptey, R. O. (2017). Health Infrastructure and Economic Growth in Sub-Saharan Africa. In R. Das (Ed.), *Social, Health, and Environmental Infrastructures for Economic Growth* (pp. 82–98). Hershey, PA: IGI Global. doi:10.4018/978-1-5225-2364-2.ch005

Adetiloye, K. A., Eke, P. O., & Taiwo, J. N. (2017). Public-Sector Project Abandonment Decision: A Test of the Ricardian Equivalence Theory on the Failed Lagos Metroline in Nigeria. In R. Das (Ed.), *Social, Health, and Environmental Infrastructures for Economic Growth* (pp. 188–215). Hershey, PA: IGI Global. doi:10.4018/978-1-5225-2364-2.ch010

Adhikary, M., & Khatun, M. (2016). Issues of Convergence: Some Evidences of SAARC Countries. In R. Das (Ed.), *Handbook of Research on Global Indicators of Economic and Political Convergence* (pp. 119–143). Hershey, PA: IGI Global. doi:10.4018/978-1-5225-0215-9.ch006

Akhter, T., & Palit, A. (2016). Effects of Neoliberal Globalization on Readymade Garment Industry of Bangladesh: A Case Study for Chittagong. In R. Das (Ed.), *Handbook of Research on Global Indicators of Economic and Political Convergence* (pp. 538–557). Hershey, PA: IGI Global. doi:10.4018/978-1-5225-0215-9.ch023

Akincilar, A. (2017). Do Judgmental Factors Lead to a Good Decision on Investing in a Currency or Mislead the Financial Player?: An Application in Turkey. In J. Stanković, P. Delias, S. Marinković, & S. Rochhia (Eds.), *Tools and Techniques for Economic Decision Analysis* (pp. 43–62). Hershey, PA: IGI Global. doi:10.4018/978-1-5225-0959-2.ch003

Allegreni, F. (2017). Crowdfunding as a Marketing Tool. In W. Vassallo (Ed.), *Crowdfunding for Sustainable Entrepreneurship and Innovation* (pp. 187–203). Hershey, PA: IGI Global. doi:10.4018/978-1-5225-0568-6.ch011

Altındağ, E. (2016). Current Approaches in Change Management. In A. Goksoy (Ed.), *Organizational Change Management Strategies in Modern Business* (pp. 24–51). Hershey, PA: IGI Global. doi:10.4018/978-1-4666-9533-7.ch002

Ambani, P. (2017). Crowdsourcing New Tools to Start Lean and Succeed in Entrepreneurship: Entrepreneurship in the Crowd Economy. In W. Vassallo (Ed.), *Crowdfunding for Sustainable Entrepreneurship and Innovation* (pp. 37–53). Hershey, PA: IGI Global. doi:10.4018/978-1-5225-0568-6.ch003

Amoako, G. K., Adjaison, G. K., & Osei-Bonsu, N. (2016). Role of Strategic Change Management in Emerging Markets: Ghanaian Perspective. In A. Goksoy (Ed.), *Organizational Change Management Strategies in Modern Business* (pp. 328–351). Hershey, PA: IGI Global. doi:10.4018/978-1-4666-9533-7.ch016

Arsenijević, O. M., Orčić, D., & Kastratović, E. (2017). Development of an Optimization Tool for Intangibles in SMEs: A Case Study from Serbia with a Pilot Research in the Prestige by Milka Company. In M. Vemić (Ed.), *Optimal Management Strategies in Small and Medium Enterprises* (pp. 320–347). Hershey, PA: IGI Global. doi:10.4018/978-1-5225-1949-2.ch015

Basu, I. (2017). Role of Infrastructure Development to Empower Women: An Over-Determined View. In R. Das (Ed.), *Social, Health, and Environmental Infrastructures for Economic Growth* (pp. 39–56). Hershey, PA: IGI Global. doi:10.4018/978-1-5225-2364-2.ch003

Ben Rejeb, W. (2017). Empirical Evidence on Corporate Governance Impact on CSR Disclosure in Developing Economies: The Tunisian and Egyptian Contexts. In D. Jamali (Ed.), *Comparative Perspectives on Global Corporate Social Responsibility* (pp. 116–137). Hershey, PA: IGI Global. doi:10.4018/978-1-5225-0720-8.ch006

Blomme, R. J., & Morsch, J. (2016). Organizations as Social Networks: The Role of the Compliance Officer as Agent of Change in Implementing Rules and Codes of Conduct. In A. Goksoy (Ed.), *Organizational Change Management Strategies in Modern Business* (pp. 110–121). Hershey, PA: IGI Global. doi:10.4018/978-1-4666-9533-7.ch006

Boachie, C. (2017). Decision Making under Risk and Uncertainty in the Oil and Gas Industry. In J. Stanković, P. Delias, S. Marinković, & S. Rochhia (Eds.), *Tools and Techniques for Economic Decision Analysis* (pp. 181–207). Hershey, PA: IGI Global. doi:10.4018/978-1-5225-0959-2.ch009

Candelise, C. (2017). The Application of Crowdfunding to the Energy Sector. In W. Vassallo (Ed.), *Crowdfunding for Sustainable Entrepreneurship and Innovation* (pp. 266–287). Hershey, PA: IGI Global. doi:10.4018/978-1-5225-0568-6.ch015

Carvalho, G., Simões, M., & Duarte, A. P. (2017). Export-Led Recovery in Portugal: Can It Also Sustain Growth? In J. Stanković, P. Delias, S. Marinković, & S. Rochhia (Eds.), *Tools and Techniques for Economic Decision Analysis* (pp. 129–150). Hershey, PA: IGI Global. doi:10.4018/978-1-5225-0959-2.ch006

Chakrabarti, G., & Sen, C. (2016). Green Convergence in Emerging Nations: The Determinants and the Possibilities. In R. Das (Ed.), *Handbook of Research on Global Indicators of Economic and Political Convergence* (pp. 448–473). Hershey, PA: IGI Global. doi:10.4018/978-1-5225-0215-9.ch020

Chakraborty, S. (2016). Economic Convergence and Real Dimensions: The Case of Shelter Deprivation. In R. Das (Ed.), *Handbook of Research on Global Indicators of Economic and Political Convergence* (pp. 338–363). Hershey, PA: IGI Global. doi:10.4018/978-1-5225-0215-9.ch015

Chan, D., & Kumar, S. (2017). Social Media Strategies for Small and Medium Scale Enterprise in the Klang Valley Region of Malaysia. In N. Ahmad, T. Ramayah, H. Halim, & S. Rahman (Eds.), *Handbook of Research on Small and Medium Enterprises in Developing Countries* (pp. 377–400). Hershey, PA: IGI Global. doi:10.4018/978-1-5225-2165-5.ch018

Chatterjee, N. (2017). An Assessment of Infrastructural Facilities in the Dryland Areas of West Bengal. In R. Das (Ed.), *Social, Health, and Environmental Infrastructures for Economic Growth* (pp. 234–268). Hershey, PA: IGI Global. doi:10.4018/978-1-5225-2364-2.ch012

Chatterjee, N., & Dinda, S. (2016). Convergence of Forest Resources in Jangalmahal, West Bengal. In R. Das (Ed.), *Handbook of Research on Global Indicators of Economic and Political Convergence* (pp. 511–537). Hershey, PA: IGI Global. doi:10.4018/978-1-5225-0215-9.ch022

Chatterjee, T., & Dinda, S. (2016). Health Status and Convergence in Developing Open Economies: Is Health Status Converging in Developing Economies? In R. Das (Ed.), *Handbook of Research on Global Indicators of Economic and Political Convergence* (pp. 364–381). Hershey, PA: IGI Global. doi:10.4018/978-1-5225-0215-9.ch016

Chaudhury, A. R. (2016). How Does Inequality of Opportunity Persist from Education to Earning?: Some Recent Evidences from India. In R. Das (Ed.), *Handbook of Research on Global Indicators of Economic and Political Convergence* (pp. 314–337). Hershey, PA: IGI Global. doi:10.4018/978-1-5225-0215-9.ch014

Cinelli, S. A. (2017). Real Estate Crowdfunding: 2015 and Beyond. In W. Vassallo (Ed.), *Crowdfunding for Sustainable Entrepreneurship and Innovation* (pp. 238–265). Hershey, PA: IGI Global. doi:10.4018/978-1-5225-0568-6.ch014

Cinelli, S. A. (2017). The World's Oldest Profession - Now and Then: Disruption of the Commercial Banking Model. In W. Vassallo (Ed.), *Crowdfunding for Sustainable Entrepreneurship and Innovation* (pp. 78–89). Hershey, PA: IGI Global. doi:10.4018/978-1-5225-0568-6.ch005

Çolakoğlu, S., Chung, Y., & Tarhan, A. B. (2016). Strategic Human Resource Management in Facilitating Organizational Change. In A. Goksoy (Ed.), *Organizational Change Management Strategies in Modern Business* (pp. 172–192). Hershey, PA: IGI Global. doi:10.4018/978-1-4666-9533-7.ch009

Damnjanović, A. M. (2017). Knowledge Management Optimization through IT and E-Business Utilization: A Qualitative Study on Serbian SMEs. In M. Vemić (Ed.), *Optimal Management Strategies in Small and Medium Enterprises* (pp. 249–267). Hershey, PA: IGI Global. doi:10.4018/978-1-5225-1949-2.ch012

Daneshpour, H. (2017). Integrating Sustainable Development into Project Portfolio Management through Application of Open Innovation. In M. Vemić (Ed.), *Optimal Management Strategies in Small and Medium Enterprises* (pp. 370–387). Hershey, PA: IGI Global. doi:10.4018/978-1-5225-1949-2.ch017

Das, R. C., Das, A., & Martin, F. (2016). Convergence Analysis of Households' Consumption Expenditure: A Cross Country Study. In R. Das (Ed.), *Handbook of Research on Global Indicators of Economic and Political Convergence* (pp. 1–28). Hershey, PA: IGI Global. doi:10.4018/978-1-5225-0215-9.ch001

Das, U., Das, R. C., & Ray, K. (2016). Convergence and Equality of Road Infrastructure: A Cross Country Analysis. In R. Das (Ed.), *Handbook of Research on Global Indicators of Economic and Political Convergence* (pp. 170–183). Hershey, PA: IGI Global. doi:10.4018/978-1-5225-0215-9.ch008

Dastaviz, A. H. (2016). Integration of Competing Values and Knowledge Organisational Activities in a New Model. *International Journal of Knowledge-Based Organizations*, *6*(4), 50–61. doi:10.4018/IJKBO.2016100105

Datta, P. K., Tiwary, H., & Chakrabarti, S. (2017). MGNREGS of India: Complementarities Between Employment and Infrastructure. In R. Das (Ed.), *Social, Health, and Environmental Infrastructures for Economic Growth* (pp. 57–81). Hershey, PA: IGI Global. doi:10.4018/978-1-5225-2364-2.ch004

Davidson, D. K., & Yin, J. (2017). Corporate Social Responsibility (CSR) in China: A Contextual Exploration. In D. Jamali (Ed.), *Comparative Perspectives on Global Corporate Social Responsibility* (pp. 28–48). Hershey, PA: IGI Global. doi:10.4018/978-1-5225-0720-8.ch002

de Burgh-Woodman, H., Bressan, A., & Torrisi, A. (2017). An Evaluation of the State of the CSR Field in Australia: Perspectives from the Banking and Mining Sectors. In D. Jamali (Ed.), *Comparative Perspectives on Global Corporate Social Responsibility* (pp. 138–164). Hershey, PA: IGI Global. doi:10.4018/978-1-5225-0720-8.ch007

De Ruiter, M., Blomme, R. J., & Schalk, R. (2016). Reducing the Negative Effects of Psychological Contract Breach during Management-Imposed Change: A Trickle-Down Model of Management Practices. In A. Goksoy (Ed.), *Organizational Change Management Strategies in Modern Business* (pp. 122–142). Hershey, PA: IGI Global. doi:10.4018/978-1-4666-9533-7.ch007

Dedousis, E., & Rutter, R. N. (2016). Workforce Localisation and Change Management: The View from the Gulf. In A. Goksoy (Ed.), *Organizational Change Management Strategies in Modern Business* (pp. 301–327). Hershey, PA: IGI Global. doi:10.4018/978-1-4666-9533-7.ch015

Demiray, M., & Aslanbay, Y. (2017). The Crowdfunding Communities and the Value of Identification for Sustainability of Co-Creation. In W. Vassallo (Ed.), *Crowdfunding for Sustainable Entrepreneurship and Innovation* (pp. 155–174). Hershey, PA: IGI Global. doi:10.4018/978-1-5225-0568-6.ch009

Demiray, M., Burnaz, S., & Aslanbay, Y. (2017). The Crowdfunding Market, Models, Platforms, and Projects. In W. Vassallo (Ed.), *Crowdfunding for Sustainable Entrepreneurship and Innovation* (pp. 90–126). Hershey, PA: IGI Global. doi:10.4018/978-1-5225-0568-6.ch006

Dikeç, A., Kane, V., & Çapar, N. (2017). Cross-Country and Cross-Sector CSR Variations: A Comparative Analysis of CSR Reporting in the U.S., South Korea, and Turkey. In D. Jamali (Ed.), *Comparative Perspectives on Global Corporate Social Responsibility* (pp. 69–95). Hershey, PA: IGI Global. doi:10.4018/978-1-5225-0720-8.ch004

Duruji, M. M., & Urenma, D. F. (2016). The Environmentalism and Politics of Climate Change: A Study of the Process of Global Convergence through UNFCCC Conferences. In R. Das (Ed.), *Handbook of Research on Global Indicators of Economic and Political Convergence* (pp. 398-429). Hershey, PA: IGI Global. 10.4018/978-1-5225-0215-9.ch018

Erne, R. (2016). Change Management Revised. In A. Goksoy (Ed.), *Organizational Change Management Strategies in Modern Business* (pp. 1–23). Hershey, PA: IGI Global. doi:10.4018/978-1-4666-9533-7.ch001

Ertürk, E., Yılmaz, D., & Çetin, I. (2016). Optimum Currency Area Theory and Business Cycle Convergence in EMU: Considering the Sovereign Debt Crisis. In R. Das (Ed.), *Handbook of Research on Global Indicators of Economic and Political Convergence* (pp. 67–91). Hershey, PA: IGI Global. doi:10.4018/978-1-5225-0215-9.ch004

Eryılmaz, M. E., & Eryılmaz, F. (2016). Change Emphasis in Mission and Vision Statements of the First 1000 Turkish Organizations: A Content Analysis. In A. Goksoy (Ed.), *Organizational Change Management Strategies in Modern Business* (pp. 352–362). Hershey, PA: IGI Global. doi:10.4018/978-1-4666-9533-7.ch017

Frączkiewicz-Wronka, A., Tkacz, M., & Arando, S. (2017). The Business Model of a Public Social Partnership: Contextual Determinants. In M. Lewandowski & B. Kożuch (Eds.), *Public Sector Entrepreneurship and the Integration of Innovative Business Models* (pp. 108–138). Hershey, PA: IGI Global. doi:10.4018/978-1-5225-2215-7.ch005

Friedrich, P., & Chebotareva, M. (2017). Options for Applying Functional Overlapping Competing Jurisdictions (FOCJs) for Municipal Cooperation in Russia. In M. Lewandowski & B. Kożuch (Eds.), *Public Sector Entrepreneurship and the Integration of Innovative Business Models* (pp. 73–107). Hershey, PA: IGI Global. doi:10.4018/978-1-5225-2215-7.ch004

Gan, P. L., Mahmud, I., Ramayah, T., & Zuhora, F. T. (2017). Understanding Attitude towards Green IT among Professionals in IT Service SMEs in Bangladesh. In N. Ahmad, T. Ramayah, H. Halim, & S. Rahman (Eds.), *Handbook of Research on Small and Medium Enterprises in Developing Countries* (pp. 48–66). Hershey, PA: IGI Global. doi:10.4018/978-1-5225-2165-5.ch003

Ganesan, Y., Haron, H., Amran, A., & Ooi, S. K. (2017). Corporate Social Responsibility in SMEs: The Role of Non-Audit Services. In N. Ahmad, T. Ramayah, H. Halim, & S. Rahman (Eds.), *Handbook of Research on Small and Medium Enterprises in Developing Countries* (pp. 345–359). Hershey, PA: IGI Global. doi:10.4018/978-1-5225-2165-5.ch016

Ghosh, D., & Dinda, S. (2017). Health Infrastructure and Economic Development in India. In R. Das (Ed.), *Social, Health, and Environmental Infrastructures for Economic Growth* (pp. 99–119). Hershey, PA: IGI Global. doi:10.4018/978-1-5225-2364-2.ch006

Ghosh, S. (2017). Changes in Infrastructural Condition of Slums in India: A State Level Analysis. In R. Das (Ed.), *Social, Health, and Environmental Infrastructures for Economic Growth* (pp. 14–38). Hershey, PA: IGI Global. doi:10.4018/978-1-5225-2364-2.ch002

Gonzalez, R. V. (2016). Knowledge Management Process in Multi-Site Provision of Service. *International Journal of Knowledge Management, 12*(2), 20–37. doi:10.4018/IJKM.2016040102

Greco, T. (2017). Horizontal Crowdfunding Platforms: Socio-Economic Impact and Exogenous/Endogenous System of Rules. In W. Vassallo (Ed.), *Crowdfunding for Sustainable Entrepreneurship and Innovation* (pp. 127–139). Hershey, PA: IGI Global. doi:10.4018/978-1-5225-0568-6.ch007

Greco, T. (2017). Vertical and Community-Based Crowdfunding Platforms. In W. Vassallo (Ed.), *Crowdfunding for Sustainable Entrepreneurship and Innovation* (pp. 140–154). Hershey, PA: IGI Global. doi:10.4018/978-1-5225-0568-6.ch008

Hack-Polay, D., & Qiu, H. (2017). Doing Good Doing Well: Discussion of CSR in the Pulp and Paper Industry in the Asian Context. In D. Jamali (Ed.), *Comparative Perspectives on Global Corporate Social Responsibility* (pp. 226–240). Hershey, PA: IGI Global. doi:10.4018/978-1-5225-0720-8.ch011

Halim, H. A., Ahmad, N. H., Hanifah, H., & Ramayah, T. (2017). The Impediments to Entrepreneurial Ventures among the Bottom of Pyramid Community in Northern Malaysia. In N. Ahmad, T. Ramayah, H. Halim, & S. Rahman (Eds.), *Handbook of Research on Small and Medium Enterprises in Developing Countries* (pp. 67–81). Hershey, PA: IGI Global. doi:10.4018/978-1-5225-2165-5.ch004

Hanifah, H., Halim, H. A., Ahmad, N. H., & Vafaei-Zadeh, A. (2017). Innovation Culture as a Mediator Between Specific Human Capital and Innovation Performance Among Bumiputera SMEs in Malaysia. In N. Ahmad, T. Ramayah, H. Halim, & S. Rahman (Eds.), *Handbook of Research on Small and Medium Enterprises in Developing Countries* (pp. 261–279). Hershey, PA: IGI Global. doi:10.4018/978-1-5225-2165-5.ch012

Haro-de-Rosario, A., del Mar Gálvez-Rodríguez, M., & Caba-Pérez, M. D. (2017). Determinants of Corporate Social Responsibility Disclosure in Latin American Companies: An Analysis of the Oil and Gas Sector. In D. Jamali (Ed.), *Comparative Perspectives on Global Corporate Social Responsibility* (pp. 165–184). Hershey, PA: IGI Global. doi:10.4018/978-1-5225-0720-8.ch008

Hassaan, M. (2016). Sustainability Reporting in Transitional Economies. In R. Das (Ed.), *Handbook of Research on Global Indicators of Economic and Political Convergence* (pp. 184–204). Hershey, PA: IGI Global. doi:10.4018/978-1-5225-0215-9.ch009

Hassan, A., & Lund-Thomsen, P. (2017). Multi-Stakeholder Initiatives and Corporate Social Responsibility in Global Value Chains: Towards an Analytical Framework and a Methodology. In D. Jamali (Ed.), *Comparative Perspectives on Global Corporate Social Responsibility* (pp. 241–257). Hershey, PA: IGI Global. doi:10.4018/978-1-5225-0720-8.ch012

Hossain, M. M., & Ibrahim, Y. (2017). Working Capital Financing by Banks in Small Enterprises: Problems and Challenges for Bangladesh. In N. Ahmad, T. Ramayah, H. Halim, & S. Rahman (Eds.), *Handbook of Research on Small and Medium Enterprises in Developing Countries* (pp. 137–158). Hershey, PA: IGI Global. doi:10.4018/978-1-5225-2165-5.ch007

Indiran, L., Khalifah, Z., Ismail, K., & Ramanathan, S. (2017). Business Incubation in Malaysia: An Overview of Multimedia Super Corridor, Small and Medium Enterprises, and Incubators in Malaysia. In N. Ahmad, T. Ramayah, H. Halim, & S. Rahman (Eds.), *Handbook of Research on Small and Medium Enterprises in Developing Countries* (pp. 322–344). Hershey, PA: IGI Global. doi:10.4018/978-1-5225-2165-5.ch015

Issa, T., & Pick, D. (2017). Teaching Business Ethics Post GFC: A Corporate Social Responsibility of Universities. In D. Jamali (Ed.), *Comparative Perspectives on Global Corporate Social Responsibility* (pp. 290–307). Hershey, PA: IGI Global. doi:10.4018/978-1-5225-0720-8.ch015

Ivana, B., & Vrkić, F. (2017). Crisis Communication and Crisis Management during the Crisis: Case Study of Croatia. In J. Stanković, P. Delias, S. Marinković, & S. Rochhia (Eds.), *Tools and Techniques for Economic Decision Analysis* (pp. 208–224). Hershey, PA: IGI Global. doi:10.4018/978-1-5225-0959-2.ch010

Ivančević, K. (2017). Insurance as an Optimization Tool for Risk Management in Small and Medium-Sized Enterprises. In M. Vemić (Ed.), *Optimal Management Strategies in Small and Medium Enterprises* (pp. 178–197). Hershey, PA: IGI Global. doi:10.4018/978-1-5225-1949-2.ch009

Jain, P. (2017). A Crowd-Funder Value (CFV) Framework for Crowd-Investment: A Roadmap for Entrepreneurial Success in the Contemporary Society. In W. Vassallo (Ed.), *Crowdfunding for Sustainable Entrepreneurship and Innovation* (pp. 288–309). Hershey, PA: IGI Global. doi:10.4018/978-1-5225-0568-6.ch016

Jalali, A., Thurasamy, R., & Jaafar, M. (2017). The Moderating Effect of Social Capital in Relation to Entrepreneurial Orientation and Firm Performance. In N. Ahmad, T. Ramayah, H. Halim, & S. Rahman (Eds.), *Handbook of Research on Small and Medium Enterprises in Developing Countries* (pp. 82–115). Hershey, PA: IGI Global. doi:10.4018/978-1-5225-2165-5.ch005

Jana, S. K., & Karmakar, A. K. (2016). Food Security in Asia: Is There Convergence? In R. Das (Ed.), *Handbook of Research on Global Indicators of Economic and Political Convergence* (pp. 382–397). Hershey, PA: IGI Global. doi:10.4018/978-1-5225-0215-9.ch017

Jana, S. K., & Karmakar, A. K. (2017). Infrastructure, Education, and Economic Development in India: A State Level Analysis. In R. Das (Ed.), *Social, Health, and Environmental Infrastructures for Economic Growth* (pp. 1–13). Hershey, PA: IGI Global. doi:10.4018/978-1-5225-2364-2.ch001

Jankovic-Milic, V., & Džunić, M. (2017). Measuring Governance: The Application of Grey Relational Analysis on World Governance Indicators. In J. Stanković, P. Delias, S. Marinković, & S. Rochhia (Eds.), *Tools and Techniques for Economic Decision Analysis* (pp. 104–128). Hershey, PA: IGI Global. doi:10.4018/978-1-5225-0959-2.ch005

Jayapal, P., & Omar, A. (2017). The Role of Value Co-Creation on Brand Image: A Conceptual Framework for the Market Performance of SMEs in Malaysia. In N. Ahmad, T. Ramayah, H. Halim, & S. Rahman (Eds.), *Handbook of Research on Small and Medium Enterprises in Developing Countries* (pp. 185–207). Hershey, PA: IGI Global. doi:10.4018/978-1-5225-2165-5.ch009

Kaplan, J., & Montiel, I. (2017). East vs. West Approaches to Reporting Corporate Sustainability Strategies to the World: Corporate Sustainability Reporting: East vs. West. In D. Jamali (Ed.), *Comparative Perspectives on Global Corporate Social Responsibility* (pp. 49–68). Hershey, PA: IGI Global. doi:10.4018/978-1-5225-0720-8.ch003

Kasemsap, K. (2016). The Roles of Organizational Change Management and Resistance to Change in the Modern Business World. In A. Goksoy (Ed.), *Organizational Change Management Strategies in Modern Business* (pp. 143–171). Hershey, PA: IGI Global. doi:10.4018/978-1-4666-9533-7.ch008

Kasemsap, K. (2017). Encouraging Internationalization and Entrepreneurial Orientation in Small and Medium Enterprises. In N. Ahmad, T. Ramayah, H. Halim, & S. Rahman (Eds.), *Handbook of Research on Small and Medium Enterprises in Developing Countries* (pp. 233–259). Hershey, PA: IGI Global. doi:10.4018/978-1-5225-2165-5.ch011

Kesti, M. O., Leinonen, J., & Kesti, T. (2017). The Productive Leadership Game: From Theory to Game-Based Learning. In M. Lewandowski & B. Kożuch (Eds.), *Public Sector Entrepreneurship and the Integration of Innovative Business Models* (pp. 238–260). Hershey, PA: IGI Global. doi:10.4018/978-1-5225-2215-7.ch010

King, D. R. (2016). Management as a Limit to Organizational Change: Implications for Acquisitions. In A. Goksoy (Ed.), *Organizational Change Management Strategies in Modern Business* (pp. 52–73). Hershey, PA: IGI Global. doi:10.4018/978-1-4666-9533-7.ch003

Kishna, T., Blomme, R. J., & van der Veen, J. A. (2016). Organizational Routines: Developing a Duality Model to Explain the Effects of Strategic Change Initiatives. In A. Goksoy (Ed.), *Organizational Change Management Strategies in Modern Business* (pp. 363–385). Hershey, PA: IGI Global. doi:10.4018/978-1-4666-9533-7.ch018

Kleverlaan, R. (2017). How to Launch a Successful Crowdfunding Campaign. In W. Vassallo (Ed.), *Crowdfunding for Sustainable Entrepreneurship and Innovation* (pp. 224–237). Hershey, PA: IGI Global. doi:10.4018/978-1-5225-0568-6.ch013

Kożuch, B., & Jabłoński, A. (2017). Adopting the Concept of Business Models in Public Management. In M. Lewandowski & B. Kożuch (Eds.), *Public Sector Entrepreneurship and the Integration of Innovative Business Models* (pp. 10–46). Hershey, PA: IGI Global. doi:10.4018/978-1-5225-2215-7.ch002

Laha, A. (2016). Association between Governance and Human Development in South Asia: A Cross Country Analysis. In R. Das (Ed.), *Handbook of Research on Global Indicators of Economic and Political Convergence* (pp. 254–273). Hershey, PA: IGI Global. doi:10.4018/978-1-5225-0215-9.ch012

Lavassani, K. M., & Movahedi, B. (2017). Applications Driven Information Systems: Beyond Networks toward Business Ecosystems. *International Journal of Innovation in the Digital Economy*, *8*(1), 61–75. doi:10.4018/IJIDE.2017010104

Lerro, A. M. (2017). Legal Aspects and Regulation in Crowdfunding: Comparisons across Countries. In W. Vassallo (Ed.), *Crowdfunding for Sustainable Entrepreneurship and Innovation* (pp. 204–223). Hershey, PA: IGI Global. doi:10.4018/978-1-5225-0568-6.ch012

Lewandowski, M. (2017). Public Organizations and Business Model Innovation: The Role of Public Service Design. In M. Lewandowski & B. Kożuch (Eds.), *Public Sector Entrepreneurship and the Integration of Innovative Business Models* (pp. 47–72). Hershey, PA: IGI Global. doi:10.4018/978-1-5225-2215-7.ch003

Lousã, M. D., & Monteiro, J. A. (2015). Explanatory Model of Adoption, Development and Utilization of Administrative Workflow Systems. *International Journal of Sociotechnology and Knowledge Development*, *7*(4), 31–52. doi:10.4018/IJSKD.2015100103

Maciejczak, M., & Słodki, A. (2017). Initial Price Strategies of Polish Micro and Small Enterprises: An Application of Game Theory for Industrial Organization of the SME Sector. In M. Vemić (Ed.), *Optimal Management Strategies in Small and Medium Enterprises* (pp. 126–143). Hershey, PA: IGI Global. doi:10.4018/978-1-5225-1949-2.ch007

Magala, S. J. (2017). Between Davos and Porto Alegre: Democratic Entrepreneurship as Crowdsourcing for Ideas. In M. Lewandowski & B. Kożuch (Eds.), *Public Sector Entrepreneurship and the Integration of Innovative Business Models* (pp. 1–9). Hershey, PA: IGI Global. doi:10.4018/978-1-5225-2215-7.ch001

Malega, P. (2017). Small and Medium Enterprises in the Slovak Republic: Status and Competitiveness of SMEs in the Global Markets and Possibilities of Optimization. In M. Vemić (Ed.), *Optimal Management Strategies in Small and Medium Enterprises* (pp. 102–124). Hershey, PA: IGI Global. doi:10.4018/978-1-5225-1949-2.ch006

Malek, N. A., & Takala, J. A. (2017). Regression Analysis for Environmental Practices: Participation among Finnish SMEs. In M. Vemić (Ed.), *Optimal Management Strategies in Small and Medium Enterprises* (pp. 44–59). Hershey, PA: IGI Global. doi:10.4018/978-1-5225-1949-2.ch003

Malik, A. (2016). The Role of HR Strategies in Change. In A. Goksoy (Ed.), *Organizational Change Management Strategies in Modern Business* (pp. 193–215). Hershey, PA: IGI Global. doi:10.4018/978-1-4666-9533-7.ch010

Mandal, C., & Gupta, A. C. (2016). A Comparative Study on World-Wide Carbon Emission Convergence: An Empirical Analysis. In R. Das (Ed.), *Handbook of Research on Global Indicators of Economic and Political Convergence* (pp. 430–447). Hershey, PA: IGI Global. doi:10.4018/978-1-5225-0215-9.ch019

Manzoor, A. (2017). Sustainable Infrastructures: A New Infrastructure Investment Strategy. In R. Das (Ed.), *Social, Health, and Environmental Infrastructures for Economic Growth* (pp. 145–164). Hershey, PA: IGI Global. doi:10.4018/978-1-5225-2364-2.ch008

Mazumdar, D. (2016). The Problems of Development Gap between Developed and Developing Nations: Is There Any Sign of Convergence? In R. Das (Ed.), *Handbook of Research on Global Indicators of Economic and Political Convergence* (pp. 29–50). Hershey, PA: IGI Global. doi:10.4018/978-1-5225-0215-9.ch002

Milošević, O. (2017). Critical Review of SME Regulation Optimization in Serbia: A Reflection on Harmonization with the EU Acquis. In M. Vemić (Ed.), *Optimal Management Strategies in Small and Medium Enterprises* (pp. 79–101). Hershey, PA: IGI Global. doi:10.4018/978-1-5225-1949-2.ch005

Molnar, R. M. (2017). Structural Change Management for Sustainable SME Development: Applying Classical Management Tools. In M. Vemić (Ed.), *Optimal Management Strategies in Small and Medium Enterprises* (pp. 348–369). Hershey, PA: IGI Global. doi:10.4018/978-1-5225-1949-2.ch016

Monahov, A. (2017). The Effects of Prudential Supervision on Bank Resiliency and Profits in a Multi-Agent Setting. In J. Stanković, P. Delias, S. Marinković, & S. Rochhia (Eds.), *Tools and Techniques for Economic Decision Analysis* (pp. 63–103). Hershey, PA: IGI Global. doi:10.4018/978-1-5225-0959-2.ch004

Mukherjee, S. (2017). Anatomy and Significance of Public Healthcare Expenditure and Economic Growth Nexus in India: Its Implications for Public Health Infrastructure Thereof. In R. Das (Ed.), *Social, Health, and Environmental Infrastructures for Economic Growth* (pp. 120–144). Hershey, PA: IGI Global. doi:10.4018/978-1-5225-2364-2.ch007

Mukhopadhyay, D., & Mandal, A. K. (2017). Infrastructure Development and Changing Market Penetration of Consumer Durables in Rural India: An Empirical Investigation. In R. Das (Ed.), *Social, Health, and Environmental Infrastructures for Economic Growth* (pp. 269–289). Hershey, PA: IGI Global. doi:10.4018/978-1-5225-2364-2.ch013

Mukhopadhyay, P., Sinha, M., & Sengupta, P. P. (2017). Importance of Sustainable Rural Development through Agrarian Reforms: An Indian Scenario. In R. Das (Ed.), *Social, Health, and Environmental Infrastructures for Economic Growth* (pp. 290–306). Hershey, PA: IGI Global. doi:10.4018/978-1-5225-2364-2.ch014

Musa, E. (2017). Crowdsourcing Social Innovation: Towards a Collaborative Social Capitalism. In W. Vassallo (Ed.), *Crowdfunding for Sustainable Entrepreneurship and Innovation* (pp. 54–77). Hershey, PA: IGI Global. doi:10.4018/978-1-5225-0568-6.ch004

Nekaj, E. L. (2017). The Crowd Economy: From the Crowd to Businesses to Public Administrations and Multinational Companies. In W. Vassallo (Ed.), *Crowdfunding for Sustainable Entrepreneurship and Innovation* (pp. 1–19). Hershey, PA: IGI Global. doi:10.4018/978-1-5225-0568-6.ch001

Neogi, C. (2016). Productivity Convergence and Asian Trade Blocks. In R. Das (Ed.), *Handbook of Research on Global Indicators of Economic and Political Convergence* (pp. 92–118). Hershey, PA: IGI Global. doi:10.4018/978-1-5225-0215-9.ch005

Niederer, P. M. (2017). Principles in Crowdfunding Benefits and Validation Tools: How to Ensure Campaign Success. In W. Vassallo (Ed.), *Crowdfunding for Sustainable Entrepreneurship and Innovation* (pp. 175–186). Hershey, PA: IGI Global. doi:10.4018/978-1-5225-0568-6.ch010

Omiunu, O. G. (2017). Deploying ICT to Enhance Small Businesses and Achieving Sustainable Development: A Paradigm to Reducing Poverty and Unemployment and Enhancing a Sustainable National Development in Nigeria. In N. Ahmad, T. Ramayah, H. Halim, & S. Rahman (Eds.), *Handbook of Research on Small and Medium Enterprises in Developing Countries* (pp. 208–232). Hershey, PA: IGI Global. doi:10.4018/978-1-5225-2165-5.ch010

Osman, M. N. (2017). Internet-Based Social Reporting in Emerging Economies: Insights from Public Banks in Egypt and the UAE. In D. Jamali (Ed.), *Comparative Perspectives on Global Corporate Social Responsibility* (pp. 96–115). Hershey, PA: IGI Global. doi:10.4018/978-1-5225-0720-8.ch005

Özgeldi, M. (2016). Role of Human Resources in Change. In A. Goksoy (Ed.), *Organizational Change Management Strategies in Modern Business* (pp. 216–229). Hershey, PA: IGI Global. doi:10.4018/978-1-4666-9533-7.ch011

Patra, S. (2016). Role of SAARC in Convergence of South Asian Economies. In R. Das (Ed.), *Handbook of Research on Global Indicators of Economic and Political Convergence* (pp. 144–169). Hershey, PA: IGI Global. doi:10.4018/978-1-5225-0215-9.ch007

Patra, S. (2017). Energy Challenges and Infrastructure Development in South Asia. In R. Das (Ed.), *Social, Health, and Environmental Infrastructures for Economic Growth* (pp. 165–187). Hershey, PA: IGI Global. doi:10.4018/978-1-5225-2364-2.ch009

Puaschunder, J. (2017). The Call for Global Responsible Inter-Generational Leadership: The Quest of an Integration of Inter-Generational Equity in Corporate Social Responsibility (CSR) Models. In D. Jamali (Ed.), *Comparative Perspectives on Global Corporate Social Responsibility* (pp. 276–289). Hershey, PA: IGI Global. doi:10.4018/978-1-5225-0720-8.ch014

Radosavljevic, M., & Andjelkovic, A. (2017). Multi-Criteria Decision Making Approach for Choosing Business Process for the Improvement: Upgrading of the Six Sigma Methodology. In J. Stanković, P. Delias, S. Marinković, & S. Rochhia (Eds.), *Tools and Techniques for Economic Decision Analysis* (pp. 225–247). Hershey, PA: IGI Global. doi:10.4018/978-1-5225-0959-2.ch011

Rahman, S. A., Ahmad, N. H., & Taghizadeh, S. K. (2017). On the Road to SME Sector Development in Bangladesh: A Guideline Based on Current Challenges and Opportunities. In N. Ahmad, T. Ramayah, H. Halim, & S. Rahman (Eds.), *Handbook of Research on Small and Medium Enterprises in Developing Countries* (pp. 117–136). Hershey, PA: IGI Global. doi:10.4018/978-1-5225-2165-5.ch006

Raimi, L. (2017). Leveraging CSR as a 'support-aid' for Triple Bottom-Line Development in Nigeria: Evidence from the Telecommunication Industry. In D. Jamali (Ed.), *Comparative Perspectives on Global Corporate Social Responsibility* (pp. 208–225). Hershey, PA: IGI Global. doi:10.4018/978-1-5225-0720-8.ch010

Rajamanickam, S. (2016). Exploring Landscapes in Regional Convergence: Environment and Sustainable Development in South Asia. In R. Das (Ed.), *Handbook of Research on Global Indicators of Economic and Political Convergence* (pp. 474–510). Hershey, PA: IGI Global. doi:10.4018/978-1-5225-0215-9.ch021

Ray, K., Das, R. C., & Das, U. (2016). Convergence Aspect of Capital Formation: A Study on Major Countries. In R. Das (Ed.), *Handbook of Research on Global Indicators of Economic and Political Convergence* (pp. 51–66). Hershey, PA: IGI Global. doi:10.4018/978-1-5225-0215-9.ch003

Richet, J. (2016). Internal Communication Failure in Times of Change. In A. Goksoy (Ed.), *Organizational Change Management Strategies in Modern Business* (pp. 289–300). Hershey, PA: IGI Global. doi:10.4018/978-1-4666-9533-7.ch014

Riemann, U. (2016). The Power of Three: A Blended Approach of Project-, Change Management, and Design Thinking. In A. Goksoy (Ed.), *Organizational Change Management Strategies in Modern Business* (pp. 74–94). Hershey, PA: IGI Global. doi:10.4018/978-1-4666-9533-7.ch004

Rossetti di Valdalbero, D., & Birnbaum, B. (2017). Towards a New Economy: Co-Creation and Open Innovation in a Trustworthy Europe. In W. Vassallo (Ed.), *Crowdfunding for Sustainable Entrepreneurship and Innovation* (pp. 20–36). Hershey, PA: IGI Global. doi:10.4018/978-1-5225-0568-6.ch002

Saglietto, L., David, D., & Cezanne, C. (2017). Rethinking Social Capital Measurement. In J. Stanković, P. Delias, S. Marinković, & S. Rochhia (Eds.), *Tools and Techniques for Economic Decision Analysis* (pp. 248–268). Hershey, PA: IGI Global. doi:10.4018/978-1-5225-0959-2.ch012

Sanchez-Ruiz, L., & Blanco, B. (2017). Process Management for SMEs: Barriers, Enablers, and Benefits. In M. Vemić (Ed.), *Optimal Management Strategies in Small and Medium Enterprises* (pp. 293–319). Hershey, PA: IGI Global. doi:10.4018/978-1-5225-1949-2.ch014

Savic, M., & Zubovic, J. (2017). Modeling Labor Market Flows on the Basis of Sectoral Employment in Europe. In J. Stanković, P. Delias, S. Marinković, & S. Rochhia (Eds.), *Tools and Techniques for Economic Decision Analysis* (pp. 151–169). Hershey, PA: IGI Global. doi:10.4018/978-1-5225-0959-2.ch007

Scholtz, B., Koorsse, M., & Loleka, S. (2017). Understanding and Adoption of E-Finance in Small and Medium Enterprises (SMEs) in Developing Countries: A Study of Bangladesh and South Africa. In N. Ahmad, T. Ramayah, H. Halim, & S. Rahman (Eds.), *Handbook of Research on Small and Medium Enterprises in Developing Countries* (pp. 159–184). Hershey, PA: IGI Global. doi:10.4018/978-1-5225-2165-5.ch008

Šebestová, J., & Palová, Z. (2017). Support of Social Innovations: Case of the Czech Republic. In M. Lewandowski & B. Kożuch (Eds.), *Public Sector Entrepreneurship and the Integration of Innovative Business Models* (pp. 165–187). Hershey, PA: IGI Global. doi:10.4018/978-1-5225-2215-7.ch007

Seliga, R. (2017). Public Sector Marketing in Poland. In M. Lewandowski & B. Kożuch (Eds.), *Public Sector Entrepreneurship and the Integration of Innovative Business Models* (pp. 214–237). Hershey, PA: IGI Global. doi:10.4018/978-1-5225-2215-7.ch009

Šević, A., & Marinković, S. (2017). Investment Decision Making: Where Do We Stand? In J. Stanković, P. Delias, S. Marinković, & S. Rochhia (Eds.), *Tools and Techniques for Economic Decision Analysis* (pp. 1–23). Hershey, PA: IGI Global. doi:10.4018/978-1-5225-0959-2.ch001

Şimşit, Z. T., Günay, N. S., & Vayvay, Ö. (2016). Organizational Learning to Managing Change: Key Player of Continuous Improvement in the 21st Century. In A. Goksoy (Ed.), *Organizational Change Management Strategies in Modern Business* (pp. 95–109). Hershey, PA: IGI Global. doi:10.4018/978-1-4666-9533-7.ch005

Širůček, M., & Křen, L. (2017). Application of Markowitz Portfolio Theory by Building Optimal Portfolio on the US Stock Market. In J. Stanković, P. Delias, S. Marinković, & S. Rochhia (Eds.), *Tools and Techniques for Economic Decision Analysis* (pp. 24–42). Hershey, PA: IGI Global. doi:10.4018/978-1-5225-0959-2.ch002

Soniewicki, M. (2017). The Importance of Market Orientation in Creating a Competitive Advantage of Micro, Small, and Medium-Sized Companies in the Internationalization Process. In M. Vemić (Ed.), *Optimal Management Strategies in Small and Medium Enterprises* (pp. 1–21). Hershey, PA: IGI Global. doi:10.4018/978-1-5225-1949-2.ch001

Staszewska, B. M. (2017). Local Public Enterprise Business Model as Multiple Value Creation System. In M. Lewandowski & B. Kożuch (Eds.), *Public Sector Entrepreneurship and the Integration of Innovative Business Models* (pp. 188–213). Hershey, PA: IGI Global. doi:10.4018/978-1-5225-2215-7.ch008

Stefanova, J. S., & Wenner, Z. (2017). Entrepreneurship and Enterprise Value Creation in Support of Smart, Sustainable, and Inclusive Growth in the European Union. In M. Vemić (Ed.), *Optimal Management Strategies in Small and Medium Enterprises* (pp. 268–292). Hershey, PA: IGI Global. doi:10.4018/978-1-5225-1949-2.ch013

Taghizadeh, S. K., Rahman, S. A., & Ramayah, T. (2017). Innovation-Driven Planned Behaviour Towards Achieving the Wellbeing of the Malaysian SMEs. In N. Ahmad, T. Ramayah, H. Halim, & S. Rahman (Eds.), *Handbook of Research on Small and Medium Enterprises in Developing Countries* (pp. 280–296). Hershey, PA: IGI Global. doi:10.4018/978-1-5225-2165-5.ch013

Thavinpipatkul, C., Ratana-Ubol, A., & Charungkaittikul, S. (2016). Transformative Learning Factors to Enhance Integral Healthy Organizations. *International Journal of Adult Vocational Education and Technology*, *7*(1), 65–83. doi:10.4018/IJAVET.2016010105

Theodoridis, A., Ragkos, A., Angelidis, P., Batzios, C., & Samathrakis, V. (2017). Typologies as Management Tools: Understanding the Environmental Attitudes and Economic Prospects of Mussel Farmers in Greece. In J. Stanković, P. Delias, S. Marinković, & S. Rochhia (Eds.), *Tools and Techniques for Economic Decision Analysis* (pp. 170–180). Hershey, PA: IGI Global. doi:10.4018/978-1-5225-0959-2.ch008

Thongpoon, S., Ahmad, N. H., & Mahmud, I. (2017). Sustainable Approach towards Thai SMEs: The Effects of Country Philosophy of Sufficiency Economy and Government Support. In N. Ahmad, T. Ramayah, H. Halim, & S. Rahman (Eds.), *Handbook of Research on Small and Medium Enterprises in Developing Countries* (pp. 1–22). Hershey, PA: IGI Global. doi:10.4018/978-1-5225-2165-5.ch001

Timilsina, B. (2017). Overcoming the Barriers of Strategic Planning, Implementation, and Monitoring in Turbulent Business Environment: A Qualitative Study on Finnish SMEs. In M. Vemić (Ed.), *Optimal Management Strategies in Small and Medium Enterprises* (pp. 226–248). Hershey, PA: IGI Global. doi:10.4018/978-1-5225-1949-2.ch011

Tongiani, M. G., & Zhao, S. (2017). Traditional Italian Food Products on the Chinese Market: Best Practices for Italian Small and Medium Enterprises. In M. Vemić (Ed.), *Optimal Management Strategies in Small and Medium Enterprises* (pp. 22–43). Hershey, PA: IGI Global. doi:10.4018/978-1-5225-1949-2.ch002

Torlak, N. G. (2016). Improving the Role of Organisational Culture in Change Management through a Systems Approach. In A. Goksoy (Ed.), *Organizational Change Management Strategies in Modern Business* (pp. 230–271). Hershey, PA: IGI Global. doi:10.4018/978-1-4666-9533-7.ch012

Tran, B. (2016). Gendered Social-Networking Organizations: A View of the Sexed Mentorship Relationships. *International Journal of Organizational and Collective Intelligence*, *6*(2), 26–49. doi:10.4018/IJOCI.2016040103

Uyen, N. T., & Zainal, S. R. (2017). Non-State SMEs in Vietnam: Understanding Strategic Situation and Implications for Organizational Performance. In N. Ahmad, T. Ramayah, H. Halim, & S. Rahman (Eds.), *Handbook of Research on Small and Medium Enterprises in Developing Countries* (pp. 297–321). Hershey, PA: IGI Global. doi:10.4018/978-1-5225-2165-5.ch014

Vargas-Hernández, J. G. (2016). Critical Analysis of the Influence of Transnational Capitalism on Institutions and Organizations. In R. Das (Ed.), *Handbook of Research on Global Indicators of Economic and Political Convergence* (pp. 237–253). Hershey, PA: IGI Global. doi:10.4018/978-1-5225-0215-9.ch011

Vargas-Hernández, J. G. (2016). Strategic-Spatial Analysis of the Implementation of Business Opening Politics of Mexico. In R. Das (Ed.), *Handbook of Research on Global Indicators of Economic and Political Convergence* (pp. 274–313). Hershey, PA: IGI Global. doi:10.4018/978-1-5225-0215-9.ch013

Vargas-Hernández, J. G., Muratalla-Bautista, G., & Cruz, I. D. (2017). Point of View of Economical Organization at Manzanillo's Harbor. In R. Das (Ed.), *Social, Health, and Environmental Infrastructures for Economic Growth* (pp. 307–324). Hershey, PA: IGI Global. doi:10.4018/978-1-5225-2364-2.ch015

Vemić, M. B. (2017). A Further Look at Working Capital Optimization in Medium-Sized Firms: Concepts and Evidence. In M. Vemić (Ed.), *Optimal Management Strategies in Small and Medium Enterprises* (pp. 144–177). Hershey, PA: IGI Global. doi:10.4018/978-1-5225-1949-2.ch008

Vemić, M. B. (2017). Financial Innovation in Medium-Sized Enterprises Optimizes Their Gravitation Towards Capital Markets: Financial Future in Perspective. In M. Vemić (Ed.), *Optimal Management Strategies in Small and Medium Enterprises* (pp. 198–224). Hershey, PA: IGI Global. doi:10.4018/978-1-5225-1949-2.ch010

Villegas, M., & McGivern, M. H. (2015). Codes of Ethics, Ethical Behavior, and Organizational Culture from the Managerial Approach: A Case Study in the Colombian Banking Industry. *International Journal of Strategic Information Technology and Applications*, *6*(1), 42–56. doi:10.4018/IJSITA.2015010104

Virkar, S. (2016). Can Codes of Ethical Conduct Work?: Evaluating the Effectiveness of Privatised Corporate Governance in a World of Political and Economic Convergence. In R. Das (Ed.), *Handbook of Research on Global Indicators of Economic and Political Convergence* (pp. 206–236). Hershey, PA: IGI Global. doi:10.4018/978-1-5225-0215-9.ch010

Windsor, D. (2017). Defining Corporate Social Responsibility for Developing and Developed Countries: Comparing Proposed Approaches. In D. Jamali (Ed.), *Comparative Perspectives on Global Corporate Social Responsibility* (pp. 1–27). Hershey, PA: IGI Global. doi:10.4018/978-1-5225-0720-8.ch001

Wolf, R., & Thiel, M. (2017). CSR in China: The Road to New Sustainable Business Models. In D. Jamali (Ed.), *Comparative Perspectives on Global Corporate Social Responsibility* (pp. 258–275). Hershey, PA: IGI Global. doi:10.4018/978-1-5225-0720-8.ch013

Wronka-Pośpiech, M. (2017). Applying Business Solutions to Social Problems: Social Co-Operative and Its Business Model – Evidence from Poland. In M. Lewandowski & B. Kożuch (Eds.), *Public Sector Entrepreneurship and the Integration of Innovative Business Models* (pp. 139–164). Hershey, PA: IGI Global. doi:10.4018/978-1-5225-2215-7.ch006

Yap, N. T., & Ground, K. E. (2017). Socially Responsible Mining Corporations: Before (or in Addition to) Doing Good, Do No Harm. In D. Jamali (Ed.), *Comparative Perspectives on Global Corporate Social Responsibility* (pp. 185–207). Hershey, PA: IGI Global. doi:10.4018/978-1-5225-0720-8.ch009

Yordanova, S. D. (2017). Optimizing Virtual Communities in Tourism to Facilitate Development of Small and Medium-Sized Enterprises. In M. Vemić (Ed.), *Optimal Management Strategies in Small and Medium Enterprises* (pp. 60–78). Hershey, PA: IGI Global. doi:10.4018/978-1-5225-1949-2.ch004

Yusoff, A., Ahmad, N. H., & Halim, H. A. (2017). Agropreneurship among Gen Y in Malaysia: The Role of Academic Institutions. In N. Ahmad, T. Ramayah, H. Halim, & S. Rahman (Eds.), *Handbook of Research on Small and Medium Enterprises in Developing Countries* (pp. 23–47). Hershey, PA: IGI Global. doi:10.4018/978-1-5225-2165-5.ch002

Zel, U. (2016). Leadership in Change Management. In A. Goksoy (Ed.), *Organizational Change Management Strategies in Modern Business* (pp. 272–288). Hershey, PA: IGI Global. doi:10.4018/978-1-4666-9533-7.ch013

About the Author

Albena Antonova is researcher and lecturer at Sofia University, Bulgaria since 2004. She works mainly in the field of practical ICT applications and currently teaches courses related to emerging technologies, digital transformation, social innovations, serious games and knowledge management. She was involved in a number of international research and application projects. Some of her recent projects are in the field of digital transformation of SME, Social Energy, Serious Gaming, e-learning and m-learning implementations, green ICT and others. Her main research interests include knowledge management and knowledge management systems, emerging technologies business impact, TEL models and methods, e-Business, technology entrepreneurship and start-up, knowledge sharing, open innovations and living labs. She has more than 30 publications in the field.

Index

R

S

T

V

Stay Current on the Latest Emerging Research Developments

Become an IGI Global Reviewer for Authored Book Projects

The overall success of an authored book project is dependent on quality and timely reviews.

In this competitive age of scholarly publishing, constructive and timely feedback significantly decreases the turnaround time of manuscripts from submission to acceptance, allowing the publication and discovery of progressive research at a much more expeditious rate. Several IGI Global authored book projects are currently seeking highly qualified experts in the field to fill vacancies on their respective editorial review boards:

Applications may be sent to:
development@igi-global.com

Applicants must have a doctorate (or an equivalent degree) as well as publishing and reviewing experience. Reviewers are asked to write reviews in a timely, collegial, and constructive manner. All reviewers will begin their role on an ad-hoc basis for a period of one year, and upon successful completion of this term can be considered for full editorial review board status, with the potential for a subsequent promotion to Associate Editor.

If you have a colleague that may be interested in this opportunity, we encourage you to share this information with them.

www.ingramcontent.com/pod-product-compliance
Lightning Source LLC
Chambersburg PA
CBHW050936160926
51501CB00061B/172
* 9 7 8 1 5 2 2 5 6 2 7 0 2 *